Making
Kingdom
Disciples

MAKING
Kingdom
DISCIPLES

A NEW FRAMEWORK

CHARLES H. DUNAHOO

FOREWORD BY ALLEN D. CURRY

P&R
PUBLISHING

P.O. BOX 817 • PHILLIPSBURG • NEW JERSEY 08865-0817

Page design and typesetting by Lakeside Design Plus

Printed in the United States of America

Library of Congress Cataloging-in-Publication Data

Dunahoo, Charles H., 1940–
    Making kingdom disciples : a new framework / Charles H. Dunahoo ; foreword by Allen D. Curry.
        p. cm.
    Includes bibliographical references and index.
    ISBN 0-87552-640-3
    1. Discipling (Christianity) I. Title.

BV4520.D86 2005
248.4—dc22

                                                                    2004051005

*To the staff and committee of
Christian Education and Publications,
who co-labor with me in teaching these
foundational kingdom concepts and share
the convictions expressed in this book*

Contents

Foreword

Many will ask why another book on discipleship? Don't we have enough treatments of this subject? I believe not. Most contemporary works on discipleship deal with the process of making disciples. In fact, many people reduce making disciples to a few tried and true formulas: get someone into a consistent pattern of having a quiet time with Bible reading and prayer, witnessing to friends and neighbors, and moving toward leading others into the same patterns of behavior. Then you'll have a disciple of Christ. But does this really produce a disciple?

In the simplest definition a disciple is someone who follows Christ. If we had followed Jesus during his earthly pilgrimage, what would we have heard? We would have heard about the kingdom of God or heaven. This was central to the message Jesus preached, and this was the message he expected his disciples to embrace. For Jesus, being a disciple involved much more than a few behavioral patterns. It required a complete reordering of one's life around living in the kingdom, with Jesus as the King.

Because Jesus preached the coming of the kingdom, the book you have in your hand is necessary and important. Discipleship involves a process, but more importantly it requires a substantial change in the way one views life.

Charles Dunahoo has provided the church with a book on discipleship that deals with the central theme in the ministry of Jesus. The kingdom model of discipleship pays attention to the process of discipleship while emphasizing the content. Disciples of Jesus not only have a quiet time in which they study the Word, but they find their lives transformed. They learn to think differently from those in the world. Dunahoo patiently walks us through the problems of epistemology and shows how the Christian approach to the truth differs from the world of postmodernism. One cannot be a disciple if he does not think in the categories of the kingdom.

Because a disciple of the kingdom thinks differently, he will view the world in a dramatically new and fresh manner. Everyone has a worldview, but the Christian worldview centers on the kingdom of God. Jesus the King rules over all that exists. Disciples with a kingdom mind-set press for the entire world to acknowledge the kingship of Jesus. This is not some pie-in-the-sky, by-and-by notion; it is a here-and-now way of thinking. Fewer and fewer North Americans look at life from the perspective that Jesus is the ruler of the entire universe. Without this perspective one cannot truly be described as a disciple of Christ.

Lest you think this work avoids the practical down-to-earth process of becoming a disciple, let me assure you that it really presents a model for becoming a full-orbed disciple of Christ. For example, if you are to be a disciple, then you will live in relationship to God in terms of the covenant. Living in covenant requires one to live in rule-governed relationships. Dunahoo points us in the direction of covenantal living, even showing us how to read the Bible covenantally.

The church owes Charles Dunahoo a debt of gratitude for providing us with a fresh approach to discipleship. He gives not only the how, but more importantly the what of being a follower of Jesus.

Allen D. Curry

Preface

Why another book? So many fine books already have been written on the subject of discipleship. However, over the years as I have read and recommended hundreds of books to church leaders, I have not found a book that does exactly what I want to do in this volume. While much of what I write here can be found in other books, and often more eloquently stated, I have not seen this particular configuration of topics related to Christian discipleship. So I decided to pull together what I have learned, read, and experienced as a pastor, youth worker, and education and training coordinator for my denomination, and present the big picture rather than develop a method. I intend this book to be an overview, a primer, of the kingdom model of making disciples, and hope it will serve to improve the ministry of both professionals and laypeople.

My life purpose has been to minister to pastors and teachers. I encourage them to be more involved in the discipling process. (Most perceive themselves to be more involved than they are.) Pastors need to facilitate coordinated teaching plans that can be followed by all the teachers and departments within the church. *The educational process must be intentional* if it is to open the great treasures of the Christian faith in a life-transforming way. This cannot be done from the pulpit alone, and it cannot be done by a haphazard approach to discipleship.

A major premise of this volume is that you and I are placed on earth at this moment in history to serve God's purpose. It is no accident that we are living now. The apostle Paul told the Athenians that God determines our allotted periods and the boundaries of our dwelling places (Acts 17:26b). In 1 Corinthians 12 he further states in reference to the church, the body of Christ, that God orchestrates the whole, each part just as he wants it. Why has the sovereign God who controls all things determined for us to be here at this time? The Westminster Shorter Catechism's brilliant statement reminds us that "man's chief end is to glorify God and to enjoy him forever." Or as Paul said of David in a sermon presented to the Antiochian people, "He had served the purpose of God in his own generation" (Acts 13:36). We are here to serve God's purpose in history. There is no doubt about that.

Though the principles in this book are not generation-specific, my real concern as I write is for this generation of young people who are being reared in a context that does not encourage or support a Christian framework, even in the most general sense. The generation X-ers or baby busters and the millennial generation of children and youth are being lost from the church and maybe from the Christian faith. Marva Dawn in her book *Is It a Lost Cause?* asserts that the effort to reach the younger generations in this postmodern world does not have to be a lost cause. But to reach them, the church and the family have to understand those two generations and be willing to adjust without sacrificing solid substance, either in relationships or in truth. One of Dawn's earlier books, *Reaching Out Without Dumbing Down*, challenges us not to dumb down what we teach to our children. Philosopher Diogenes Allen cautions about removing substance from knowledge and truth. These two generations are the most academically educated of all, but for the most part are biblically illiterate. If Christian communities and parents are willing to pay the price and learn the ropes, then we might indeed see a generation won to Christ. Humanly that will not happen, but we serve a sovereign God who does not renege on his promises.

My prayer is that God will convey to you something of the urgency and passion I have to make the most of every moment. Two Scripture passages that constantly challenge me are Romans 13:11, "The present time is of the highest importance—it is time to wake up to reality"

(Phillips), and 1 Chronicles 12:32, which describes the men of Issachar as having "understanding of the times, to know what Israel ought to do."

To serve God's purpose in this generation we must understand both his purpose and this generation. Some people do one well, and some do the other, but to be effective for the Lord we need to have both in tandem. To do less is to betray our calling because to understand his Word, we have to understand our world, and to understand our world, we have to understand his Word. To understand his Word and his purpose, we must understand the Word in its original context, understand it as it has developed historically, and then understand it in our context today. These three horizons are intricately connected. Consequently, when we do not explore all three, we miss what God is saying to us.

My goal in this book is to integrate the discipling process with a "kingdom of God" perspective. Chapter by chapter we will work toward achieving that goal. Each chapter will help us define part of what is necessary if we are to meet the final challenge of ministering to today's generation. Part 1 will speak to knowing the Word (the framework for ministry), Part 2 will speak to knowing the world (the context for ministry), and Part 3 will present biblical models for application. I will end with concrete ways to use this book to serve God's purpose today. Each chapter will include topics for personal reflection or group discussion. There will also be a suggested reading list of materials related to the topic covered in the chapter.

Part 1

Being a disciple of the kingdom and effectively ministering in a postmodern world require a saving knowledge of God, an accurate knowledge of his Word, a proper knowledge of the world around us, and a true knowledge of ourselves. John Calvin wrote in the first chapter of the first book of the *Institutes of the Christian Religion* that our knowledge of God and our knowledge of ourselves are so interfaced that we cannot separate them. Our knowledge, experience, and understanding of reality are impacted by ourselves as knowers and by our role within God's covenant community. In chapter 2, on epistemology, we will discuss how we know what we know. Though difficult, that chapter will be foundational to the rest of the book. To be true disciples of Jesus Christ we cannot put our brains out of commission or turn them off when we approach the Word.

In addition, as believers in Christ we must be conscious in all we do that we are kingdom people. Chapter 3 will address the concept of the kingdom of God, which determines who we are as well as how we are to live and think. "Kingdom of God" people are to be different from the world. We are a part of the world because of God's plan, but we are to be different from it.

The Sermon on the Mount (Matt. 5–7) describes internal and external characteristics that should be obvious in our lives. Jesus says in that sermon that those characteristics and behaviors will make a difference in the world around us. But if that is true, why does our culture demonstrate a decreasing Christian influence? With some exceptions, it seems that Christians have little moral, spiritual, educational, or philosophical influence. Both Christian and secular writers warn of a coming societal collapse. George Barna said in *The Second Coming of the Church*, published in 1998, that we had five years to turn the church around or it would slip into utter insignificance. Those five years have now passed, and some of his concerns have been realized as the church continues its declining course. This book will examine some of the reasons and remedies for that decline.

Chapter 4 will deal with the Christian's world-and-life-view. We will discuss what a worldview involves and how to develop one. The Bible states that when we become Christians our hearts of stone become hearts of flesh, but it also teaches us to love God with our body, soul, and *mind* as well. During the latter part of the nineteenth century and the entire twentieth century there was little stress on encouraging and teaching Christians to think. (While the classic education model tended to teach people to think, it synthesized a Western Enlightenment model that does not fit our postmodern world. Nor does it accurately reflect the Hebrew-Christian approach. (Consider, for example, the primacy of reason over revelation.) We will discuss the need for Christians to think and to develop a consistent worldview that pulls the pieces of life together into a coherent framework.

Not only have today's Christians been convinced that thinking in general is not necessary for salvation and life, but many believe that doctrine and theology in particular are only for professional theologians. Chapter 5 deals with biblical doctrine within the historic Reformed tradition. The apostle Paul stated our role clearly when he said that what we teach must be in accord with sound doctrine (Titus 2). However, in our Reformed and evangelical circles, we tend to teach doctrine in a dogmatic way without relating it to life and community, or we do not teach doctrine at all. In this chapter I will show that both approaches will finally produce the same results, and we will have no foundation to hold us up under the pressures of a postmodern world. Teaching sound doctrine in a practical manner that touches people in their individual and communal lives has never been more needed. Without the blend of the two we will never penetrate the rising generation and help them to embrace Christ and come into the Christian community.

Chapter 6, which focuses on the covenants, will highlight the need to see that Christianity is the religion of truth fleshed out in vertical and horizontal relationships. The personal Triune God created us in his image to relate to him in a personal way and then to relate to one another within the community of faith. Modernism's strong emphasis on individualism has taken its toll in the Christian community. It led to our individualistic, self-reliant culture. I believe that covenantal thinking and living are what our postmodern world, particularly the rising generation, is looking for in their lonely, fragmented, and dislocated lives.

Part 2

Chapter 7 will begin to describe our present cultural setting. If we are to serve God's purpose in this generation, we must understand the times. God has created history, and it is moving to his appointed end. Contrary to Eastern thought, we do not believe history is merely cyclical. Yet within our sequential linear understanding of history moving toward a cataclysmic conclusion, there is obviously a cyclical pattern that enables us to learn from the past to understand the present and have a point of reference for thinking about the future.

Things are not the same today as they were two hundred, five hundred, or two thousand years ago. For example, I have always had a love and appreciation for the Puritans, but we cannot live in their world. We cannot live in Paul's world, or Calvin's or Luther's. For one thing, language, the heart of culture, has changed, and that change accelerated greatly during the twentieth century as a result of modernity's search for the newest and the best. We are shaped enormously (though often unconsciously) by the pop culture around us. Our lifestyle, our worship practices, our obsession with comfort, and our short-order consumer thinking are reflections of modernity.

Chapter 8 will focus chiefly on postmodernism. Though introduced in the last part of the nineteenth century and accelerated in the twentieth century, postmodernism has clearly surfaced in our culture as the later generations appeared. It has brought with it a new and different model for interpreting and understanding reality. Two book titles reflect something of the change connected with postmodernism: Walter Anderson's *Reality Isn't What It Used to Be* and Richard Middleton and Brian Walsh's *Truth Is Stranger than It Used to Be*.

I discuss postmodernism because it is not a passing fad. It is a total paradigm shift that manifests itself in many ways, not the least of which is our current-day focus on pluralism, relativism, tolerance, and pop culture. It has ramifications for our epistemology and our methods of communication. Postmodernists have freely and openly used language to compose their own categories and realities by deconstructing things; for instance, they deconstruct history to make it say whatever they want it to say. While the Enlightenment period and the Age of Reason exalted man's autonomous reason and experience as the final reference point, with experience playing a subservient role, postmodernism promotes man's experience to the primary position. Postmodernism is the first model that offers reality without absolutes and universals.

Chapter 9 will address the topic of generations. Understanding the world requires an understanding of people in their respective generations, each of which has certain distinguishing characteristics that give us insights into what and how its members think and why they live as they do. Starting with the builders of pre–World War II time and going on to the present millennial generation (children and youth born between 1980 and 2000), we will seek to understand how to minister effectively to all the generations. We will focus on generation X (the baby busters) and the millennial generation. These are the two generations leaving the church in large numbers, if in fact they were ever there. These are the first two generations of postmodernism that have no true knowledge of God because they are biblically illiterate. Our challenge is to reach these rising generations and communicate the gospel of truth to them in a way that draws them into the Christian community instead of pushing them away.

Part 3

The final section contains materials for use in personal or small-group inductive Bible study. We will discuss briefly the role of hermeneutics or Bible interpretation. As we study the Word of God, it is important to incorporate the pieces of the puzzle set forth in this book.

The Christian community has a challenge to engage in a strategy that will help turn the tide of massive biblical illiteracy in our culture. We cannot do that using yesterday's methods. The scientific method of doing theology, which developed first in the early university model and expanded with modernism's paradigm, does not fit this postscientific, nonrational age. We are Reformed but always reforming by the Word of God. The Bible is always our "only infallible rule of faith and life," but we have to understand it today. Though the Bible was written over a period of time long ago, and though the canon of Scripture closed with the Book of Revelation, the Word, according to the Westminster Confession of Faith (1.8), must be translated into the "vulgar," the common language of the people. Just as we cannot study the Bible effectively and properly apart from knowledge of the past, neither can we be effective without studying it in the language of the people in our day. I believe this implies more than just a modern Bible translation. Like the Lord himself, his Word is alive and powerful. It is his written Word for us today. Though postmodernism tends to be suspicious of authority, exclusivism, absolutes, and universal truth, the Bible is truth for all peoples and all times. God expects us to co-labor with him in communicating his Word to this world.

Chapter 10 examines what we can learn from Paul's interaction with the Athenians in Acts 17: his understanding of their culture combined with an uncompromised proclamation of the gospel in terms relevant to his listeners. Chapter 11 contains an overview of Ecclesiastes highlighting how it answers questions and concerns typical of the postmodern mind-set. Chapter 12 uses an episode from Abraham's life (Gen. 13) to illustrate the importance of reading Scripture covenantally to avoid the pitfalls of moralism and legalism.

I write from my commitment to Reformed theology and to a Calvinistic worldview. Those two disciplines will enable me to communicate more effectively God's truth in this day, as Calvin did in his day. If I can encourage Christians, and particularly Christian leaders, to think biblically and strategically, then this book will have served a useful purpose.

If this book causes uneasiness or disturbs your comfort zone, then I trust it will also encourage and challenge you to think. I am well aware, as someone has said, that "if you make people think they are thinking, they will love you; but if you make them think, they may hate you." Hate is not my objective. Thinking about God with our minds and loving him with our hearts are. Time is of the essence. We have a job to do that is humanly impossible. My prayer is that God will marshal our forces together to build his church and to extend his kingdom.

PART 1

Knowing the Word:
The Framework for Discipleship

1

An Overview of the Kingdom Model

Before Jesus ascended into heaven, he gave his final command to his church about their assignment during the interim between his ascension and his return at the end of the age. He said, "All authority in heaven and on earth has been given to me. Go therefore and make disciples of all nations, baptizing them in the name of the Father and of the Son and of the Holy Spirit, teaching them to observe all that I have commanded you. And behold, I am with you always, to the end of the age" (Matt. 28:18–20).

The importance of those words cannot be overstated. They express God's revealed will for his church until he returns at the consummation of all things. The church's mission is to make disciples by evangelizing and educating the believers. In turn, the believers are to be transformed into the likeness of Christ, demonstrated by a life of Christlike service within the kingdom of God.

This survey chapter will present a vision for what I believe is God's plan for disciple making, which I call the kingdom approach, but in that approach we need to understand the church's role. Recent studies and trends suggest that making disciples is not being done with any great effectiveness; for example, less than 10 percent of professing Christians

4

self-consciously embrace a biblical world-and-life-view. So states George Barna in *The Second Coming of the Church*.[1] That statement is backed up by a host of others who have evaluated the church's effectiveness.

Among them George Gallup Jr. and D. Michael Lindsay summarize what they see as major trends in religious life in the United States:

- Widespread popularity of religion
- Glaring lack of Bible knowledge
- Inconsistencies of belief
- Superficiality of faith
- Belief in but not trust in God
- Failure of organized religion to make a difference[2]

Religion and religious practices are relegated to the private sector of life. The difference between the lifestyles of Christians and non-Christians is negligible. Gallup and Lindsay conclude that Christians are not making that much of a difference in society, but neither is religion in general.

Contrast the situation in America with the counsel the apostle Paul gives:

> And so, dear Christian friends, I plead with you to give your bodies to God. Let them be a living and holy sacrifice—the kind he will accept. When you think of what he has done for you, is this too much to ask? Don't copy the behavior and customs of this world, but let God transform you into a new person by changing the way you think. Then you will know what God wants you to do, and you will know how good and pleasing and perfect his will really is. (Rom. 12:1–2, NLT)

A look at our culture reveals that a younger generation is coming along that is the most biblically illiterate generation in our history. We are living in a disconnected culture where people are experiencing more and more loneliness and isolation. Neither those inside nor those outside the church see the institutional church positively because it is not addressing the issues or offering substantive solutions to life's problems and challenges. Therefore, we may be facing the death of the institutional church as we know it. If not, then we may witness in the next decade an over-hauling of the present institutional church that will make it look far different from the church today. Postmodernism, the overarching philosophy today, is a life-view paradigm that is seeking to remove foundations and redefine reality in nonfoundational, relativistic terms. Christians are not being equipped to be salt and light in this world, and many have either retreated or walled themselves off from the world and thus are viewed by the world as insignificant and irrelevant.

On the basis of observations as coordinator of Christian education and publications for my denomination, I conclude that the biblical model for making disciples is not being followed. At this point it is important to look closely at the word "disciple," for it has various connotations. In this book I will define the term as follows:

> Generic definition: A disciple is someone who accepts a set of beliefs, and embraces a holistic, total, and intentional approach to life based on those beliefs.

> Kingdom definition: a kingdom disciple is someone who thinks God's thoughts after him and applies them to all of life.

In the Christian sense, the aim of every disciple is to "take every thought captive to obey Christ" (2 Cor. 10:5), especially remembering the proverb, "As [a man] thinks in his heart, so is [or lives] he" (Prov. 23:7, NKJV; "he is like one who is inwardly calculating," ESV).

In the late 1980s I was sitting in the office of my friend Norman Harper, dean of the Graduate School of Christian Education at Reformed Theological Seminary in Jackson, Mississippi. During our conversation he remarked, "You know, Charles, one of our biggest problems is that our teaching elders do not have a vision for Christian education." He had published a book several years earlier entitled *Making Disciples: The Challenge of Christian Education at the End of the 20th Century*. In that book he defined a disciple as "someone who self-consciously strives to live all life under the Lordship of Jesus Christ." He further wrote, "The making of disciples is the ultimate purpose of all true education."

We talked further about those ideas in following years when Harper was serving on the Presbyterian Church in America's Christian Education and Publications Committee before his departure for heaven. I have frequently recalled his comments since then. As the twentieth century drew to a close and I reflected on the trends and statistics, his words began to crystallize in a new way for me.

Jim Petersen, international vice president of Navigators, an organization that focuses on making disciples, made a similar comment. In his book *Lifestyle Discipleship: The Challenge of Following Jesus in Today's World*, his very first sentence in chapter 1, which is entitled "Discipleship and Our Contemporary Culture," is, "Thirty years of discipleship programs and we are not discipled."

I could go on and on citing similar quotes leading me to conclude that both Harper and Petersen, from two slightly different perspectives, are right. As I have studied trends related to the church and the broader religious and philosophical scene, and as I have had much firsthand experience working with local church leaders, researchers like George Barna, George Gallup Jr., and Robert Wuthnow have convinced me that we are operating from a questionable, maybe even faulty, paradigm of making disciples. Actually, three of the four approaches that I will shortly describe are not totally wrong, but taken individually, or even combined with one another, they fall short of what I believe is the right one; therefore they are not producing the results that God intends. In that sense they are wrong, if used by themselves.

Simply put, we have been operating, often unintentionally, with more of a man-centered rather than a God-centered approach to making disciples, and it is not working. Although there may be much activity and movement that suggest otherwise, the statistics are real. I use "man-centered" to mean either man corporately or man individually. We must operate with the right paradigm—not a man-centered but a God-centered model; not a narrow isolationist or separatist approach, but a "kingdom of God" approach. What is the difference?

The late Francis Schaeffer, to whom I am deeply indebted, suggested that there is an overarching philosophy that impacts every area of life. In his book *The God Who Is There* he diagrams a series of steps where philosophy, at the top of the stairs, begins to work its way down and impacts every area of life, even theology and the church. (See figure 1.1 for a slight variation of Schaeffer's original.) This gives us a sense of the approach we must follow in making disciples.

FIGURE 1.1. STEPS OF PHILOSOPHICAL INFLUENCE

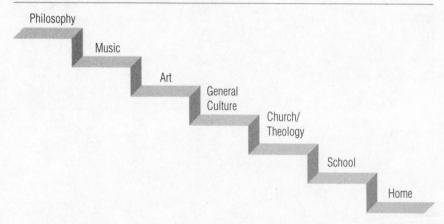

Now the modernistic period, with its Enlightenment philosophy, was exacting. Everything had to fit somewhere. Logic and reason ruled the day until postmodernism, which began full force in the 1960s as the new model, was even more exacting with its disdain for words, logic, and reason. Barna may have sounded a bit like an alarmist when he said in 1998 that we have about five years to turn this ship around,[3] but he had valid reasons to say that we need to do that. Maybe Michael Regele in his book *The Death of the Church*, speaking of the visible church as we know it, was also correct in his thesis that the church must die in order to live. Let us take a look at the ways in which the church is striving to make disciples today and then at what God actually has in mind.

AN OVERVIEW OF THE KINGDOM MODEL

Three Inadequate Approaches

For the sake of clarity I will say there are three main approaches being used today under the rubric of making disciples (see figure 1.2). I do not intend to communicate that the three approaches are wrong, but merely reductionistic and incomplete.

FIGURE 1.2. MODELS FOR DISCIPLE MAKING

APPROACH		FOCUS	CONTEXT	ORIENTATION	CHARACTERISTICS
Model 1: Program-based	People-centered	Informational/ content	Person in community setting (large group)	Program, Activity	Fosters "Christian ghetto"
Model 2: Individual		Formational/ relationships	Person to person, one on one	Felt needs	Checklist for spiritual growth; may occur apart from church membership
Model 3: Small group		Formational/ relationships	Person in small group	Society	Focuses on formation in a small-group setting; may tend to down play the role of corporate worship
Model 4: Kingdom	God-centered	Transformational (includes information and formation) Content Relationships Application Service and ministry	Any or all of the above	Kingdom	Total transformation of life and thought; focuses on the big picture of God and his kingdom

The first approach is a program-based model and focuses on man as part of a corporate entity. The second approach focuses on man the individual and his felt needs. The third places man in the context of small-group relationships and focuses more on society. These approaches zero in on man and his relation to God, with a secondary focus being man and his relationship to his fellow man.

Approach 1: The Program-based Model

The first model was primarily used before the 1950s. I call it an "informational or program-based model." It emphasizes sharing the most information with the most people, focusing on man in his community setting and his activities. This model stresses profession of faith in Christ as well as church membership and attendance. When people participate in church activities, worship, fellowship dinners, Sunday school, and small groups, they find it easy to openly declare their Christian faith. That others are doing the same creates a plausibility structure or a safe environment. For that group, the church becomes almost like a little Christian Shangri-La.

In church the Bible is read and biblical themes are taught, but outside that group environment people tend to put their faith on hold. This model often becomes a programmed (informational) approach to making disciples. We have learned from people like Marshall McLuhan that the methods can easily become the message and thus alter the message's original intent. That is why we must strongly insist that if our message is correctly defined, we must also use methods that will consistently enable us to communicate the message without changing its content or intent.

Approach 2: The Individual Model

During the early twentieth century, the church was divided between liberals and conservatives, with the liberals seeking to make a broad social application of its message at the expense of the proper gospel focus, and the conservatives reacting and withdrawing from the world and its challenges. This, along with the ineffectiveness of Approach 1, led to the development of a new model in the late 1940s and early 1950s. This second model was more of a "para-church" model. I call it the "individual model."

10

The individual model focuses on man and his relation to God, stressing the one-on-one relationship of the disciple to the discipler. In this model people accept Christ, usually because of someone's witness, and then either that person or someone else comes along to help the new Christian grow in Christ. This model calls for the new believer and his discipler or mentor to meet one-on-one or in a very small group. The focus is usually on reading the Bible, memorizing Scripture, learning to share the gospel, and prayer. This approach generally encourages the development of a neat list of things that we have to do to be a disciple. The individual model's effectiveness depends on the effectiveness of the one-on-one instruction received. This approach is stronger to the extent that it overlaps the program-based model, weaker to the extent that it stands alone. People like Billy Hanks, Bill Shell, and others have talked and written about the need to integrate this method with the church's method. As a matter of fact, all of us know people who profess to be Christians but who see no need for the church in their Christian experience. This model easily reinforces that concept.

Approach 3: The Small-Group Model

The third approach works within small groups. Like the second approach, it is what Robert Pazmiño calls a formational model, focusing on people, either one-on-one or in small groups. This particular relational model began in the 1960s. During the 60s and early 70s there were a host of groups growing up everywhere. Somewhat out of a reaction to rugged individualism and the need for more intense interpersonal relations, the "groupie" mentality emerged throughout the culture. The movement developed with the emergence of sensitivity groups and transactional psychology. At the same time groups such as Alcoholics Anonymous were experiencing some success. Their approach was based on building intense relationships where people in a small group generally made more progress than people alone or in a crowd.

In the small group there are usually activities such as sharing, praying, and studying the Bible or discussing a biblical topic. Since much of the Judeo-Christian history centered on small groups, this model naturally found a place in the life of God's people. House churches are well known to those who study early church history. As one writer expressed, "We have a need to belong, not to an undifferentiated mob, but to a handful of people with whom we can share our thoughts and feelings and with whom we can work to create something of lasting value."[4]

Robert Wuthnow writes that 40 percent of American adults currently take part in small diverse groups that meet regularly and offer care and support; two-thirds of them are connected to churches or synagogues.[5] This small-group model (built around the "felt needs" in a person's life) focuses on relationships and caring much more than on program or content.

Approach 4: The Kingdom Approach

The kingdom approach, which more fully lends itself to what I call the God-centered framework, not only incorporates these three models, but places them in the context of God's kingdom. It is informational, formational, and *transformational!* Not until we reach the transformational stage will we be discipled in the biblical sense of being transformed into a new person by changing the way we think, bringing every thought into captivity to obeying Christ, as Paul wrote in Romans 12 and 2 Corinthians 10, and not copying the behavior and customs of this world. This refers not just to our devotional or church life, but all of life. In the words of Abraham Kuyper, "There is not a square inch within the domain of our human life of which the Christ, who is the Sovereign over all, does not say, 'Mine.'"[6] All of life is a religious activity to be lived unto God.

The primary objectives of the kingdom approach of disciple making include knowing, understanding, and applying God's Word to all life. It also involves living lives more obedient to God's commands. Transforming the way a person thinks and lives is a key in serving and ministering to those who are the image bearers of God both inside and outside the church community. Bringing all thoughts captive to Christ is also essential. This kingdom model produces Christians with a self-conscious understanding of an all-pervasive philosophy of life. As Wuthnow emphasizes, the lordship of Christ will be reflected in how we use our money and other material resources for the kingdom.

The kingdom model does not separate faith and life (as though such were possible). It focuses on integrating God's truth into all areas of life, and because of that, it is not merely an academic, informational, or intellectual concept. The kingdom model applies to, serves, and ministers to all areas.

While Bible study is basic in the kingdom paradigm, we must also study all legitimate areas of life under the lordship of Christ—mathematics, science, history, law, psychology, and sociology. This model does not suggest that the church plays a lesser role in the process, for the church is the heart of the kingdom model. But the kingdom model paradigm is broader than the institutional church. (Chapter 3 will discuss the relationship of the church to the kingdom.)

Thus the kingdom approach is more comprehensive than the first three approaches above, although it should embrace aspects of all three. A God-centered or kingdom approach focuses on a right view of God, his relation to man, and man's to him, man's relationship to his fellow man, and to the world around him.

In the kingdom approach, Christian education not only deals with different institutions—home, church, state, and school—their relationships with one another and the world around us, it also deals with other spheres of life, such as science, history, mathematics, and law; therefore, *we are to have a Christian world-and-life-view*.

One thing that makes the kingdom framework important is its focus on the transformation of the individual, and its recognition of his or her uniqueness as an image bearer of God. There is no stereotyping in the kingdom, rather, we are to demonstrate our uniqueness as we minister and serve the Lord in our context. The kingdom model respects the individual's giftedness. Wherever we are in life, we are to serve the Lord's purpose; that is our reason for being.

Another thing that makes the kingdom focus important is that it offers a particular challenge to the rising generations to know the Word of God, to know the world around us, and to know ourselves. As we grow in that knowledge, we are reminded that Christian education is discipleship and discipleship is obedience to God in all things, because Christ is Lord of all.

While there may be a handful of colleges teaching from this kingdom perspective, such as Calvin College and Covenant College, not many churches in America, to my knowledge, are doing this. The approach used by Francis Schaeffer in L'Abri, Switzerland (though he also used the small group and one-to-one method) probably comes as close as any that I am familiar with to basing discipleship on the kingdom model (though that is my designation).

At this point I do not want to get into any how-to methods. Rather, I want to focus on understanding the kingdom framework or setting, which will in turn provide for us a way to develop our methodology. Parts 1 and 2 of this book will identify some necessary components of the method and describe some of the anticipated results, but in reality the kingdom framework will vary from individual to individual or group to group. I have evaluated too many programs that have attempted to create the impression that theirs is the right method of making disciples. There are many useful methods, but whatever way we choose to implement the process, we must not use a method that will compromise or alter the message of the gospel.

Also, I want to underscore that the kingdom model incorporates the gospel of truth. It starts and ends with the self-attesting Jesus Christ. "In him all things hang together." "In all things Christ preeminent." The kingdom model must not sacrifice the gospel, for without the gospel there is no substance to our efforts to make disciples. If one's world-and-life-view does not start with the self-attesting Christ of Scripture, then it will be an exercise in futility. On the other hand, the kingdom model involves more than Bible study, sharing, praying, and witnessing in the evangelistic sense; and it takes place within various settings. It is one thing to know the Bible content and another to know how to use that knowledge in everyday life.

AN OVERVIEW OF THE KINGDOM MODEL

I do not hesitate to refer to Christian education as disciple making. Contrary to the inadequate approaches we have described, Christian education is not merely program-centered or informational; neither is it only person-centered or formational; nor is it limited to any one institution or life area. It is God-centered, total-life-oriented, hence transformational. This is a process intentionally designed to help us think, act, and live differently. But the kingdom model does not produce stereotypes or cookie cutter disciples. As a matter of fact, operating within the kingdom model, we may reach different conclusions about many things, but there will be unity as regards the system involved. Christians may reach somewhat different conclusions on ethical issues. Some kingdom Christians may see things differently in the political arena, but all will operate with a world-and-life-view perspective as those options are dealt with. That's why my early quote from Jim Petersen is so important.

Transformation of life is our aim in making disciples. You cannot be discipled within the kingdom framework and not have your life orientation changed. You will develop a biblical world-and-life-view that is constantly reforming your thinking and living because that is the aim of the kingdom model.

A Further Word about the Word

God intends for those in his kingdom to be people of the Word in all of life. He intends for us to use the Word as our infallible guide to finally evaluate the broader area of truth. As the psalmist said, "*In your light do we see light*" (Ps. 36:9). He intends for us to learn his truth in all areas, using the Bible as our guide.

While we must pay particular attention to the Word of God in Scripture, because it is his word written, we must also seek to understand God's truth in all of life. We must remember there is no dichotomy between God's general and special revelation.

Therefore, we define Christian education as *a process of transmitting a world-and-life-view built on God's truth. That is the kingdom approach that must center on Jesus Christ and his Word.* "Education is the divinely instigated and humanly cooperative process whereby persons grow and develop in life, that is, in godly knowledge, faith, hope and love through Christ."[7] Norman De Jong holds that it is superfluous to use the adjective "Christian" with the word "education" simply because true education is education in truth and all truth is from God. Any education that is not Christian is not true education.[8] Education is a religious exercise, but not all religion in this fallen world is Christian. That is why we need to use God's Word as the foundation of all knowledge and education.

Recall here Paul's words in Romans 12:1–2 about being transformed into new persons by changing the way we think. Sadly, if the statistics are correct, our models of making disciples may be making people more spiritually aware, but they are not changing the way people think and live. Remember Barna's 10 percent—the number of professing Christians who have a self-conscious world-and-life-view. Also, James Engels and Will Norton suggest in *Contemporary Christian Communications: Its Theory and Practice* that there are converts to Christ whose worldviews have not changed at all since becoming a Christian. And following up on Charles Malik's statement that evangelism has the twofold task of saving the soul and saving the mind, J. P. Moreland and William Lane Craig comment: "Our churches are unfortunately overly populated with people whose minds, as Christians, are going to waste. As Malik observed, they may be spiritually regenerate, but their minds have not been converted; they still think like non-believers."[9]

The Bible states, "All things were created through him and for him"; thus in everything he [is] preeminent" (Col. 1:16, 18). It is legitimate for any institution (home, church, school) to study God's truth and to engage in Christian education, both formally and informally. But individuals must also be involved. Not only is this legitimate, but it must be done if there are to be a restoration and reclaiming of all things to the glory of Christ.

The kingdom approach to disciple making is aimed at transforming all of life, including ours, to the Lord. It intentionally communicates a lifestyle that is Christlike in every area, aiming at the sanctification process and the total transformation that Paul writes about in Romans 12:1–2.

Finally, we need to note a strategic point made in the Great Commission, Matthew 28:19–20 (see appendix 1). In those famous verses, Jesus connects disciple making with baptism. Because baptism is one of the two sacraments belonging to the church, we believe that he is here connecting disciple making with the church. "Teaching them to observe all that I have commanded you" is also clearly connected with the church.

Topics for Reflection or Discussion

1. Which of the three inadequate approaches to disciple making is most familiar to you; how has it impacted your life, particularly your worldview?

2. Which of the models described in this chapter does your church use for discipleship? It may vary somewhat from our description. If so, can you see the difference?

3. We noted that the three inadequate approaches are either informational or formational in focus, while the kingdom approach aims at transformation. How can we integrate the other two concerns into the kingdom approach?

4. The kingdom of God is the subject of chapter 3. Be certain that you understand the differences and similarities between the kingdom approach to making disciples and each of the other three described. What are some of the real differences? Keep in mind that the kingdom model requires a different paradigm than do the other three models described.

5. At this point in your reading how would you design a discipleship program in your church? Keep in mind that it may require a paradigm shift. Refer to your design throughout your reading of this book and make corrections where necessary.

Suggested Reading

De Jong, Norman. *Teaching for a Change.* Phillipsburg, N.J.: P&R Publishing, 2001. This book calls for education that aims for life transformation rather than merely transmitting information or content. Thus the purpose of De Jong's work is likewise making kingdom disciples, though in a school context.

Harper, Norman. *Making Disciples: The Challenge of Christian Education at the End of the 20th Century.* Memphis: Christian Studies Center, 1981. One of the key books on Christian education and disciple making within the kingdom. This book reflects a solidly biblical, Reformed view of the kingdom of God and the relation between the covenant of grace and the educational (disciple-making) process.

Pazmiño, Robert W. *Foundational Issues in Christian Education.* Grand Rapids: Baker, 1997. Realizing that Christian education does not take place in a vacuum, Pazmiño discusses seven foundational issues. He understands the need to balance continuity and change. Without altering the foundation, the book challenges us to "consider the new wineskins" for Christian education. Too often to be contemporary means to forget the basics. Or fearing new trends, we often react with, "But this is the way we have always done it." Here is indeed a "foundational" book.

———. *Principles and Practices of Christian Education: An Evangelical Perspective.* Grand Rapids: Baker, 1992. A good sequel to the above. Pazmiño elaborates on the transformational aspect of Christian education. He emphasizes the need for personal corporate transformation, as well as relating the process to specific people in their contexts.

2

Epistemology: What and How We Know

Why a chapter on epistemology so early in this book? Francis Schaeffer states, "Epistemology is the central problem of our generation; indeed, the so-called 'generation gap' is really an epistemological gap, simply because the modern generation looks at knowledge in a radically different way from the previous ones."[1] Epistemology is the study or theory of knowledge, particularly the how and what of the knowing process. God's concern incorporates both the *hows* and *whats* of our knowledge. Both are so interfaced with how we live that we must have some general understanding in this area.

In this chapter we will focus on helping the people we are discipling in two ways: first, they must have a solid base for knowing what they believe and why; and second, they must understand, as John said in 1 John 1:8, that God's truth is to be personalized "within us." Therefore, in this chapter we will concentrate on truth and knowledge as they relate both to God, the source of truth, and to us, the recipients of it. Our ultimate desire in making disciples is not only that God's truth be a part of our lives, but that we also practice it (1 John 1:6) faithfully and consistently.

A disciple is someone who lives not merely on faith, but also on knowledge and understanding. Thinking is not an afterthought. It is part of who we are, made in God's image and likeness. Imagine what happens with everything if our epistemology is off base. We can never really be certain of what we know or of the process of knowing it. That is a brief commentary on today's postmodern culture, where truth is whatever one wants it to be. Talking about truth is like trying to pick up Jell-O. As we will see, if truth is only what we want it to be or only what is true for me, then truth really makes no difference. As believers, just because we start with God's objective truth doesn't mean our subjective experience won't get off track, yet, we are more likely to succeed starting with God than if we start elsewhere.

Sometime ago I received an email with this sad, humorous, but all too true story about three umpires. I have since seen the same story quoted in Anderson's *Reality Isn't What It Used to Be*, and in J. Richard Middleton and Brain J. Walsh's book *Truth Is Stranger than It Used to Be*. The three umpires were drinking a beer after a baseball game and carrying on this conversation. One umpire says, "There's balls and there's strikes, and I call 'em the way they are." Another umpire said, "There's balls and there's strikes, and I call 'em the way I see 'em." The third umpire said, "There's balls and there's strikes, and they ain't nothing until I call 'em."

When Pilate asked Jesus, "What is truth?" (John 18:38), his question revealed a fundamental flaw that has been repeated over and over. We are in a state, especially today, where the answer given to that question has been so vague and unclear that the postmodernist tendency suggests the question is no longer relevant. What Jesus said to provoke Pilate's question has all too often been ignored; as a result, truth has been thought of merely as some abstract proposition that exists out there in some nebulous realm called objectivity. "I am the truth." If we read carefully Jesus' words, then we see that truth, hence knowledge, is not an impersonal concept, but is related to the person of Jesus Christ.

If what I know, or think I know, does not correlate to the person of Christ, then it is off base. Pilate's question is found in the Gospel of John, the same Gospel that begins with these words: "In the beginning was the Word, and the Word was with God, and the Word was God. He was in the beginning with God" (John 1:1–2). Each time the term "Word" is used in those verses, it is translated from the Greek word *logos*. From that term we derive not only our translation "Word" but also the term "logic." Most commentaries and word studies tend to focus on the logical, rational side of this term (i.e., its connotation of knowledge), but do not do justice to the personal aspect. The Word was and is God. God is a person. God is the personification of truth and knowledge. We have erred in trying to make knowledge something outside of and apart from relationships. John has not only said that the Word is God, but in verse 14 he says that the Word becomes flesh. This "person," referred to as the Word, is God, and God becomes flesh.

As we think about epistemology, it is essential that we do so in relation to God. There is no truth and knowledge apart from him. We are not God. He is outside of us and above his creation; therefore, we refer to his transcendence. Yet, as the biblical God, he is very present among us, hence his immanence. That is why there are both a subjective and an objective aspect to knowing, but never an impersonal one. Michael Polanyi the scientist and Lesslie Newbigin the philosopher-theologian did not invent the idea of personal knowledge. That started with the personal God.

The neoorthodox theologians of the first half of the twentieth century had the right idea; they simply went too far and landed on the subjective, existential side of the knowing equation that made truth dependent on man and his experience. However, we must not separate in some artificial scholastic manner the subjective and the objective in the knowing process, for God is truth and the source of all true knowledge.

To know God, the Truth, requires a personal faith commitment. All the God-talk we can manufacture is nothing if we do not know him. The challenge is to correlate what we believe to be true with what is actually true. We must be aware that our perceptions, assumptions, and descriptions come through our personal grids and filters. Often, how we perceive a text is so colored by our personal grids that we may miss the real point. If that is the case, we are wrong. This means that we must be sure that our personal grid or filters are ultimately faithful to biblical revelation.

As a young minister wanting to teach this concept, I used the phrase "epistemologically self-conscious" in one of my sermons. My general practice is not to use jargon or technical terms unless essential to the point; however, when it is necessary to use these words to instruct, I do so but then immediately define them. I defined "epistemologically self-conscious" as "being aware of what we know and how we know what we know." One of the older church members missed that definition and was quite exercised that I would use such a technical term. Sometimes it is necessary to use technical terms, and this is one of those times.

W. Jay Wood's thoughts on the nature of epistemology are worth quoting here:

> Careful oversight of our intellectual lives is imperative if we are to think well, and thinking well is an indispensable ingredient in living well. According to this tradition, only by superintending our cognitive life (the way, for example, we form, defend, maintain, revise, abandon and act on our beliefs about important matters) can we become excellent as thinkers and, ultimately, excellent as persons.[2]

It is my desire as God's disciple to be "epistemologically self-conscious" for two personal reasons. One is the scriptural teaching that "as [a man] thinks in his heart, so is he" (Prov. 23:7, NKJV; "he is like a man who is inwardly calculating," ESV). In Matthew 12:34 and 15:18 Jesus similarly refers to the impact of what comes out of the heart. Two, we can be extremely and unconsciously gullible, especially in our pop-culture environment, thus embracing ideas that are wrong and deadly.

In Romans 12 Paul begs us to be thinking beings. I like Romans 12 for many reasons, but mainly because as he begs us to be thinking beings, he goes on to say that thinking is not merely an academic exercise. It impacts our life and ministry. So, when we are mentally lazy, to use Wood's description, our lives quickly reflect that. As a result, there is not much depth to our faith, leaving us in a state of vulnerability.

Our country has gone through embarrassing and devastating situations with certain elected officials, and even with "church" representatives. The question has arisen whether a person's morals are private or whether they affect the whole of life. America is largely a country of adults who have not matured to adulthood morally and intellectually. Part of the problem is that we have not been given the epistemological framework to add depth to our faith and work it out into the rest of life.

In chapters 8 and 9 we will deal with postmodernism and the "generations." There are five generations presently living today, and nowhere is there more of a pronounced difference between the generations than in the area of how we know what we know. Schaeffer insightfully noted that the so-called generation gap is really an epistemological gap. He was right because as we examine postmodernism, focusing on the baby busters (generation X-ers) and the millennials, who are the first two postmodern generations, we observe a definite paradigm shift in knowledge, as well as in the knower and what is known.

To place this in some historical perspective is always valuable because understanding where we come from can help us understand both where we are and where we are going. We can divide history into three sections or eras. The first is the *premodern* period that began before the Protestant Reformation of the sixteenth century and lasted until a brief time after that. The second is the *modern* period from the early eighteenth century until the mid-twentieth century. The third period is the *postmodern* period beginning with the mid-twentieth into the twenty-first century. The reason for this particular division relates to truth, authority, and knowledge. What and how we know (epistemology) differ in each of these periods.

In *premodern* times the criteria of knowledge, truth, and authority were based on revelation and faith in God. Regardless of whether one was a Christian or not, God was at the center in the premodern model. Faith and believing were the beginning points of the knowing pattern.

There was a relationship between the knower and the known. Reason, logic, and empiricism were trusted to a lesser degree. This was also a time of much superstition and the belief in magic. Nonetheless, there was the idea of universal truth, which emanated from God through revelation. There was a clear distinction in premodern times between God the Creator and man the creature, made in God's image and likeness. God was over and above his creation, yet personally related to it.

With the arrival of the *modern period*, a shift in the epistemological paradigm occurred. Though this period, often referred to as the Enlightenment period or the Age of Reason, still allowed for the existence of God and revelation, the focus shifted from revelation to reason. Man became the final reference point. Instead of thinking God's thoughts after him, as in premodern times, man now assumed the role of an original thinker, and God, if and when included in the process, became the reflective thinker. This was the time of the scientific and industrial revolutions. Reason, logic, and the empirical scientific method of investigation became king, and man put his faith in those things.

The epistemological methodology focused on objectivity: knowledge is something out there, literally removed from the knower. A deep cleavage developed between God and knowledge, and hence between man and knowledge. There was a definite attempt to separate the knower from the known. Everything in the realm of knowledge had to be factual. It had to fit within the rational laws of logic, and it had to be understood and explained by man. Though there was the inclusion of the empirical and to a lesser degree the experiential, the main focus was on the objective knowledge discovered by man. Though man was the final determiner, what he knew was out there, outside of self.

(Incidentally, much of our evangelical and Reformed paradigm for doing Bible study, exegesis of texts, and theology itself reflects the scientific method developed in this modern era. This is evident in everything from calling theology the queen of the sciences to using the empirical method and scientific investigation to develop much of eighteenth-, nineteenth-, and twentieth-century theology. Many of our fathers in the faith used those same cultural tools. I am a bit puzzled at times when I hear or read that we should not use cultural tools in theology, yet we turn around and quote those men of great theological acumen who used them regularly. Clearly, culture colors our epistemology.)

The *postmodern era* brings us to another obvious shift in the paradigm. There was a huge swing surfacing in the twentieth century, especially from the 1950s. Hints of this coming shift were already abroad with the existential philosophers who were looking inward, focusing on man, his being, and his experience as a standard of truth and knowledge. The factual, logical, rational, scientific empiricism of the modernists such as David Hume and René Descartes was rejected, and knowledge was concentrated more and more on the knower, the self, and personal experience. Hence, without being too simplistic, truth and knowledge have become whatever we want them to be, and that is generally based on our experience and certainly our choice. In this culture, one might even feel free to manipulate or deconstruct history and reconstruct it to make it say what he wants it to say, or to use words to mean whatever he wants them to mean.

Like the modernist, postmodern man takes center stage and is the reference point of knowledge. But unlike the modern focus on a realm of objective knowledge and truth, these rational, logical aspects are now passé. Postmodern man has chosen simply to operate on the axiom that truth is whatever we want or need it to be for any particular occasion. Truth may vary from person to person, context to context, and moment to moment. That is why I likened postmodern epistemology to Jell-O. It is hard to grasp anything solid because there are no universals or absolute truths in this paradigm. Karl Marx's statement "All that is solid melts into air," is descriptive of postmodernism. Revelation, if it is entertained at all, is so subjectively determined that God can be whatever we want him to be, even nothing if we so choose.

The tragedy of the developments of the last four hundred years, especially in the West, is that truth and knowledge have been divorced from the person of God. That divorce has been subtle and yet obvious. But to talk about truth as something inside us that doesn't correlate to anything outside of our own lives is just as wrong as talking about truth as something totally objective and outside ourselves.

N. T. Wright seems to be on the right track when he says that knowledge is never independent of the knower.[3] To know something is to sustain some kind of relationship with what we know. That is why we spoke earlier about the personal side to knowledge. What we know has its base in something objective, something outside ourselves, but once we say "I" or "we" know, we are involved in the personal and subjective side of the equation. That does not imply that what we call knowledge does not exist apart from our knowing it, but only that we can know it personally.

One of the reasons today's generation has such a problem with authority is that for them it is a concept either divorced from God or associated with something less than a biblical revelation of God. Or it is merely related to a concept of tradition that doesn't seem to have much to offer today's generation, because it is so impersonal.

God-Interpreted Thinking

The only consistently satisfying approach to epistemology and the entire theory of knowledge comes from starting with the personal God who is the truth and the revealer of truth to his people. Every other position will come up short of correlating to reality. Only that which begins with God will satisfy our need to know the truth.

The psalmist said, "How precious to me are your thoughts, O God! How vast is the sum of them!" (Ps. 139:17). Because we are made in God's image and likeness, we cannot help but think about God even though in sin we try to suppress the truth. Even in our attempt to deny him, as the atheists claim to do, we have to first affirm him to deny him.

Our thoughts of God are not always precious because they are not always right. We are living in a biblically illiterate time. George Gallup Jr., George Barna, and others have clearly documented that. To think precious thoughts about God that are true and right, we cannot merely think our thoughts. We must think his thoughts after him. We must start with

God and think about him as he reveals himself in the world around us, but especially in his written Word. What we think and know about God must correspond to what He knows and reveals to us, or we will be off track.

Remember our opening quote from Schaeffer. If we are off base in our epistemology, then everything else will be off. God is the basis of what and how we know. We must have a right knowledge of God and know how to facilitate the knowing process on that basis. That will ultimately meet the deepest needs of our life.

God has taken the initiative and unveiled himself to us so we may know him who is the truth. That is why we cannot separate objective truth from the subjective person or knower. We cannot know God simply objectively because he is the personal Triune God. Knowledge of him requires a relationship with him.

To illustrate this concept: one of the frequently discussed issues in today's Christian world is creation. Did God create us, or were we the result of some evolutionary process of chance? Did we evolve from the primordial slime moving through different stages of existence until finally becoming an upright, thinking, and feeling being? While the Bible was not given to be a textbook on science, it was written to communicate truth. Therefore, if we believe anything contrary to the written Word, then what we believe and claim to know is in error. Genesis 1 states that God created in six days. Without getting sidetracked into the different possible definitions of "day" in the Bible, if we conclude that God created in four days or twelve days, then we are in error because that does not correlate to what God says in the Scripture.

God has communicated his truth to us in two books, the book of nature (creation) and the Bible, sometimes called the book of his work and the book of his word. We often refer to these as general revelation and special revelation. We can and must be faithful to our original responsibility to "be fruitful, multiply, and subdue the earth." That requires that we be students of both books. In that process we must not make either book into what God never intended it to be and do. In the book of nature, we study, observe, experiment, and gain evidences in our search for truth. But to keep our study and conclusions on target, we must correlate what we learn from those areas with what God says in his Word in order to check our conclusions. He has given us his Word and Spirit to help us stay on course. There is no contradiction between the two books. Though God's truth is multifaceted, his truth is one unified whole with no loose ends. All truth is God's truth, and that truth will not contradict itself.

That we are able to know God has many implications. For instance, because he is the Creator God and we are his creatures, we can never know everything that God knows. That means that we can never know anything exhaustively. Just think how refreshingly satisfying that is! Only God has comprehensive and complete knowledge. Unlike the Greeks who maintained that to know anything, we must know everything, the Christian says that even though we cannot know all that there is to know because we see through a glass darkly, because we are finite, and because we are sinners, yet we can know truth.

God knows all things originally and truly, and we can know him; therefore we can know things analogically and derivatively. But what does knowing analogically mean? Robert Reymond explains it like this:

> There are three possibilities as they relate to knowledge . . . we can know things univocally (the same) or equivocally (different) or analogically (partly alike and partly not alike). If I assert that an analogy may be drawn between an apple and an orange, do I not intend to suggest that the apple and the orange, obviously different in some respects, are the same in at least one respect?[4]

Knowing by analogy is the best way to explain and preserve the Creator/creature distinction. The further marvel of it all is that God has chosen to reveal "true truth" to us. As the truth himself, he has chosen to do this anthropomorphically, that is, in human terminology, in order that we might be able to study, understand, and explain reality. As long as what we know corresponds to what he knows, we can have a satisfying confidence in what we know, though we know in part, as Paul said in 1 Corinthians 13.

On the other hand, the eclectic approach of the postmodernists proves utterly chaotic as they try to come to truth and knowledge without a universal reference point. There is no unifying element in postmodernism, and that is why truth is so relative and reality and truth are "stranger than they used to be." Postmodernists are always trying to fill the void of no universals with what I call "momentary, fleeting universals or absolutes." (Of course those do not exist.) What they see, experience, and conclude about things is not trustworthy because their grid is faulty. They cannot be certain that they have seen reality as it really is.

One of the most descriptive terms of man's attempt to understand reality, truth, and knowledge today is "solipsism," that is, making reality to be whatever he wants it to be. Therefore, being what Lesslie Newbigin has referred to as students of truth and knowledge, we have also become the judges of truth and knowledge. Yet our biases and filters color our judgments; hence, we do not always see things clearly. A Hawaiian prophet once said, "You create a universe by perceiving it."[5]

A Reliable Checks-and-Balances Approach

Truth, though subjectively experienced, must involve more than our interpretation. We must seek to eliminate our personal biases as much as humanly possible. What we know or claim to know is a result of what we believe. Our knowledge is so based on our senses, our experiences, and traditions that it is difficult, if not impossible, to evaluate what we know without a reliable reference point.

We need a checks-and-balances approach to what we know and why. When I first began to read Francis Schaeffer, I wondered why he used the phrase "true truth." I came to realize that in our postmodern world we tend to use words esoterically that are vital to the communicating process. If truth is whatever one wants it to be, then words can mean whatever one wants them to mean. Schaeffer used the phrase "true truth" to remind us that truth must be related to God. Regardless of what we call truth, if it does not correspond to God's truth, then it is not true truth.

If this postmodern generation wants to talk about experiences, benefits, and pluses in life, to know God and truth is the best benefit one could have to that end. He is not only a friend who sticks closer than a brother; he is the reference point that defines reality, truth, and life. How that plays out is that he has given us a primary and secondary plumb line, a standard of measure of truth. The primary is in his written Word. Hence we say that he is our final reference point as he speaks in his Word and by his Spirit. The Bible becomes our criterion for measuring truth. It is our rule of faith and practice, as the Westminster divines reminded us. Also, God has given us another check and balance in the knowing process, and that is each other. Though some have been hesitant in evangelical circles to include the community in the knowing process, we must not make that mistake. Along with his Word and Spirit, God has placed us in the body of Christ as a secondary measure. In the believing community we must learn how to work together, tradition and all, to help us know the truth. Second Peter 1:20 states, "*No prophecy of Scripture comes from someones own interpretation.*"

While God reveals to us objective truth, we cannot know it purely objectively. But God never intended that we should. Or as the philosophers, following Immanuel Kant, might say, we cannot know a thing in itself, but we can know because the sovereign God has revealed his truth to us. The knower and the known must not be divorced. Remember, as we have said, that all knowing involves subjective personal knowing; hence knowledge involves the personal. Actually, it is an illusion to believe that the knower and the known can be separated. Therefore, using God's checks and balances, we must work to assure ourselves that our filters are not distorting God's knowledge and truth. True knowledge cannot be separated from God, nor can it be known apart from our knowing it. That is not intended to imply that truth is not truth until we know it. But it does suggest that we cannot know truth with pure objectivity. That is why those primary and secondary checks and balances are essential in the knowing process.

With the transitions from premodern to modern to postmodern we have seen how each paradigm led to the next. At the beginning of the progression we have what is called the thesis, which states what something is. Then we have the antithesis, the opposite of the thesis. If something is true, its opposite is false. This method of epistemology stood through premodern and most of modern times. However, during the later modern period a new scheme called the synthesis was introduced and made popular by the German idealist George W. F. Hegel. A synthesis is basically a result of the collision between the thesis and antithesis. With the introduction of the synthesis, no longer was it sufficient to say that if one thing is true, then the opposite is not true. But if one thing is true and the opposite is not true, there may arise from that confrontation a new truth called the synthesis. From there the process starts over. From the synthesis a new thesis and a new antithesis arise. Hence truth is always evolving. As an example, take the thesis that white is white. The antithesis is that white is black. The synthesis is gray, produced by the collision of white and black. Then the gray collides with whatever rises to oppose it, and this produces something different.

Thesis + Antithesis = Synthesis = Thesis + Antithesis = Synthesis

This dialectic is just a short step from postmodernism, which bypasses the thesis and antithesis (jumping straight to the synthesis) by embracing the attitude that truth is what is expedient or we determine it to be. Recognizing that no people or culture is neutral or objective, and having no way to transcend subjectivism and thereby settle conflicting claims (because "there are no metanarratives"), postmodernists resign themselves to a knowing process wherein truth is relatively determined from moment to moment, from place to place.

All of this illustrates why it is essential to understand that in the realm of knowledge and truth and in the knowing process God must be the final reference point. If he is not, we are left without a standard whereby

32

we may know reality. We must begin with the personal Triune God in what we know and how we know what we know. We must see the personal aspect of the knowing process and understand why knowing God truly is essential to all true knowledge.

Cornelius Van Til wrote a series of science articles for the *Banner* during the 1930s. In one of his articles he uses the following illustration to point to the necessity of God in true knowledge:

> I see a cow. I say it is an animal. But what is an animal? To answer that question fully I should be able to say what life is, for a cow is a living thing. I watch the cow eat grass. Does grass live too? Yes it does. The grass grows out of the ground. Does the ground live also? No it does not. But some say that it does. At any rate I see that the lifeless is indispensable for the living. Hence I cannot say what life is unless I can also say what the ground is. I cannot really say what a cow is until I can tell what the whole of physical reality is. But now comes a still greater difficulty. We are ourselves a part of this reality. That might seem at first sight to give us the advantage of an inside view. But it would certainly have the disadvantage of only an inside view.... Suppose there is a God. He will have the best "outside" view of us."[6]

Van Til goes on to develop the idea of the indispensability of our knowledge of God and his knowledge of us. Our knowledge of ourselves, he maintains, would be wholly wrong if it did not correspond to his knowledge of us. Then Van Til demonstrates that this kind of knowledge between God and man is also essential in knowing anything in his creation. While it is true that I do not have to know what a cow is in order to benefit from its dairy by-products, to know the cow, I must know God and I must know myself. They are all interrelated. But even with that I must also understand that I can never exhaustively know what a cow is. If there is just one area where we can know anything without God, then God is not God. If I claim to know anything that does not correspond to what God knows, then I need a course correction.

Common Grace in Epistemology

If we cannot know anything without God, how can an unbeliever ever know anything? That is a valid question. God is so wise and sovereign that he knows when, where, and how to help man along with the process of epistemology. He used men like Abraham Kuyper, Herman Bavinck, Cornelius Van Til, and others to help us understand a doctrine called "common grace," which builds on the truth that God created man in his image and likeness. Though the fall into sin greatly damaged that image, and though sin robbed man of the truth as God had given it, he did not completely lose his likeness to God in the fall; therefore, that image remains the point of contact between God the Creator and man the creature. It is also the point of contact between human beings.

John Calvin often has been quoted as saying that everyone has a sense of deity within him. Although he can and does suppress it, it is operating day after day. Otherwise unbelieving man could not function or accomplish anything. Van Til explains, "To not know God, man would have to destroy himself. He cannot do this. There is no realm of non-being into which man can slip in order to escape God's face and voice. The mountains will not cover him; Hades will not hide him. Nothing can prevent his being confronted with him with whom we have to do."[7] This also explains how believers and unbelievers can join together and seek to carry out God's cultural mandate. By God's common grace we operate, though not always self-consciously, on the premise that there is true knowledge because of God. It is understandable that the unbeliever would not have this self-consciousness about what he knows, but it is inexcusable that a believer would forget God's grace and exalt the knowledge of man. God is the final reference point in knowing for both believer and unbeliever alike.

The truth is that God's common grace is bestowed upon believers and unbelievers; and because fallen depraved man cannot totally deny God and his relation to him, he is still a beneficiary of God's truth, at least in the general sense. The unbeliever, though he does not know God savingly, does know God creatively, according to the apostle Paul in Romans 1:19–32. He knows certain things about God, but that knowledge is totally dependent on and determined by God's graciousness. To illustrate this: man is a depraved sinner, but because of God's gracious attitude he is not as depraved as he is capable of being. As a result, unbelieving man can join with the believers in accomplishing some of God's original design in creation. Henry Meeter summarizes: "From the writings of Scripture and from the teachings of Calvin, we learn that God does have an attitude of favor, or grace, to the non-elect, and that this common grace will one day add to their punishment, because it did not lead them to repentance and life for God."[8]

Common grace bears on epistemology in that it reminds us that an unbeliever, bent on denying the Triune God, is totally dependent on Him to know anything. As Jesus tells us in Matthew 5:45, God causes his rain to fall on the just and the unjust. He can and does reveal truth to the nonbeliever. God is the origin or author of truth. Man is created in his image and likeness; hence, man can know truth, not exhaustively or comprehensively, but truly, because of God's gracious self-revelation. Though the fall greatly impaired the image of God in man and touched every part of his life, it did not destroy that image, nor did it cause God to withdraw or to cease revealing himself to mankind in general. Though sinful man insists on denying and suppressing the truth, God nonetheless in his gracious kindness continues to reveal himself to all mankind. And because of his common grace, even the unbelieving man operating on borrowed principles can from time to time learn certain things about God and truth that do not threaten but actually help the believing person (Einstein's discovery of the theory of relativity, for example). That general knowledge is also the important point of contact in the relationship between the believer and the unbeliever, and it is on that basis that we can love our enemies and work with them patiently and cautiously because they too are made in the image and likeness of God.

Conclusion

As we reflect upon history, from creation, especially the Garden of Eden, until today, we find two basic schools of epistemology in operation. Though there are variations, there are, in the end, only the two schools. The first school holds that knowledge starts with the Triune God. Our entire knowledge is based upon him and his revelation. When using our rational capabilities or empirical senses in the knowing process, we do so with the understanding that what we think and observe is dependent upon God's revelation. That was the original position in creation. When God's grace later overruled the entrance of sin, he created a legacy that has continued until this day through both Testaments, through people like Augustine, Thomas Aquinas (to a lesser degree), John Calvin, Abraham Kuyper, Cornelius Van Til, John Frame, Greg Bahnsen, and many other Christian thinkers.

The second school was introduced in the opening of Genesis in the garden when Adam and Eve were successfully tempted by the serpent to embrace the second theme: man does not need to depend totally, if at all, on God for knowledge and truth. Therefore, man has the ability, apart from God, to have true knowledge. God's revelation is not a necessary ingredient. Man can use his rational and logical facilities as well as his empirical senses and experiences to know the truth. Man can actually make truth to be whatever he wants it to be. That lineage began in the garden with Satan's temptation and continues to be obvious through the Testaments and throughout history with people like Plato, Aristotle, Descartes, John Locke, Immanuel Kant, Friedrich Nietzsche, and postmodernists.

Knowledge, truth, and authority hold up only if God is the way, the truth, and the life. If he is, and we believe him to be so, then our knowledge must come from him, and what we know must correspond to what he knows. By his Word and Spirit and with the faithfulness of the Christian community, we can work together to gain a greater and more accurate understanding of truth.

As we try to understand and further clarify our roles in God's service, I believe that the postmodern period, while off base in its ideology regarding truth, knowledge, and authority, is forcing us to think more relationally and experientially in all areas. Epistemology is one of those areas

---

where the pendulum had swung too far by following a more classical or traditional Enlightenment model. Relationships and experience are vital in the learning process. We must keep our biblical focus in epistemology, which will bring us more and more to the realization that knowledge and truth are personal. They are intended to be believed, practiced, and applied to everyday life. Knowledge and truth are intended by God to make a difference in the way we think, live, and relate to him, to the world around us, and to one another. Those are the things that the younger generations are searching for in their quest.

TOPICS FOR REFLECTION OR DISCUSSION

1. Read Proverbs 1:1–7.
   a. What are the implications and applications of verse 7 as it relates to epistemology?
   b. Where does wisdom fit into the subject of epistemology?
   c. Read Proverbs 1:29 and discuss the relation between knowledge and the fear of God.
2. Read Romans 1:19–32.
   a. What does this passage say about God?
   b. What does it say about man?
   c. What is the significance of Paul's teaching in this passage?
   d. How does this passage underscore Schaeffer's comments regarding epistemology?
3. Read Psalm 139.
   a. This passage teaches many truths, but what implications does it have for epistemology?
   b. What does it say about God's knowledge and those who know God?
   c. What are the similar truths taught in this passage and Romans 1:19–32?
4. Read Romans 12.

a. Note how Paul, after challenging the readers not to be squeezed into the world's mold, shows them how to be salt and light. Discuss this chapter with that in mind. How have we been or can we be squeezed into the world's mold or conformed to the ways of the world? What are the results?

5. Have the entire group or subgroups discuss selected items from the list below.

a. Explain and discuss the importance of epistemology.
b. Read John 18:36–39. Discuss the dialogue between Pilate and Jesus. What is the message here?
c. What does it mean to be epistemologically self-conscious, and what is its significance?
d. How do the three periods in history relate to epistemology?
e. How does epistemology actually connect the objective part of knowing with the personal or subjective part?
f. How do truth and knowledge (epistemology) impact our concept of authority?
g. Where do reason, logic, and empiricism fit into epistemology?
h. What do the knower and the known have to do with epistemology?
i. What are the implications of the knower and the known in this process of knowing? Discuss the difference between objective and subjective.
j. How do we think God's thoughts after him?
k. What is the connection between the doctrine of common grace and epistemology?
l. What keeps us from knowing things exhaustively, and why is this important?
m. How does epistemology affect our relationships?

6. How does the knowledge of God impact our relationships vertically and horizontally, that is, with God, each other, and creation?

7. Spend time developing an action plan that will enable members of the group to use this study of epistemology in their daily lives.

8. Spend time praying for one another and the preaching and teaching of truth around the world.

Suggested Reading

Frame, John M. *The Doctrine of God.* Phillipsburg, N.J.: P&R Publishing, 2002. Several chapters relating to epistemology that complement the earlier book *The Doctrine of the Knowledge of God.*

Mark, Esther Lightcap. *Longing to Know.* Grand Rapids: Brazos, 2003. An approach similar to that suggested in this chapter. She writes clearly with valuable insights into epistemology, particularly the personal side of knowledge.

Van Til, Cornelius, *The Defense of the Faith.* Philadelphia: Presbyterian and Reformed, 1955. A standard classic dealing with apologetics and epistemology.

Wood, W. Jay. *Epistemology: Becoming Intellectually Virtuous.* Downers Grove, Ill.: InterVarsity, 1998. A popular, easy read on the topic of epistemology. Some good insights into the personal and relational aspects of epistemology.

3

The Kingdom of God

In *The Other Six Days*, R. Paul Stevens deals with the idea of the priesthood of all believers and seeks to nullify the dichotomy within the church that has developed since the end of the first century A.D. His position is that God's people are one people with no separate clergy-laity dichotomy though there is a distinction in gifts and offices. Within the one people we have different roles and assignments, but we are all one among equals, the people of God.

Despite what others may say, it is important for a disciple, especially a new disciple, to understand that as a believer he or she is a member of the kingdom of God as well as the church. This kingdom concept has implications for theology, mission, and ministry. A disciple's life involves all three areas, and how accurately we understand our place will determine how we live as disciples.

Three misconceptions about *theology* have developed down through church history. First, theology is a conceptual, abstract, or theoretical category with its practice tacked on somewhere afterwards. Second, professionals study theology so they can dumb it down for the ordinary church member. Third, since the Enlightenment period, theology has become a specialized science rather than a way of life for all of God's people. These misconceptions, which will be discussed further in chapter 5, must be acknowledged and corrected.

In *mission* that same mindset applies: that to serve the Lord one either has to be a preacher or missionary, requiring either ordination or commissioning for such a task. "Ordinary" people of God are not part of the church's active mission.

In *ministry* again the implications are present. Only the professionals do the work of ministry, or as Stevens says, the ordinary Christian is the object (receiver) of ministry but not the subject (doer) of ministry. This clearly suggests that ministry is not something the ordinary Christian does.

Part of my reason for writing this book is the growing concern that we do not appear to have a biblical perspective on what being a disciple really is. Without that clear idea, the right way to make disciples is only a shot in the dark. Therefore, lacking that clear definition, we have had to develop various, often random, programs and methods for church growth and "discipling" the people. It is no wonder that the statistics mentioned earlier underscore the lack of a holistic perspective on what a disciple is.

Cornelius Plantinga in *Engaging God's World* has said, "Given Jesus' summons, his followers have always understood that to be a 'Christ person' is to be a 'kingdom person.' Working in the kingdom is our way of life. And many followers have concluded that we need powerful Christian education to learn how to serve the kingdom most intelligently."[1]

Throughout this book I want to keep before us that a disciple is someone who not only follows Jesus but who also cares for or has a heart for the things that God does in all of life. I stand against the idea that a disciple is someone who goes through a limited checklist of activities. A kingdom disciple cannot be satisfied by his personal prayer life or Bible study or personal witnessing, as though they had some special elevated place within the Christian life. Many Christians have the notion that there are both legitimate sacred and legitimate secular aspects to life. Many methods of "discipling" have fed that notion. But if we have the right kingdom perspective, then we will know that there is no area of life about which God is not concerned and over which he is not the sovereign Lord. The apostle Paul says, "So, whether you eat or drink, or whatever you do, do all to the glory of God" (1 Cor. 10:31).

Following God's Word in the disciple-making process, it is essential to think biblically about the kingdom of God. Sadly, our studies, research, and experience tell us that people have no clear concept of the kingdom of God. While some see it merely as synonymous with the church, others see no connection between the kingdom and the church. There is also the confusion regarding the present kingdom and the "not yet" aspect of the kingdom. Yet the idea of the kingdom is absolutely basic to Christianity. The kingdom of God or the kingdom of heaven was Jesus' main theme in the Gospels. He began his ministry on the theme "the kingdom of heaven is at hand" (see Matt. 4:17). He told Nicodemus in John 3 that unless he was born again, he would not see the kingdom of God. This is basic!

The kingdom of God approach for making disciples will have a transforming impact on all of our life and not simply a part. So we must understand what the kingdom of God is. We must not bypass this in the early stages of making disciples.

In the New Testament we read the phrases "kingdom of God" and "kingdom of heaven." Without going into lengthy exegetical discourse or biblical history, we note that those terms refer to the same thing. (One reason for the two different phrases is that the Jews were so hesitant to use the word "God," they often substituted something else, like "heaven," or they simply left a blank for God.) In using the idea of the kingdom, the Bible seeks to underscore the kingship of Jesus Christ, in terms of both the total creational *realm* over which he is sovereign and his *reign* over all dimensions of his subjects' lives.

One of the distinguishing characteristics of the kingdom model of making disciples is that it focuses on God not man. Jesus, not man, is the King of his kingdom. We are his people obligated to honor, bow down to, and serve the King. When we think about the idea of kingdom (realm and reign), there is no area of life where we are not to serve him. Unless we begin the discipling process with our focus on God, we will focus on man, and that is to focus on formation rather than transformation. That, we believe, is what is wrong with so many of the methods and models that have been and are being used. Disciples are to focus on the Lord in all things and not on ourselves as his disciples.

Also, along with focusing on the Lord God as the center of the process, the kingdom model will help us understand how to relate to others and to the world around us. It will enable us to understand both the continuity and the discontinuity of the church and the kingdom. It will remind us that the kingdom is present now, but it will also come in its fullness at the end of the age. Beyond these things, the kingdom model will also keep us from misunderstanding what the Christian life really is: present and future.

In the next chapter we will discuss a biblical world-and-life-view. If we have a right concept of the kingdom of God, a biblical world-and-life-view will be a natural outcome. A. A. Milne, famous for his *Winnie the Pooh* stories, wrote a novel entitled *Two People*, which focuses on Mr. Pump. Mr. Pump was a haberdasher and a very devoutly religious man. He was so religious in fact that he would not dare carry his religion into the marketplace because it was too sacred. To illustrate this, he had two hats, one for his marketplace role and another for his Sunday morning churchgoing role. He would not dare confuse the two hats because Sunday was for the Lord's work and Monday through the end of the week was for the marketplace. He stated, "After all, no man can serve two masters at one and the same time." Mr. Pump was right in seeing a *distinction* between the church and the marketplace, but he was wrong to create a sacred/secular *division* by suggesting that the two do not mix.

This story serves to help us understand that in this life we do have somewhat of a dual role. On the one hand it does appear that Christians wear two hats, but on the other hand, and more correctly, we wear only one hat. We are to be "in the world but not of the world." We are members of both God's kingdom and his church. We may say that we wear two hats because there is a difference between the two; however, on the other hand we clearly wear only one hat because Christ is Lord over all.

There are many well-meaning churchgoers who think like Mr. Pump. They think that they are to serve the Lord on Sunday, but one has to be a professional clergyman or staff member to serve the Lord during the week in some church-related ministry. Selling clothes, keeping house, and teaching school are not religious or sacred activities, but secular occupations that have no religious connotation.

Understanding the all-inclusiveness of the kingdom will remind us that everything we do is a religious activity and is to be done to the glory of God. Having adopted this mind-set, I suggested on many occasions a ministry approach that we were beginning to implement in my last pastorate. We called it an "every member a minister" program. Of course our aim was not that we wanted every Christian to become a minister or missionary commissioned to serve the Lord in a professional sense. We were intentionally trying to communicate that serving the Lord by using our spiritual gifts is not merely a Sunday activity or reserved for church professionals. It is a daily process for all of God's people. The implications are obvious. No matter what we are doing on any day of the week, we are to serve the Lord.

The present evidence suggests the kingdom concept is not being communicated to new Christians from the outset or even to mature Christians down the road; therefore, the Christian life has been split into Mr. Pump's sacred and secular realms. One way this faulty notion plays out is in our thinking the local pastor or the foreign missionary is more spiritual in his daily routine than is the person in the marketplace or on the home front because he is serving the Lord. But the Bible does not teach such an arbitrary separation. All Christians, regardless of their work, are to do all to the glory of God. Religious activities are a seven-days-a-week process. There is no dimension that is secular or nonreligious, for all of life is sacred with spiritual implications.

Over the years I have counseled with those either frustrated with or burned out in their work, feeling no satisfaction from what they have been doing. No small number have asked, Is this God's way of telling me that I need to quit my job, go to seminary, and become a preacher or a missionary? Most if not all the counselees expressed a real desire to serve the Lord, but felt they were not doing that in their present occupation; it was only a secular occupation. In those situations my procedure has always been to review the kingdom model of vocation with them before dealing with the possibility of a change. There have been several occasions where we determined that God was leading in a different direction and initiating some change but not necessarily toward seminary or the foreign mission field. On the other hand, there have been those who concluded that full-time Christian employment in ministry was indeed the way to go. Still others decided to remain in their professions but with a new attitude.

What Is the Kingdom?

What is the kingdom of God or kingdom of heaven? It is vital for us to understand this, if we are to implement the kingdom of God model for making disciples. I will try to keep the response basic but not simplistic. I will suggest further reading at the end of the chapter for those wishing to do more study on the topic. There are important aspects such as the antithesis between the kingdom of God and the kingdom of the world that I will not deal with in this chapter but that must be included in our thinking about the kingdom. I hope to demonstrate that antithesis and tension throughout this book, especially in Part 2.

In regard to our question, note first that the psalmist has answered very clearly in Psalm 103:19, "The LORD has established his throne in the heavens, and his kingdom rules over all." The psalmist states here a basic belief of the Christian faith: God is the Creator and sovereign over all his creation. The reference to "his kingdom" indicates that it is all-inclusive.

The essence of the kingdom of God concept is mostly, now, a reference to God's *rule* and *reign*. "His kingdom" in verse 19 further suggests that as the King, God is the lawgiver and authority over his kingdom, which includes his people. From the Old Testament it is clear that the prophets, especially men like Daniel and Isaiah, saw God ruling over his kingdom now, though not yet in its fullness.

Second, because God the lawgiver is the personal theistic God, we must understand the *relational* aspect of the kingdom, which is both present and yet to come. As people of his kingdom, we come to realize that he touches our lives at every level. There is no area that does not belong to him.

Third, in the New Testament the apostle Paul refers to the future aspect of the kingdom: "Therefore God has highly exalted him and bestowed on him the name that is above every name, so that at the name of Jesus every knee should bow, in heaven and on earth and under the earth, and every tongue confess that Jesus Christ is Lord, to the glory of God the Father" (Phil. 2:9–11).

Both the Old and New Testaments present the idea that the kingdom of God is coming. Yet in fact, with the coming of Jesus Christ, it has already come (Mark 1:15). We also remember, however, that it will come in its fullness when Christ comes again at the end of the age. That is the moment when Philippians 2:10–11 will be finally and completely realized.

We need to keep the past, present, and future aspects of the kingdom in mind, especially the present and future, because some have said that what we have now, regarding the kingdom, is all that we are going to have. Others have maintained that the kingdom's coming is a totally future event with no present reality.

One of the things that I was glad to have learned early on in my Christian life was that the establishing of the kingdom, present and future, is entirely of God's doing. Meredith Kline refers to God's intrusion between the creation and consummation (the end); it is in God's intrusion, during that interval between the beginning and the end, that he establishes his kingdom.[2] You remember the story. God told Adam that he would certainly die if he ate of the tree of knowledge of good and evil. When we read that Adam disobeyed and ate of the tree, we expect God's judgment immediately to fall. But instead, God intruded and said, in effect,

46

"I will pronounce my final judgment in my own time. Meanwhile, I am going to set into motion a plan of redemption that will undo the damage caused by Adam's sin." This is something only God could do; man is the recipient of God's grace.

For purposes of this book we realize that the kingdom of God has come. It is present with us because Christ has come and is here in his Spirit. Yet God's kingdom is also a future eschatological event ("not yet"). There is more to come, a time when God will "put all things in subjection under his feet" (1 Cor. 15:27). Is it any wonder that Jesus taught us to pray for his kingdom to come on earth as it is in heaven? Geerhardus Vos referred to the two consecutive stages of the coming of the kingdom, the first being a more gradual process and the second a more cataclysmic and instantaneous event connected with the return of Christ and the final consummation.

Because of the present and future implications, one of the first things we want to be certain of is that Christians understand the doctrine of the kingdom of God. In addition, as we will later see, this kingdom idea of being a disciple certainly offers the kind of challenge the younger generations are looking for in their lives. One of their criticisms about Christians is that they are no different from non-Christians. They see that for many people, being a Christian merely means going to church and singing the hymns. These skeptical young people need to see the present significance and future hope the kingdom of God brings.

The Relation of the Kingdom to the Church

As we talk about the kingdom's relation to the church and vice versa and the relation of both to the world, we must recognize that the church focuses on a specifically narrower concept of the Christian life. Its mission is connected with things like the means of grace, the Word and the sacraments. It also focuses on the special "family" relationships among fellow believers. The kingdom, by contrast, suggests a much broader or wider aspect of the Christian life because it involves all areas of life and not just the church. This concept can be represented with two circles (see figure 3.1).

FIGURE 3.1. THE KINGDOM AND THE CHURCH

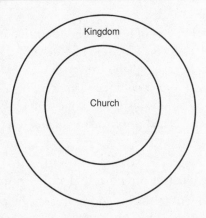

By looking at the church, people should see more clearly than in any other place what the kingdom of God is like because it is the heart of the kingdom. The kingdom, as the outer circle suggests, is not limited in its dominion. Christ is the King and head of the church, her Lord and master, but he is also the Lord of the universe. As Christians, belonging to Christ's church, move out into the broader area of the kingdom as salt and light, God intends that their lives make an impact in every area of life. As kingdom people our Christianity cannot be divorced from anything within the realm of God's kingdom.

Someone has said that there appears to be more world in the church than church in the world. This observation has some weight. Christians are not to be like the world; we are to be in the world but not of the world. All the kingdom parables in the New Testament, as well as the Beatitudes in the Sermon on the Mount (Matt. 5), underscore that kingdom people are different in their approach to life. In family life, Christians are to be different. In politics or education or law, or any other marketplace activity, Christians are to be different. This clearly means that God intends that those belonging to his body, the church, the disciples of Christ, not think of themselves merely as social transformers. He intends for his dis-

THE KINGDOM OF GOD

48

ciples rather to think of themselves first as Christians in all that they do. This will, in turn, position Christians to have a transforming effect on the world around them.

Douglas Bannerman has written,

> But from the standpoint of our present discussion it may be enough to say that practically the kingdom of God in this world is just the Church at work. It means "all those throughout the world who profess the true religion, together with their children,"—that is according to the Westminster Confession, the catholic Church visible—regarded especially in their life and work, their influence direct and indirect in the world.[3]

The circles in the illustration indicate that the church is neither separate from nor equivalent to the kingdom. It is the heart of the kingdom. Raymond Zorn states it well in *Church and Kingdom*: "For the present, we wish only to note that the Church, though an integral part of the Kingdom, may not however be identified with the Kingdom." Then quoting F. J. A. Hort, Zorn writes,

> We may speak of the *Ecclesia* (church) as the visible representative of the Kingdom of God, or as the primary instrument of its sway, or under some other analogous forms of language. But we are not justified in identifying the one with the other, so as to be able to apply directly to the *Ecclesia* whatever is said in the Gospels about the Kingdom of Heaven or of God.[4]

This means in practical terms that the kingdom of God expands into all of life and exerts influence in the world as Christians here on earth serve God's purpose by living out their Christian life. This means the kingdom of God grows as Christians grow spiritually and live out in the external environment their internal faith in the Lord Jesus Christ. Zorn again says it well: "The people of God were not to be in isolation from, but in the world's midst to serve and represent their King, subduing and bringing it under the obedience of his rule."[5] The apostle Peter said it like this: "But you are a chosen race, a royal priesthood, a holy nation, a people for his own possession, that you may proclaim the excellencies of him who called you out of darkness into his marvelous light" (1 Peter 2:9). As was true of Israel in Old Testament times, so is the church today to be a kingdom of priests and a holy nation that bears witness to the truth of the gospel in the entire world and in all areas of life.

The Kingdom and the Church, Alike and Different

Understanding the relationship between the church and the kingdom, of which we have only skimmed the surface, will help us to see clearly what God expects from both the role and the responsibility of the church. It also will enable us to understand the broader kingdom's role. This understanding will keep us from either separating or equating those roles and responsibilities.

The reason this understanding is so vitally basic in the discipleship process is that it helps the Christian know how to live as a member of Christ's body, the church, but also how to live in the broader kingdom realm. It is easy to see, as you study this area, why the confusion may exist. As we stated above, some have believed and maintained that the kingdom and the church are one and the same while others have said that they have no connection. Some have said that our focus should be totally on the church while others want to talk only of the kingdom of God as a future eschatological event.

In reference to the circles of our diagram we can borrow from Aristotelian terminology: the kingdom is the genus, and the church is the species. The church is more narrowly focused while the kingdom is all-inclusive. We will see this more clearly as we continue.

Herman Ridderbos, the author of the important textbook *The Coming of the Kingdom*, writes,

> The *basileia* [kingdom] is the great divine work of salvation in its fulfillment and consummation in Christ; the *ekklesia* [church] is the people elected and called by God and sharing the bliss of the *basileia*. Logically

the *basileia* ranks first, and not the *ekklesia*. The former, therefore, has a much more comprehensive content. It represents the all-embracing perspective, it denotes the consummation [end] of all history, brings both grace and judgment, has cosmic dimensions, fills time and eternity.[6]

Ridderbos concludes that the church and the kingdom are distinct yet are unthinkable without each other.

As Edmund P. Clowney has taught so clearly, the church is a ministry community. It involves ministry to God, to its members, and to the world. It involves a ministry of order, of mercy, and of the Word.[7] The church preaches the gospel of Jesus Christ to the world. It brings people together for worship, instruction, fellowship, and ministry within that church family and then equips them to move out into the broader area as kingdom people to represent the Triune God in all of life. So while the church is the heart of God's kingdom, it is not the totality of the kingdom. As George Eldon Ladd has written, "The kingdom is the rule of God; the church is a society of men."[8] It is through the society, the church, that the gospel is proclaimed by word and deed. The church, as a society, is not to become enmeshed in kingdom activities outside the church's role. For example, the church does not establish political parties, nor does it take up the sword for punishment of evildoers.

It is important for Christians to be involved in higher education, politics, economics, and all the legitimate categories of life, but not in the name of the church. Those are kingdom areas. God intends for Christians to be spiritually trained and equipped by the church. God's covenant family is then able to move out as salt and light into the broader kingdom areas. In the kingdom disciples have an opportunity to bear witness to the truth of the gospel. They are also ready to carry out the first commission given in Genesis 1, the cultural mandate. A disciple must know how to distinguish his or her role and position in the church from broader kingdom activities.

When people look at the community of the church, they should have a glimpse of what the kingdom of God is like. In one sense the church is invisible in that only God knows the true members. But the church also has the visible aspect of those who make a public profession of their faith in Christ. I once read in this connection that when people see the church, they should see a model of God's kingdom to come because he intends it to be a replica of the final kingdom.

Jacques Ellul underscores a dual point in his insightful book *The Presence of the Kingdom*. First, when people see the church on Fourth and Main, they should see the presence of the kingdom. Of course Ellul is not referring to the brick and mortar church building but to the people and what they represent as the church. Second, theology has very little to offer to the world today because the laypeople have privatized their faith and like Mr. Pump dare not mix their religious faith with daily routines of life. Ellul concludes that when the gospel is preached today, it does not reach the world because the church is not the salt and light throughout all of life that God intends it to be. "The position of the laymen's life is essential, both to the church and to the world. Consequently it is essential that this position should be clearly understood."[9]

Implications and Applications of the Kingdom for Christians

I am grateful for men like Abraham Kuyper, Herman Bavinck, and Geerhardus Vos for their emphasis on and development of this concept of the kingdom of God. They have helped us to see more clearly the role of the church and the kingdom and their relation to each other. Some of those Dutch theologians developed a concept called "sphere sovereignty," with an emphasis on keeping the different spheres separate from one another while relating all the spheres to God's sovereignty. Some would say that the church has its separate sphere of responsibility. Its specific role is to preach the gospel and promote redemptive living. The home has its separate role; the school has its unique calling; and the state has its sphere. According to sphere sovereignty, the government should not run the school, nor should the church attempt to run the government. Some have taken this so literally that they debate whether churches should run Christian schools (more so during the 1900s than today). Sphere sovereignty is helpful in understanding roles, but it does not imply that there is no connection or overlap between the different spheres. If their focus is God, they will actually support each other.

Living in our Western, North American culture, we have had a tendency to create the impression both by word and deed that while our Christian faith is important, it should not be brought out into the public arena. I remember the controversy surrounding the nomination of John F. Kennedy as a candidate for the presidency in the 1960s. One of the concerns was that he was Roman Catholic. It was believed that that relationship would interfere with his role as president, if elected. His response attempted to assure the people that his religion would not influence his politics, as though such a position were possible.

I am eager that we Christians, kingdom disciples, see and understand that we have a diversity of roles in this life. We must be able to make the distinction among them while not attempting to hide or to keep our religious convictions out of the picture.

With today's obvious emphasis on the privatization of religious beliefs, the confusion about political correctness, and equating church and state separation with separation of religion and state, we have increasingly witnessed a withdrawal of open religious expression from the marketplace. This has served to feed the notion that there are a sacred area of life and a secular area, as mentioned above, and the two should always remain separate and distinct. That misunderstanding makes it difficult to discuss the topic of "church and state separation" because we inevitably confuse the church with religion, which we cannot separate from the state.

Understanding the kingdom of God helps us to see that we cannot put aside our religious convictions. No matter what activity we engage in, it is integrally related to our faith. That is acceptable as long as we do not attempt to violate the line of separation between church and state. The church as such should not become politically partisan. That is not the church's role. However, that does not mean that Christians should not be politically oriented. Civil government, politics, is a kingdom role, not a church function. The church's role is a spiritual one, which, if carried out effectively, will equip its members to live in the broader kingdom as representatives of the King.

One of the fallacies of some of the movements in the 1980s was that if we could only elect a few Christians to legislate morality, then we could get things back on the right track. However, the right approach was to get ordinary everyday Christians to become involved in the political arena of life, acting from their Christian faith, and then we would begin to see some social difference. One of the things that caused the church to lose its orthodox moorings in the 1900s was redefining the church's role around social reform. That was a kingdom task, not the church's role.

I remember a negative reaction I had in the 1960s when preachers wearing their clerical collars led or participated in civil rights demonstrations. This identified those kingdom activities with the church in people's minds. I also remember speaking to a gathering of Christian school leaders along with a young man who had been serving as an aide in Washington, D.C. He stated that the number of Bible studies in which some of our legislators participated would encourage us. But I also recall him saying how discouraging it was to see some of those same legislators dealing with issues without considering what they had learned in those studies.

I do not think we should start a Christian political party, as some have suggested. However, I do think kingdom living requires Christians to be involved in the civil arena of life—not in the name of the church, but in the name of the Lord and King Jesus. As a Reformed evangelical Presbyterian, I would like to see more of us involved in the political realm of life, not flaunting our Presbyterianism or church affiliation but rather being true to our Christian beliefs.

One mark that distinguishes American Presbyterian confession from that of the original British confession is the position on the church's relationship to the state. In chapter 31 of the American version of the Westminster Confession of Faith, the confessional position of orthodox Presbyterian denominations, we read, "Synods and councils are to handle, or conclude nothing, but that which is ecclesiastical; and are not to intermeddle with civil affairs which concern the commonwealth, unless by way of humble

54

petition in cases extraordinary; or by the way of advice, for satisfaction of conscience, if they be thereunto required by the civil magistrate."

As I was concluding this chapter, I happened to hear about a circuit court decision regarding the Pledge of Allegiance. The court ruled that the pledge is unconstitutional because it contains the phrase "one nation, under God." The following morning I heard an interview with the man who raised the issue and challenged the use of the pledge in the government school system. He claimed to be patriotic: he was not against his country but against the phrase "under God." His explanation was that we should not mix "government and religion." This is a real issue especially in the pluralistic culture of North America. But as we have suggested and will elaborate on later, because man is the image of God, and hence a religious being, he is necessarily religious in all that he does.

Education is another area that illustrates the importance of understanding the relationship between the church and the kingdom. While it is true that the family is the basic unit of society, the church does have an educational assignment to teach, train, and equip God's covenant people to think and live Christianly (redemptively). Many of us in Reformed churches take vows, when baptism is administered to covenant children, to assist the parents in the rearing of their covenant children. This does not mean that the church is to take over the role of the parents in their children's education. However, as many biblical passages make clear, educating God's covenant children, while primarily the responsibility of the parents, involves the broader covenant community.

There was a time, not too long ago, when people believed that it was just as wrong for the church to usurp the parents' role, as it was for the state to develop schools to educate the children. Today, in rethinking the concept of the covenant family many have come to realize that the church assists the parents by helping to coordinate, facilitating, and encouraging the educational process, but not by taking the parents' place.

If the church's role is ecclesiastical and spiritual, preaching and teaching the Scriptures to God's people, then the church as an institution should be extremely wary of becoming involved in the plethora of social issues that need to be addressed today. The church's role is not to promote social reform or societal transformation, but rather to equip its people to move out into the kingdom realm in the name of Christ to claim all areas for the Lord. As the church, it has no authority over non-believers. A correct understanding of the relation between kingdom and church would offset both the claim by some that the church is "so heavenly minded that it is no earthly good" and the claim on the other hand that the church is going where it has no business.

Further, understanding the kingdom of God will keep us from some abstract scholastic concept about the Christian life, and instead remind us that being a Christian is a whole new way of seeing, thinking, living, and serving the King, Jesus. Scriptures like the Beatitudes in Matthew 5, as well as the kingdom parables of Jesus, remind us that kingdom people have an entirely different orientation to life and reality from that of those not born into the kingdom. That's why the conclusions to many of the kingdom parables (e.g., the prodigal son) tend to catch the audience off guard because they expect another ending. Kingdom people, however, see reality through God's spectacles or glasses, as John Calvin has said; therefore, we have a different perspective on things.

Understanding the kingdom will also remind us that while the kingdom has come because Christ has come, it will not come in its fullness until the end of the age when Christ returns. The apostle Paul says in 1 Corinthians 15:28 that "when all things are subjected to him, then the Son himself will also be subjected to him who put all things in subjection under him, that God may be all in all." At that moment the church will have been delivered up to the kingdom, and the completeness or the fullness of God's rule and realm will have come.

Christian disciples, be of good cheer. There is more to come. See the challenge—until then live as kingdom-minded people with a dual role as members of the church, Christ's body, and citizens of his kingdom.

Topics for Reflection or Discussion

1. How does this chapter relate the kingdom of God to the disciple-making process?
2. Discuss the story of Mr. Pump. Relate it to the "secular" and "sacred" dichotomy.
3. Identify some of the misconceptions that surround the kingdom of God and discuss their implications.
4. What is the relation of the church to the kingdom of God? Why should such a distinction be made? Include in the discussion the role of the church and the role of the kingdom as they relate to discipleship.
5. In practical terms, what does it mean to be a citizen of the kingdom of God?
6. In some models of discipleship, the focus is generally on evangelism, Bible study, and prayer. As important and essential as they are, God's instruction regards those activities as just a part of his intent for the totality of the kingdom. Discuss this kingdom perspective in light of discipleship.
7. Jesus' teaching on the kingdom is central to his message. He even teaches us to pray for the kingdom to come. In that light, where does the kingdom concept fit in the presentation of the gospel message?
8. How does the concept of the kingdom encourage Christians to be salt and light?

Suggested Reading

Clowney, Edmund P. *The Church*. Downers Grove, Ill.: InterVarsity, 1995. "Must" reading on the church's role as it relates to the kingdom by one of the best authorities on the topic of the church.

Ellul, Jacques. *The Presence of the Kingdom*. Colorado Springs: Helmers and Howard, 1989. Helpful, challenging, and thought-provoking insights that serve as an introduction to his many writings on various topics. While

Ellul writes in a more sociological motif and more from a neoorthodox theological position, it is worth the time and effort to read him.

Ridderbos, Herman. *The Coming of the Kingdom.* Philadelphia: Presbyterian and Reformed, 1962. One of the most extensive studies on the kingdom's present and future states. Its understanding of present and future aspects, along with its unfolding of Scripture, particularly the parables, makes this book one of a kind.

Vos, Geerhardus. *The Teaching of Jesus Concerning the Kingdom of God and the Church.* Grand Rapids: Eerdmans, 1951. A brief but very difficult to read summary on the topic of the kingdom of God. It is worth reading because Vos was a pioneer in developing the concept of the kingdom of God, particularly in its relation to the church.

Zorn, Raymond O. *Church and Kingdom.* Philadelphia: Presbyterian and Reformed, 1962. A concise, easy-to-read book that follows the path of this chapter.

4

A Christian World-and-Life-View

In the twentieth century more and more areas of life, including academia, felt the withdrawal and absence of a substantive Christian presence. The average Christian settled for being a simpleminded believer. "Believe on the Lord Jesus Christ, and you will be saved" was all that mattered. But many Christians have missed the whole story about the Christian life. In reality true life-changing conversion happens only if one thinks differently about the real foundational issues of life, yet I have had numerous conversations with pastors saying how difficult it is for their people to grasp the concept of a world-and-life-view. The evidence presented by the pollsters and analysts demonstrates that there are myriads of Christians, even evangelicals, who have professed faith in Christ, accepted him in some manner of speaking as Savior and Lord, yet have not developed a Christian mind that knows how to think God's thoughts after him. Years ago I came across a reference to a man who almost thought for himself. Though that was intended to be humorous, I realized how characteristic that has been of Christians. I do not want to be too judgmental on this note, except to say that we will never effectively serve God's purpose in this generation unless we learn how to think and apply our hearts and minds to wisdom.

Too many people profess to be Christians without understanding the implications of that profession. A Christian is a believer in Jesus Christ, trusting in him for salvation now and for eternity. But a Christian is also one who has become "a new creation. The old has passed away; behold, the new has come" (2 Cor. 5:17). No longer is a Christian under the complete control of sin. Christ has freed us from sin's bondage by his death on the cross and the Holy Spirit's application of his work to our lives in the new birth and the subsequent conversion to him, making it real to us.

To be a Christian means that God has become our point of reference and framework. "In him we live and move and have our being" (Acts 17:28). As Christians we need to become more and more self-consciously aware of this truth. One way to do this is to follow the apostle Paul's instruction (2 Cor. 10:5) to bring every thought captive to the obedience of Christ or to "think God's thoughts after him." To be a Christian, not in name only, but as one who practices his or her beliefs (which is the essence of a disciple), is to think from a Christian perspective about life and reality. In becoming Christian our life becomes oriented to God who tells us to "be transformed by the renewal of your mind" (Rom. 12:2).

Christians are to focus on thinking from God's perspective. Thinking is part of the process called sanctification, which is sometimes referred to as "grow[ing] in the grace and knowledge of our Lord and Savior Jesus Christ" (2 Peter 3:18).

As we grow, we realize that everything bears witness to the sovereign God. We also begin to realize more and more that it is not about us, it is about God. The apostle Paul says, "He is before all things, and in him all things hold together.... In everything he [is] preeminent" (Col. 1:17–18). Thus we must start with God and his revelation to us and nowhere else.

The sad reality, according to observations of trends, analyses, and personal testimonies, is that people can be genuinely converted to Christ (that is, believe that Jesus is the Savior) and still not mature in the way they look at life. Another way to say this is that a person can be a Christian and not operate from a biblical world-and-life-view (also called worldview in this chapter), or even know that such a thing exists.

One reason a disciple of Christ needs to understand something of the world-and-life-view concept is that until we know that we have one, we cannot evaluate and correct it. One reason Christians are not making more of a difference in the world is that our worldviews are syncretized with other deeply engrained views that are contrary to the Christian faith. One example comes to mind to underscore this point. We live in a society that places a great deal of value, at least in word, on education. While that is not all bad, our view of education has developed primarily from the perspective that an educated person is one who has a college degree. In a sense it does not matter where the diploma is from as long as you have one. In my denomination, one of the technical requirements for applying for ordination under the normal route (there are exceptions) is that the candidate have a degree or diploma from "an approved college or university." I received my degree from a totally secular university that did not teach from a biblical world-and-life-view. Supposedly, the philosophy of education that I experienced at the university and that which I was exposed to at the seminary were diametrically opposed, though because of common grace, benefit was derived from my studies at both institutions. I had credentials that satisfied the body that approved and ordained me to the gospel ministry. This demonstrates how easily we allow the world to shape our view of what education or an educated person is.

All of this is to say that we are in a battle over worldviews, maybe more so today than in the past. A disciple of Jesus Christ cannot afford to be unaware of or indifferent to that battle. We must be trained and equipped for the warfare.

Abraham Kuyper was known, among other things, for emphasizing a Christian world-and-life-view—that was the theme of his Stone Lectures, delivered at Princeton Theological Seminary in 1898. Some of his friends in America suggested that he use the term "life-system" rather than "world-and-life-view." He did that though he favored the latter term. Yet "life-system" is a good description: it simply refers to the way we see the world. What is remarkable about Kuyper is that he not only helped others understand a biblical world-and-life-view, but he also modeled it in his own life. Whether he was functioning as a statesman, politician, theologian, scientist, or journalist, he sought to bring all areas under the lordship of Christ. They were part of his worldview or life-system.

What Is a World-and-Life-View?

Though the term "worldview" may have come into its own during the transition to the twentieth century (translated from the German word *Weltanschauung*), the concept is a biblical one. Some speak instead of a world-and-life-view, life perspectives, a philosophy of life, or a life-system.

Brian Walsh and Richard Middleton write that a world-and-life-view helps us answer the basic questions: What is real? Who am I? What is wrong? What is the solution? The answers will depend on our world-and-life-view.

In James Sire's definition, "a world view is a set of presuppositions (or assumptions) which we hold (consciously or unconsciously) about the basic make-up of our world."[1] A world-and-life-view helps us deal with fundamental issues: What is prime reality? Who is man? What happens to man at death? What is the basis of morality? What is the meaning of human history? Sire goes on to say, "Within various basic world views other issues often arise. For example: What is the nature of the external world? Who is in charge of this world—God, man, or man and God, or no one at all? Is man determined or is he free? How can we know and how can we know that we know? Is man alone the maker of values?"[2]

A world-and-life-view is not something reserved only for Christians. Every person has a worldview whether consciously or not. As some have said, it is just part of being human to have a worldview. It is part of the way God has wired us to think and live. Our worldview is a reference to how things fit together in our minds and hearts. I like to use the term "framework" or "frame of reference" for individuals. Albert Wolters defines it simply as "the comprehensive framework of one's basic belief about things."[3]

While most people do not inherently understand that they have a worldview, a grid by which they see and understand the world and reality, everyone does eventually. Of course, for some there is more of a self-conscious recognition of this than with others. Yet once we understand that everyone has one, we can more readily see a person's worldview and provide him or her with a framework when a crisis strikes.

For our purposes, we refer to a world-and-life-view as that which determines how we see things, how we understand them, and the impact they have on our lives. It is our conceptual framework from which we think, work, and live. While it is not external to us, it is like a pair of eyeglasses we wear that in turn defines the things we see and how we see them. Our worldview acts as a command center, controlling our view of reality. In one sense, our worldview is like our fingerprints. Though there are similarities between fingerprints, each person's are distinctly his. So it is with our world-and-life-view. There are likenesses with others, but our world-and-life-view is our own unique grid through which we operate.

When we look at the world, we cannot see it totally objectively, because we have certain filters that color how we see the world. Person A may see things differently from person B. One may be right and the other wrong, or both may be partially right but not necessarily exactly alike. (This is another example of why we need one another.) How we see things and interpret them is determined by our worldview.

Basic Ingredients of a Biblical World-and-Life-View

All kinds of ingredients make up one's world-and-life-view. I will mention just a few basic ones. I start with *beliefs*, particularly our basic beliefs about God, life, self, the world around, and reality in general, because these are core elements in our worldview. A pantheist, who believes God is one with everything or is everything, will think and behave differently from a deist, who believes that God is not involved in our daily lives. Also, an atheist's claim that there is no God will shape his worldview as will a Christian's belief that God is a personal being with whom we can relate.

Our view of God is influenced by a number of factors including where we were born, the family we were born into, the culture around us, and our deliberate choices. Whatever we believe about God, whether it is right or wrong, will impact our view of reality. Similarly, if we believe that bigger and newer is better than smaller and older, or if we believe that man has limitless capabilities, or that the universe is a product of time plus chance, those ingredients will be stirred into our world-and-life-view and we will understand life and act accordingly.

Another ingredient in our world-and-life-view is our *value* system, what we think something is worth, such as life, education, and health. Our hopes and our loves also play a shaping role.

Family is a major ingredient in developing our worldview. We learn not only from teachings but also from examples. Parents play an important role in how we view the world around us. Surprisingly to some because of the generational differences, survey after survey continues to show that parents are the most influential people in the lives of their children. A friend of mine shared a personal example. She had taught the doctrines of grace to her children over the years, believing them to be foundational. However, when a tragedy struck, she found herself reverting to what she had learned from her parents, that if we want God to do good things for us, we must do good, and when we experience bad things, we have done something wrong at which God is expressing his anger. In the crisis of the situation, those thoughts and feelings took control of her life. However, her children, who had been taught the doctrines of grace then rebuked her, challenged her thinking, and helped her to get her thoughts back on obedience to Christ.

Our *friends* and *environment* also feed into our worldview. For Christians, the Christian environment plays a role in the development of a world-and-life-view. The church teaches us about God and truth, and the church's people, consciously or subconsciously, model or demonstrate their understanding of life and reality before our very eyes, and that in turn influences how we view things.

We can see how influential a world-and-life-view is by examining the ingredient of belief in God. Though America was never officially Christian in its beliefs, the view of God that pervaded the early part of our country's history through the late 1800s was sympathetic to the Judeo-Christian position. It was not a private conviction; it had great marketplace impact. The Bible was a major book in our country's history. Its view of God and its general teachings were reflected in much early American culture. Today, that view of God has been replaced by a secular view that tries to teach and operate on the principle that there is no God, or if there is, it doesn't make any difference. We can see what that view is doing to our American lifestyle; that is an example of a world-and-life-view in motion.

Our *educational philosophy* will also have an impact on our worldviews. Our president has put much emphasis on the educational process in America, and he is to be commended. He professes to be an evangelical Christian. Recently he stressed that children must learn to read in order to do their work. Again commendable. However, I thought of an earlier document in our American history, the Mayflower Compact. That document included foundational thoughts about education and particularly the ability to read. In contrast to the president's emphasis the Compact stated that children must learn to read in order to read and understand the Word of God. These two emphases are not mutually exclusive, but should be connected as part of the whole growing and learning process.

To be a disciple of Christ and think God's thoughts after him, we must develop a way of looking at and interpreting the world around us that is consistent with God's knowledge of his creation. If we are not growing in our ability to think God's thoughts after him, then we are not growing in Christ. That is true of far too many professing Christians. Our world-and-life-view is far too often basically the same after becoming a Christian as it was prior to that point.

We as Christians, through our lives and witness, must know how to challenge others. In this process we must also regularly test our own worldview by the word of God in the Bible. If any part of our worldview or how we see and interpret things differs from what God says in his Word, then we must "take every thought captive to obey Christ" (2 Cor. 10:5). That is part of the spiritual growth process of renewing and transforming our minds to correlate with God's revelation.

A Christian World-and-Life-View

As we are making disciples and become even more discipled ourselves, our world-and-life-view should be taking on more and more of a biblical pattern. Because, if it is really about God, then we have to start with him and see things the way he wants us to see and understand them. The writer of Proverbs wrote, "As [a man] thinks in his heart, so is he" (Prov. 23:7, NKJV). This underscores a principle that runs throughout Scripture. Our thought processes are the control center of our lives, and at the central nerve point is our world-and-life-view. My concern as one involved in Christian education that aims at making disciples is how many people in our circles study the Bible in a vacuum. They study the Word and often testify to being blessed by it, yet also acknowledge that it has not noticeably changed the way they think, feel, and act. We generally hear that kind of confession after they have come to a more comprehensive understanding at a later time. I know in my own life, that things I have learned, even taught, have not always fit together at a particular time, but then later things seemed to click with a new and fresh perspective. That's why a world-and-life-view is never completed or finished. Like sanctification, transformational learning, including our world-and-life-view, is an ongoing process.

Why a World-and-Life-View Is Important

Arthur Holmes notes four reasons why self-consciously having a world-and-life-view is essential.[4] First, we have a built-in need to see how things fit together, to unify thought and life. We are frustrated and uncomfortable with loose ends. A worldview helps us integrate, organize, and unify our values, feelings, and ideas. Wolters talks about the "more significant feature of worldviews" as being their pattern and coherence. He says that even our inconsistencies have their patterns.

We need a worldview that is coherent and consistent, not one that is constantly changing. Trying to live with contradictions and incoherency is dehumanizing. Some of the despair of the existentialists and the dead-end streets for the postmodernists stem from that. Though postmodernists try to convince themselves and us that things do not have to make sense, that we do not have to understand, God has made us with the need to know and understand, to ask what, why, and how questions. That is why a self-conscious world-and-life-view is so important to us. But more basic than the question, Why is a world-and-life-view important? we should ask, If we all have a world-and-life-view and each of those views is different, how can I be certain that my world-and-life-view is coherent and consistent? How can I be sure that I am seeing things as I am supposed to see them? That is where the challenge to bring every thought captive to the obedience of Christ is so important.

Second, we also have a need, according to Holmes, to define the good life and find hope and meaning. Recent trends reported by several different sources point out that a person's number one felt need, which is also a real need, is to believe and know that life has meaning and purpose. Without meaning and purpose we might be where some of the early twentieth-century existentialists were—seriously considering suicide or cautioning their students against it.

God has made us with those needs. We are living in troublesome times, and part of the key to our survival is the hope for better things to come, which of course God promises to his children. Our world-and-life-view can help us to find meaning for all the things that happen. As Paul Hiebert, missiologist and anthropologist, has written, "Our world view buttresses our fundamental beliefs with emotional reinforcements so that they are not easily destroyed."[5]

Third, Holmes says that we have a need for a worldview to guide our thoughts. They cannot be simply random thoughts, at least ultimately. A world-and-life-view keeps our thoughts on a track that helps us understand why we see things the way we do. I think of Job in the Old Testament. As his world was becoming unglued, his family was dying, and his wealth was fading, Job's perspective was that God is the sovereign God, and I will trust him. Though he could not understand why these things were happening to him, he knew that God knew because he had been conditioned to think God's thoughts after him. Contrast Job's approach to his situation with that of his wife or even his friends. Their worldviews were different. Job had the right perspective about God and reality; they did not.

I also think of the Book of Ecclesiastes, where we are presented with two distinctly different perspectives about life and reality, the man who lived "under the sun" and the man who lived "above the sun." The one had a worldly view of life and the other a heavenly view. Those views influenced how they perceived and interpreted different things. The first man believed he lived in a closed universe where cycles and patterns were inalterably in place, while the second man believed that though God had set certain patterns in motion, he could intervene and change those patterns at his pleasure.

Fourth, Holmes further states that a world-and-life-view will help guide our actions. Someone has said, "Sow a thought, reap an action." "As [a man] thinks in his heart, so is he" (Prov. 23:7, NKJV; "for he is like one who is inwardly calculating," ESV); or as Jesus says in Matthew 12:34, "For out of the abundance of the heart the mouth speaks." We know that our actions are influenced by our world-and-life-view because what we do reveals what we think, and what we think is determined by our world-and-life-view.

Do you remember our premise at the beginning of this chapter? It is possible to be converted to Christ and not converted in one's world-and-life-view. Though our new birth and conversion set in motion the propensity for a biblical world-and-life-view, it must be consciously developed.

Wolters is right on track when he describes a reformational worldview as "the basic temper and attitude that should accompany the Christian as he or she tackles the societal, personal, and cultural issues of the day."[6] He is also on target in underscoring that "reformational" here means sanctification and that we are reformed according to the Word as we are transformed in our learning and living process.

James Engel has constructed a very helpful diagram pointing out that it is possible, in our view of the salvation process, to stop it prematurely, particularly at what we call conversion, and never take the convert beyond that point (see figure 4.1). The consequence of that is failure to develop

KNOWING THE WORD: THE FRAMEWORK FOR DISCIPLESHIP

a biblical world-and-life-view. The diagram has some similarity to the *ordo salutis* in Reformed theology. The process of developing an understanding of God begins at what is labeled the –8 stage and moves forward to the –1 stage, where regeneration and then conversion take place.

FIGURE 4.1. POSSIBLE INTERRUPTION IN THE SALVATION PROCESS

	SPIRITUAL DECISION PROCESS	
GOD'S ROLE	COMMUNICATOR'S ROLE	MAN'S RESPONSE
General revelation	–8	Awareness of Supreme Being
	–7	
	–6	
	–5	
	–1	
Regeneration		Conversion (faith/repentance)
New creation in Christ		
Sanctification	Cultivation +1	Growth process
	Follow-up +2	
	+3	
Eternity		

(Adapted from James Engel, *Contemporary Christian Communications: Its Theory and Practice* [Nashville: Nelson, 1979], 83.)

Basically, we would say at the outset to a new Christian, or even to an older one, that the framework or grid through which one sees and interprets life must be consistent with what God says in his Word. As a matter of fact, that is much of what is involved in the discipleship process, though it is not generally emphasized in today's methods. For Christians, the Bible plays a fundamental and essential role in the development of a proper world-and-life-view. The levels from +1 to +3 depict the process of developing what we call a biblical worldview.

How this begins to play out in people's lives is that we cannot have a worldview that is aligned to God's Word and hold to a dualistic, dichotomized view of life. There is no bifurcation into the secular and sacred realms as we saw in the previous chapter on the kingdom of God. A Christian world-and-life-view sees life in a holistic way; God is sovereign over all. All of our life has "sacred" connotations and denotations.

70

It is all one. And what we need to remember as disciples of Jesus Christ is that we are to do all to the glory of God, no matter what we do.

Some people believe that a biblical world-and-life-view will provide Christians with answers to every little detail of life. Actually, it does not. It does provide us with a framework with which we can demonstrate the image of God within us by dealing with all the issues of life from a godly perspective. While a biblical worldview doesn't tell us what to think about everything, it does help us frame the questions that we ought to be asking. Christians may come to different conclusions about some things and still be within that framework. For example, all people operating under the biblical norm to honor their parents may choose different ways to do that, according to their culture, time, and place. A biblical worldview provides us with a unifying framework but allows a diversity of conclusions. How a person dresses, what books one reads, what foods one consumes, or what relationships one develops will differ from person to person, yet each person can be operating within a biblical framework. I have some dear friends whose approach to political philosophy is different from mine, and yet I am convinced that we are all operating within a biblical world-and-life-view. I believe that is one way that God uses others to help us sharpen, clarify, and articulate our worldview.

Wolters closes his treatise on a reformational worldview with these words:

> All thoughtful Christians, in whatever area they are called to exercise their responsibilities, must take seriously the question of biblical world-view, and must guide both their thinking and their acting accordingly. To ignore the question is to deny the practical relevance of Scripture to the greater part of our workaday lives.[7]

Some Cautions Regarding Worldview

The concept of worldview suggests that we have a need to understand certain things about life and reality. There are philosophical and theological implications. For some the concept could also suggest the need to walk not by faith but rather by sight. For others it could even suggest that there is always only one right conclusion. A world-and-life-view is to be inclusive. It is a bit like the saying that "the whole is greater than the sum of its parts."

David Naugle cautions that "while philosophy may assist in the world-view process, and in fact does, it must never usurp it."[8] He warns against simply embracing one philosophy as our worldview. He also reminds us that there will always be some space between the Bible and a biblical worldview, hence our need to be always reforming according to the Word (*semper reformandi*). We must constantly work to keep a Christian per-spective; it doesn't happen automatically.

Another caution that Naugle brings to mind is the need to be careful with spiritual pride—the attitude that because I see things that you don't see, I have it all together and I cannot learn anything from you. Such an attitude does not reflect the reformational or transformational world-view that God wants us to have. Also we cannot assume that just because we have been converted our worldview is correct. We must not allow our worldview to keep us from spiritual growth. Our relationship to Christ is a growth process. Developing, refining, and reforming our worldview is also a process. If that process leads to intellectual snobbery, we need to repent.

Another caution we need to remember is that our worldview impacts our relationships to God, one another, and the world around us. If, in an effort to treat everyone equally, we embrace a pagan view that God is in all things without any distinction between him and his creation, we will relativize everyone and everything, including the Creator, reducing God and man to mere things. We will have a tendency to submit to the world, rather than exercise wise stewardship over it, worship things instead of God, and conform to the ways of the world rather than reform it.

If, on the other hand, our view of God is that he is sovereign over his creation and through Christ enters into a personal relationship with us, then we will see one another as true equals before God, in need of redemp-tion and completely dependent on him. We will honor the world for the sake of its Creator and Redeemer. Rather than becoming too enamored with or abusing it, we will understand that our role is to have dominion over it and do everything we can to remove the effects of sin in all of life.

Conclusion

While on the one hand we could say that developing a self-consciously biblical world-and-life-view is one of the components in the disciple-making process, we could say, on the other hand, that it is the framework within which we make disciples. It takes the emphasis in the discipling process beyond the individual and the church to the broader kingdom and world.

George Barna's statement that less than 10 percent of Christians embrace a biblical world-and-life-view demonstrates that, like Mr. Pump, most Christians do not mix religion and life. Religion just isn't congenial to the marketplace or any other "secular" area of life. Belief in God does not make a significant difference other than personal piety for many Christians who would call themselves evangelicals, regular church attendees, people who read the Bible and pray. Among those who hold to a high view of Scripture, less than 10 percent know how to allow it to help them construct their world-and-life-view. Clearly, then, making disciples involves more than Bible study, prayer, or even telling about the saving work of Christ.

I was pleased a couple of years ago when a high school senior approached me after I had preached in a local church and asked if I had time to help him develop a biblical world-and-life-view. He wanted to think and live as God would have him do, yet he was acutely aware of the tendency to be carried along by the currents of the world. We had a great time for the next six to nine months working through that worldview construct.

We cannot engage the world or make any real difference unless we understand our worldview because part of our task as Christians, beyond our own growth and development, is to challenge those to whom we witness to think through the right questions and answers about life and reality. Asking the right questions, working through to right answers, and keeping the process going are what developing a world-and-life-view is all about. From a Christian perspective we have to do a better job teaching and living out a biblical world-and-life-view. So, whether we view this as one of the components of the disciple-making process or the framework in which discipling is done, it must be present, or we will not make disciples who love the things of God and serve his purpose in all of life.

TOPICS FOR REFLECTION OR DISCUSSION

1. Why is it so hard for some to grasp the concept of a world-and-life-view?
2. Formulate your own a definition of "world-and-life-view" and try it on someone.
3. The Western world, in contrast to the Eastern, separates religion from other areas of life and hence fails to see Christianity as a total system. Why? Is this correct?
4. Review and expand on our discussion of why a world-and-life-view is important.
5. Watch a TV program or a movie or read a book and describe its worldview. Is it correct? If not, what is wrong?
6. How is the Christian world-and-life-view tied to thinking Christianly?
7. How would you reply to someone who asks about or challenges the place of Scripture in your worldview?
8. Discuss the relation between culture and worldview.

SUGGESTED READING

Kuyper, Abraham. *Lectures on Calvinism: The Stone Foundation Lectures.* Grand Rapids: Eerdmans, 1972 (1899). Classic lectures demonstrating a Calvinistic life-system in all areas of life.

Plantinga, Cornelius. *Engaging God's World: A Christian Vision of Faith, Learning, and Living.* Grand Rapids: Eerdmans, 2002. A study of the impact that a Christian worldview has on how we live, think, and learn.

Sire, James. *The Universe Next Door: A Basic Worldview Catalog.* Downers Grove, Ill.: InterVarsity, 1988. Excellent setting forth of a world-and-life-view.

The latest edition incorporates more information and critique of post-modernism.

———. *Naming the Elephant: Worldview as a Concept.* Downers Grove, Ill.: InterVarsity, 2004. A must read, this sequel to *The Universe Next Door* expands Sire's thoughts on worldview. I appreciate his openness to go beyond his earlier concept. He is moving in a most helpful direction in this book, and it should not be overlooked.

Walsh, Brian J., and J. Richard Middleton. *The Transforming Vision: Shaping a Christian Worldview.* Downers Grove, Ill.: InterVarsity, 1984. An exposition on the theme that if Christianity is to make any significant difference, Christians must embrace, practice, and teach a biblical world-and-life-view. The book aims at not only helping develop a biblical worldview, but also teaching it.

Wolters, Albert M. *Creation Regained: Biblical Basics for a Reformational Worldview.* Grand Rapids: Eerdmans, 1985. A definition of the nature and scope of a worldview. Wolters describes how a reformational worldview is suited to influence the world as Christians live out their faith in all of life.

5

The Reformed Faith

T he title "The Reformed Faith" will likely make the reader think of theology and doctrine. For our purposes we will define and distinguish the two like this: theology is the study of God's truth and the articulation of our understanding of it; doctrines are those essential elements that are incorporated into our theology. I will not deal with the fine points of theology; however, I will try to keep both theology and doctrine in perspective as they relate to making disciples.

Often we hear that theology is an academic exercise for professionals and classrooms, or that doctrines are too heavy and intellectual for ordinary Christians to consider. Consequently, many discipleship programs do not openly incorporate either of the two. But Stanley Grenz writes, "Doctrinal conviction provides the foundation for our attempts to determine the best way to live out our Christian commitment in the midst of the varied situations that confront us. And it motivates us to act continually in accordance with our commitment to Christ. Whenever our theological work stops short of this, we have failed to be obedient to our calling as thinking Christians. Indeed our goal must always be to link Christian belief with Christian living."[1]

In the chapter on epistemology I argued that our knowledge of everything is totally dependent on God, consciously or unconsciously. The way he chooses to teach us his truth requires that we follow his design. Francis Schaeffer wrote in *The Christian Manifesto* that "the basic problem of the Christians in this country [the U.S.] in the last 80 years or so, in regard to society and about government, is that they have seen things in bits and pieces instead of totals."[2]

I hope this chapter will help us work through some mistaken ideas that have decreased our effectiveness in making disciples. That four out of ten professing evangelical Christians do not believe in absolute truth and that more young evangelicals are embracing New Age teachings are facts that we must face.[3] Our approach to making disciples may actually be building on sand, even though we are using some of the right materials in the process. That is why, as we have stated, our design and purpose is to first establish a framework that will enable us to make disciples who will make a difference.

From my studies I remember reading an early mission statement for Harvard College. Recently while reviewing *Engaging God's World* by Cornelius Plantinga Jr., I was reminded of that mission statement: "Let every Student be plainly instructed, and earnestly pressed, to consider well [that] the maine end of his life and studies is *to know God and Jesus Christ which is eternall life*, Jn. 17:3, and therefore to lay Christ in the bottome, as the only foundation of all sound knowledge and Learning."[4] The objectives used then are the same objectives that we need before us as we seek to make kingdom disciples.

In the current approach to making disciples the message and methods have been extremely eclectic. We have taken more of a shotgun rather than a rifle approach, and people have been getting only bits and pieces instead of totals, a little here and a little there, not fitting or hanging together. That does not bother us as it should. Most of us grew up in an educational system where we studied the various individual topics in the curriculum without knowing how they fit together, if in fact they do. Our whole educational process has reflected and resulted in eclectic learning. Even our Christian schools have fallen into that pattern.

One of the reasons people do not like to think about learning or why they find learning to be such a chore is that they cannot automatically fit things together. That is frustrating because without any coherency or consistency the pieces may not make sense. When the pieces do not fit, it is hard to see the practical results of learning; hence we generally get the reaction "So what?" or "Why should I bother to learn?"

To illustrate my point: one of the biblical models of making disciples is found in Titus 2, where Paul sets forth a strategy and method. His instruction to the young pastor Titus was that in equipping the men and women who were to be involved in ministry, he had to teach them "what accords with sound doctrine." That was foundational. In chapter 1 Paul had mentioned a situation in Crete that underscored the importance of what he was saying: "For there are many who are insubordinate, empty talkers and deceivers, especially those of the circumcision party. They must be silenced, since they are upsetting whole families by teaching for shameful gain what they ought not to teach" (Titus 1:10–11). In other words, bad teaching, bad doctrine, wrong theology can divide families and, by implication, communities.

If the observations of present trends are anywhere near correct, we are at a defining moment. That is especially true where making disciples is concerned. For example, George Gallup Jr. and Michael Lindsay in their books such as *Surveying the Religious Landscape* conclude that while there are a widespread appeal and popularity of religion, there is at the same time a glaring lack of knowledge about the Bible, basic doctrines, and the traditions of the church. This has produced a superficial faith and a belief in God without a trust in him. As a result, organized religion (in our case, the Christian church) has not made much of a difference in today's culture. So they conclude that the organized church may be only one generation away from extinction (see Judg. 2:1–3).[5]

I do not mean to communicate that nothing is being done. Many Christians are attempting to make a difference in the world. There are a plethora of activities going on in churches and parachurch groups intended to disciple people. George Barna and Mark Hatch point out that there is a great deal of satisfaction on this score:

> It may come as a shock to discover that less than 1 percent of America's senior pastors list better teaching, the provision of a worldview-based teaching, or the development of a life in which faith and behavior are integrated as a top priority for their church. This may be a *non-issue* to pastors because 94 percent of them believe that "the people who attend my church are consistently exposed to preaching and teaching that intentionally and systematically lead them to develop or embrace a biblical worldview."

And yet Barna's research, which also reveals that four out of ten individuals currently involved in a Christian discipling process contend that "there is no such thing as absolute moral truth," underscores that good intent is not enough.[6] People do not know the basic Bible doctrines that are essential to a biblical worldview.

One conclusion, at least in our Reformed and evangelical communities, is that preachers are teaching the basic doctrines, but somehow the preaching and teaching are not always connecting with the people. Somehow, the preaching and teaching are not helping them develop a biblical world-and-life-view. There appears to be a disconnect between what the pastors say they are preaching and teaching, along with all the other activities in the church's ministry, and what is actually happening. I do not think we can justify the situation by pointing to Paul's summation: "I planted, Apollos watered, but God gave the growth" (1 Cor. 3:6).

Throughout my years of ministry I have observed that we make certain assumptions which may keep us from seeing clearly. I have found in working with churches that there is a strong tendency to evaluate the activities, not whether we are effectively making disciples (statistics say no) or just going through the motions. Thus we are not sure what is (or is not) happening.

The premise of this chapter is that the Reformed faith is a systematic or coherent way of framing God's truth. The doctrines that make up that faith are all-inclusive, or, to use Paul's words in Acts, "the whole counsel of God." After addressing three common misperceptions about theology and doctrine, the chapter will conclude with an overview of the doctrines that make up the Reformed system.

Three Misperceptions about Theology

Misperception # 1: Theology should be left to professional theologians. The first misperception relates to the role and use of theology and who should do theology. In the foreword to Stanley Grenz's *Created for Community: Connecting Christian Belief with Christian Living*, Leighton Ford states the problem clearly and succinctly:

> We have strangely mixed attitudes towards theology in the church today.... Laypersons, too, have different slants—ranging from "don't give me baby food; teach me how to think seriously about my faith and its implications" to "I'm not a theologian; I'm just an ordinary layperson. Just give me something to help me live day by day."[7]

Why is this the case? We have embraced a wrong view of the church and a wrong view of theology. First, a wrong view of the church. The church is the people of God for whom Christ died. There are not two, three, or four different peoples who make up the church, but one people of God. John R. Stott's *One People* and R. Paul Stevens's *The Other Six Days* are forceful and convincing presentations of this truth. There are not different categories of people in the church. But since the later first century A.D. and early second century, as Stevens points out, we have made an unbiblical dichotomy in the body of Christ. We have embraced the notion that there are the scholars, clergy, and other ministry professionals, and there are laypeople, the ordinary everyday Christians. It has been the role of the professional to study and teach. The natural result has been the long pattern of only the clergy or priests studying the Bible, doing theology, and teaching it, actually often dumbing it down for the everyday laypeople, whose role was to be taught by the professionals. The Protestant Reformation corrected this in principle, but not totally in practice.

Stevens contends that there are different roles, gifts, and assignments among the people of God, but not different categories of people. The teachers' role, whether they be called priests, clergy, or pastor-teachers, is to teach and disciple from a sound biblical foundation. They are to "equip the saints for the work of ministry," as the apostle Paul wrote in Ephesians 4:12. However, the Bible also teaches that every believer is a theologian because theology is the study and articulation of truth about God. The reason so many people cringe at this notion is that they misunderstand the Christian's role, as well as the place of theology.

Along with Stott and Stevens, Stanley Grenz and Roger Olson have been extremely helpful. Their book *Who Needs Theology?* refers to six levels of theology beginning with the "folk level" and moving to the "academic level." Although most Christians engaged in folk theology would never consider it theology, it really is. New Christians should be aware of this discipline at the outset. This is important, if for no other reason than that it will communicate that being a Christian involves more than easy believism or putting one's brain in neutral. One does not have to be trained in an academic institution to do theology and learn doctrine. Young Christians need to be taught this for a number of reasons, but the most important is to realize that, given their place in the body of Christ, what they believe and understand must be in accord with sound doctrinal teaching; their beliefs must hang together if they are to avoid things like cognitive dissonance. We must learn to live what we believe. That is transformational learning, the goal of every discipling effort.

What we have learned from the Protestant Reformation illustrates the importance of knowing doctrine. For example, are we saved because of our good works, or are our good works a result of our salvation? Another way to state this is, Are we saved by works, by works and faith, or by faith alone? Do we believe in God in order to be born again, or is our belief in God a result of being born again? One of the big issues today is, For whom did Christ die, and what did his death on the cross accomplish? Those questions are not for professionals or academics only. They affect every believer.

Misperception # 2: Theology is an abstract, not practical, exercise. The second misperception relates to what theology and doctrine are.

In a "Peanuts" comic strip Linus and Lucy are looking out the window, watching it rain. Lucy asks her brother if he thinks the rain will flood the earth. Ever the theologian, Linus answers no because in the ninth chapter of Genesis God says that would never happen again. Lucy, with much relief, says that he has taken a load off her mind, to which he responds, "Sound theology has a way of doing that." Linus, as usual, is exactly right. Sound theology is vital to being a disciple of Jesus Christ, embracing the kingdom of God perspective and the world-and-life-view.

Unfortunately, for a long time we have operated with a deficient model which promotes the idea that theology and its doctrinal components are abstract things that we need to study, discuss, learn, and maybe someday apply to our lives. A traditional seminary curriculum offers courses in Bible, historical theology, church history, systematic theology, languages, and practical or applied theology, each as separate parts of the curriculum. This has created the notion that theology is an abstract discipline or science to be studied academically, and not a practical discipline at the systematic or historical levels. The idea is like the perspective of the ancient Greeks: there are things that we can talk about or consider that do not necessarily interface with our day-to-day lives. Philosophy, like most theology, is another area that we usually view in this abstract way.

However, from a Christian perspective, we believe that doctrine is life and life is doctrine, as John Frame has pointed out so clearly in his book *The Doctrine of God.* We do not teach or learn doctrine for its own sake; neither should we develop an abstract system of theology. It must have life application. The reason Titus was told to equip his ministerial associates with sound doctrine is that their discipling of younger men and women had to be doctrinally sound. In other words, doctrine matters.

The disciple of Christ should be a student of sound doctrine. It is all a part of loving God and obeying him, as we remember that out of the heart flow all the issues of life, and as a man thinks in his heart, so is he. How we live is determined by what we think about.

82

In referring to John Calvin's methods of ministry Frame points out, "Calvin's interest was not in developing an academically respectable system of thought," but "to show the applicability of the great doctrines to everyday life."[8] Indeed, "theology helps us to formulate the message, applying the biblical teaching about God to us and to our time."[9] Theology and doctrine are a part of the warp and woof of our lives. As we stated in the chapter on epistemology, if our knowledge of God does not include the personal aspect, then our knowledge of God is faulty; and so it is with all doctrine and theology.

We shy away from doctrine and theology because we do not understand how life-impacting and transforming they are. God is concerned that we embrace right doctrine and be orthodox in our beliefs. He also intends that we not simply think straight but also be able to apply and practice doctrine. Our theology is to be a theology that is soundly life-oriented. He reveals his truth to us in such a way that our lives are transformed. If they are not, we have missed his message.

Misperception # 3: Studying theology can wait until another day. The third misperception involves how and when to incorporate theology and doctrine. Doctrines give us the foundation for what we are to believe and how we are to live. Theology gives us the form in which we fit together those doctrines. We run the risk of falling short of our objective if we avoid them in the discipleship process because we will convey that what people believe is their choice.

Of course we do not expect a new Christian, nor one who has a broader calling in life, to spend full-time studying theology and doctrines; but failure to study at all will result in a truncated understanding of what a Christian is. If beliefs are foundational to our world-and-life-view, then our Christian beliefs will improve our lives as disciples. We should not wait for some magic moment to incorporate this into the process. Studying theology and doctrine should be built in up-front, and permeate the entire process. To reiterate the quotation from Stanley Grenz that appeared at the beginning of this chapter: "Sound theological reflection will make a difference in how we live. Doctrinal conviction provides the foundation for our attempts to determine the best way to live out our Christian commitment in the midst of varied situations that confront us.... Whenever our theological work stops short of this, we have failed to be obedient to our calling as thinking Christians."[10]

An Overview of Doctrines in the Reformed System

I am aware that the word "Reformed" has not always communicated a clear message from those who send to those who receive it. Read some of George M. Marsden's books such as *Reforming Fundamentalism* to get a broader understanding of the diversity of that term. Nonetheless, it is a good term to use, if defined, to communicate something foundational in the discipleship process.

Present-day Christian historians such as Marsden and Mark A. Noll describe three distinctive approaches within the general framework called "Reformed theology." Marsden's three classifications of "Reformed" are the doctrinalists, the culturalists, and the pietists. I mention this for two reasons: first, to make the reader aware that not everyone, even in our circles, uses the term in the same way; and second, to suggest that a good part of the discipleship process will go forward if we understand the challenge we face of blending the three into one. If such a blend can be achieved, Christians may emerge better equipped for the challenge of living Christianly in our pluralistic, secular, and humanistic culture and therefore better equipped to make a difference.

As I read history, especially church history, I marvel at how God's story unfolds. However, I am also disheartened by seeing Christians so easily become their own worst enemies by allowing fine points to drive wedges between them and destroy the unity of the Christian faith and the church. I would hope and pray that somehow we can produce a new generation of disciples who know how to interact with one another, even when they do not see every jot and tittle from exactly the same perspective in our Christian belief system.

THE REFORMED FAITH

84

While I believe the Reformed faith offers the greatest potential to bring us together, it has often walled us off. We have shown the world more of a church divided than united. From my study of church history, especially since the Protestant Reformation, I believe there are more things that draw us together than should be allowed to keep us apart. As we will see in the next chapter, the covenant concept speaks more to the church as a family than as individuals; but it is not always easy to live in a family where we allow disagreements to dominate. As long as our enemy can keep us fighting within the family, he does not have to worry about our making much progress for the Lord in the world around us.

Having said that, I believe that teaching the Reformed faith (understood as a blending of Marsden's three terms) will strengthen any disciple-making process. Our doctrines will be sound, our witness will have an impact on our culture, and spiritual growth will take place in our Christian lives. If we are to teach "what accords with sound doctrine," we obviously must know sound doctrine.

What then is so special or unique about the Reformed faith? To answer that question I will describe several key doctrines. For example, within the Reformed family of Christians, the genius of the faith has been its focus on the grace of the sovereign God and its foundation on the Word of God found in the Bible. Reformed theology also emphasizes that God is the sovereign Lord and King of the universe and that man is made in the image and likeness of God (yet there is a clear distinction between creature and Creator). Other significant doctrines include man's sinfully depraved nature, meaning he cannot do anything to save himself, and Christ's redeeming work on the cross (applied to our lives by the Holy Spirit) as the only hope for salvation. The Reformed faith also clearly teaches that history will have a climax, and that there will be a new heaven and new earth wherein dwells righteousness.

The Bible

The basic process of making disciples must include an understanding of the system of truth taught in the Bible. We want each believer to understand from the very beginning that what we believe is based on what the Bible says. And while the Bible is not a systematic textbook, it does give us truths that form a system of truth that does not contradict itself but hangs together as one whole message. That understanding is essential to knowing what we believe and why, and is key to being able to articulate those beliefs when given the opportunity. Therefore, in this system we start with the Bible because it is the authority upon which we build our Christian faith.

The Reformed faith seeks to incorporate in its teachings all that God has revealed in the Bible. There are major teachings in the Bible that will give our faith coherency and consistency and not leave us guessing about the truth. Any discipling program should early on incorporate training and equipping in a number of areas.

First, the believer must understand the place and role of the Bible in a person's life. A true disciple of Jesus Christ has to take the Bible seriously as the rule of faith and practice. It teaches us what to believe and how to live. It gives us a reliable framework and foundation upon which we can build our lives. Today's postmodern world challenges the existence of truth, universals, and absolutes, claiming that authority lies either in the individual or in the group to which he belongs. The Bible contains the great metanarrative of God's creation, redemption, and consummation, his story. Today's postmodern culture denies the existence of such a story, but without it, truth is up for grabs or is simply whatever we want it to be.

Second, the Bible gives the message that Christ calls us to share with the world as we seek to carry out his Great Commission. We bear witness to his truth and testify of him. The Bible is God's word written through men in order that we might know him and his truth.

Because the Bible is God's written word in propositional form, it is more than subjective opinion; it is substantive truth. It is our point of demarcation. Whether we like it or not, we are dependent on the Bible to tell us the truth, including the gospel message. God wrote this truth through men of different backgrounds and at different times. He inspired them to write what he wanted his people to know and believe. In one sense, when we read and study the Word, we are asking God what he wants us to believe and how he wants us to live. The apostle Paul declares that the Bible is "profitable for teaching, for reproof, for correction, and for training in righteousness, that the man of God may be competent, equipped for every good work" (2 Tim. 3:16–17).

Most systematic theology books discuss six major areas that actually form the Reformed system of doctrine that should be incorporated into disciple making. They are the doctrines of God, man, Christ, salvation, the church, and last things. The Bible is the foundation of all beliefs.

God

Knowing God is what the Christian life is all about, but how we know him and what we know about him are crucial to knowing him better, and worshiping and serving him more consistently. When we speak of knowing God, we do not mean simply knowing about him.

How we know God is the issue. For example: the Reformed faith, in faithfulness to the Bible, teaches that God is the sovereign Lord and King of the universe, the Creator and Redeemer. By this God all things exist and hold together. The Reformed faith challenges us to focus our thoughts on God. What is essential here is not what we think about him but what he thinks about himself. The psalmist said, "How precious to me are your thoughts, O God! How vast is the sum of them!" (Ps. 139:17). Isaiah writes, "For my thoughts are not your thoughts, neither are your ways my ways, declares the LORD" (Isa. 55:8). The apostle Paul writes, "For from him and through him and to him are all things. To him be glory forever! Amen" (Rom. 11:36). The apostle John says, "And this is eternal life, that they know you the only true God, and Jesus Christ whom you have sent" (John 17:3). That description fits what is often referred to as the classic concept of God.

Reacting to what they thought was a too-distant classical view of God, eighteenth- and nineteenth-century liberal theologians presented God on a more horizontal plane. Early-twentieth-century neo-orthodoxy swung back to the other extreme and dealt with God as the wholly other or the transcendent God. Today's postmodern paradigm talks about God, not as the sovereign and transcendent God, but as the God who is more available and responsive to us, more of a friend, or someone who sticks close to us. There are also those who maintain that if there is a God, they cannot know him, define, or describe him; hence he is simply whatever they want God to be.

John Frame points out in his book *The Doctrine of God* that the Reformers focused their attention on salvation and faith, the hot-button issue of that day. Therefore, they did not deal so much with the doctrine of God. Even though the Reformers may not have emphasized the closeness and presence of God in actual practice, they believed in his imminence because for them, to know God, as he reveals himself, was one of the great emphases of the Reformed faith. This is vital because the Bible testifies that as image bearers we know God, and that while the knowledge of God can be suppressed because of sin, we cannot eliminate him from our frame of reference.

The real temptation that we need to guard against, as we learn from those who have gone before us, is to think of God or understand him on our terms. In following the Bible, the Reformed faith emphasizes that we must know God as he wants us to know him; we are dependent on his revelation of himself to do that.

A disciple of Christ needs to have certain things clear about God, even though "we see through a glass darkly" at this present time. We need to be clear about God's independency, his immutability, his omnipresence, and his unity. Those are things that are unique to God and not shared with any other. We need to have some familiarity with those attributes of God. If our knowledge and belief about God are wrong, then everything else will follow suit. Our life, meaning, and everything else depend upon our interpretation of God.

I have talked with people who believe that God is someone out to get them, so they had better shape up. I have talked to others who believe that God does good things for those who are good, but bad things to those who are bad. I have talked with people who believe that God is not in control of anything and makes no difference in what happens in the world or peoples' lives. In today's postmodern culture, "god" is whatever we want him or her to be. I once enrolled in a graduate class that tried to teach that we are God. These examples underscore our need to have a correct view of God, though we will never have a comprehensive one.

God's revelation of himself tells us that he is the personal Creator and Redeemer. He further reveals that while he is above his creation and not to be identified with it, he is also present within it and not removed from it. A disciple of Jesus Christ needs to know God as the ever-present personal, all-powerful, eternal spirit who is both in and above his creation. As I write this book, there is a controversy, even within evangelical circles, about who God is. Some are saying that God does not know everything, that he is not all-powerful or able to change the course of men's lives and history, that he can and will often change his mind about things. Are those things true of God? The Reformed faith and its understanding of God would say no, because that is not what God tells us in his Word.

Man

The Reformed faith also stresses the significance and importance of man because God made man in his image and likeness. Every person is to be as much like God as is humanly possible. We ought to see something of God in each other; however, we are not nor can we ever be God. While we can do Godlike things and imitate him in many ways, we are not God. We are finite beings with limitations and inabilities. Neither are we machines (though we are often treated as such in today's environment), nor are we animals. God created us with a body and soul. To understand who we are, we have to understand what we are.

God created man, male and female, in his image to carry out the purpose of his creation, namely to glorify him by loving him and doing what he commands. His commands include some things to do, for example, "Be fruitful and multiply and fill the earth and subdue it" (Gen. 1:28), and some things not to do, "Of the tree of the knowledge of good and evil you shall not eat" (Gen. 2:17). God placed Adam in the Garden of Eden on probation. He created us with freedom but also with certain boundaries. His test for us is obedience to him as our Creator God. Though God created man good and perfect, able to sin or not to sin, man chose the former.

Adam and Eve disobeyed, eating of the tree of the knowledge of good and evil. Not only did they fall into sin, Adam representing the entire human race, but their original sin was imputed to all of their descendants. At that point man began to experience death, just as God had warned. The Bible teaches that man, because of his sin, is totally depraved, not in degree, but in character and extent. There is no area of his life that is not tarnished by sin. As sinner, man is unable to do anything to change his sinful state because the freedom that he once enjoyed was lost because of sin. Outside of a relationship with Jesus Christ, man is enslaved to sin (Rom. 8:12–13).

In our sinful nature we deny and despise God, and we are unable to do anything to change that situation. The apostle Paul writes, "For the mind that is set on the flesh is hostile to God, for it does not submit to God's law; indeed, it cannot" (Rom. 8:7). Only God can alter man's sinful estate. The Bible teaches that in his lost sinful state, man needs salvation. He needs to be born again and converted to Christ but is helpless to effect any of those things.

It is essential to understand not only that man needs salvation, but that he cannot earn it for himself. He is incapable of keeping the law unto salvation. Many people have believed that salvation is left up to man. Man has to set things right, and clean up his sinful life; however, the Bible teaches that man is totally dependent on God to set things right and to redeem from sin.

The Reformed faith highlights man's responsibilities to God, others, and the world around him. That man is a sinner does not alter the fact that he bears God's image (though tarnished by the fall) and has a relationship to the rest of creation, particularly other men. We have to respect that image of God, even in the worst of sinners, including ourselves. Actually, that image becomes our point of contact for sharing the gospel and doing Godlike things for and with other human beings. This also becomes a key to later understanding our responsibility to make disciples of all nations. The image of God is universal and inseparably joined to all mankind. That is why we are told to go into all the world with the gospel and to love one another, including our enemies, because all are image bearers of God.

According to Millard Erickson, "We experience full humanity only when we are properly related to God. No matter how cultured and genteel, no one is fully human unless a redeemed disciple of God."[11] That's why we must understand that while we oppose the teachings of secular humanism, which leaves God out of the picture regarding humankind, we do respect and embrace a biblical doctrine of humanism that recognizes, acknowledges, and demonstrates the outworking of the truth that all men are image bearers of God. We cannot act or react toward people as anything less. As Francis Schaeffer said, "Man is not nothing." We must have the highest regard for human beings in our interactions even if some never believe the gospel.

Christ

The two doctrines just examined remind us that there is a Creator God who made man in his own image and likeness and placed certain requirements on man. Yet man rebelled, disobeyed God, and became a sinner, lost and spiritually dead. We have also been reminded that man, in that sinful state, can do nothing to change his condition and is under the sentence of death. However, rather than leave man in that lost and sinful condition unable to fulfill his original creation purpose, God did something to bring himself and man together again.

God sent his Son, the Second Person of the Trinity, whom we now know as the only begotten Son of God, the Lord Jesus Christ, to do what was necessary to bring about reconciliation between God and man.

Understanding who Christ is, why he came, what he did, and how that affects our lives is absolutely essential.

As the early creeds remind us, Christ was very God of very God and, since his incarnation, very man of very man. He is one person with two natures, human and divine. When Christ came to earth by way of birth to the Virgin Mary, he did not cease to be God. At no time has Christ ever been less than fully God. But what he did in the manger of Bethlehem was to take upon himself the form of a servant. He became fully man, to pay the ransom price required by our sins, which was the only way for atonement and reconciliation to happen.

One of the greatest christological passages in the Bible is found in Philippians 2:1–11. There Paul explains Christ's coming to earth as the incarnate Son of God. "He emptied himself...." In his birth Christ became what the Bible calls the second Adam to undo the sin that the first Adam had done. In his human form, he "emptied himself" or humbled himself in order to be made like those whom he came to redeem, yet he was without sin. We can be confident in his work as our mediator because he was truly the holy man of God, undefiled by sin, yet bearing the suffering and death that humans experience because of sin.

The Holy Spirit

While most of the traditional books on theology have chapters on God the Father and Christ, they do not have a separate section on the Holy Spirit, the Third Person of the Godhead (the Trinity). But we do say in the historic Apostles' Creed, "I believe in the Holy Ghost [Spirit]." Because of today's emphasis on the Holy Spirit, especially within certain circles of the Christian framework, and because of much misunderstanding, we should include an emphasis on the Holy Spirit in our kingdom approach to making disciples.

The Holy Spirit is the Third Person of the Trinity. As the Westminster Shorter Catechism (Q. 6) has it: "How many persons are there in the Godhead? There are three persons in the Godhead; the Father, the Son, and the Holy Ghost; and these three are one God, the same in substance and equal in power and glory." The Holy Spirit, along with the Son, is Lord. Actually, it is the Holy Spirit that indwells the life of a believer. It is the Holy Spirit that takes the accomplishments of Christ on our behalf and applies them to our lives. The traditional adage is still a good one: The Father plans, the Son accomplishes, and the Holy Spirit applies the redemption to our lives.

While the Holy Spirit, according to the third chapter of John's Gospel, is like the mysterious wind, and we cannot tell where he comes from or where he is going, he is very much God with us and in us. One of the things the Holy Spirit has done is to inspire the authors of the Bible to write the words of God. They were moved along by the Spirit as they wrote. This is important for disciples to understand, because, though his work is far broader than what is recorded in Scripture, he always works consistently with his Word. We are also warned that not every spirit is the right Spirit. John tells us, "Beloved, do not believe every spirit, but test the spirits to see whether they are from God, for many false prophets have gone out into the world" (1 John 4:1). The Westminster divines were careful to remind the church that the Word and the Spirit are not to be separated from one another. God always works and teaches us by his Word and Spirit (Westminster Confession of Faith, 1.6).

One extremely important thing for Christians to understand about God is that he is one God in three persons, not one God who was the Father and later became the Son, and now is the Holy Spirit. Such a position, which is known as "modalism," is contrary to the Scriptures.

Salvation

We learn from the Bible that God's way of relating to us is by covenant. The Westminster Confession of Faith states that God voluntarily condescended to relate to mankind, and his method of doing so was the covenant, which was an agreement between God and man that contained a promise from God to man, along with a condition for man to meet. The Bible teaches that God's covenant with man grew out of his covenant within the Trinity.

God's covenant with man was first presented as the covenant of life in which he said, essentially: "I will be your God, and you will be my people. If you keep my command not to eat of the tree of the knowledge of good and evil, you will live." This was a works covenant with the promise of life on condition of obedience to God's requirement. Accordingly, it is called the covenant of works.

Man did not keep his part of the covenant. Because of his disobedience the last part of God's promise was fulfilled, "In the day that you eat of it you shall surely die" (Gen. 2:17). By breaking the covenant requirements, man was brought into a state of spiritual death and darkness and could do nothing to change that situation. However, Christ, the Second Person in the Trinity, had agreed that he would come and keep the covenant on man's behalf. He would meet all the requirements of the covenant of works and thereby earn man's forgiveness and salvation, thus restoring man's relationship with God, others, and the world around us.

Because God had chosen covenant as the means by which he would relate to man, he revealed the second covenant, which we know as the covenant of grace. What God requires, though man is no longer capable of doing it, Christ came and did for us, and what he did was then attributed to man's account. Man can now relate to God only by means of the covenant of grace.

Under the covenant of grace God once again says, "I will be your God and the God of your children," not on the basis of our works of righteousness, but on the basis of what Christ has done at the cross. Therefore, while man once stood under the covenant of works unto death, by the mercy of God he now stands under the covenant of grace unto life. Louis Berkhof reminds us that even under the covenant of grace "there are requirements from God the covenant maker: 1. that they accept the covenant and covenant promises by faith and thus enter upon the life of the covenant; and 2. that, from the principle of the new life born within them, they consecrate themselves to God in new obedience."[12]

With a proper understanding of the doctrine of the covenants, a Christian learns that salvation is determined not by our own works, but on

94

the basis of Christ keeping the covenant for us. The Bible teaches that we are saved by grace through faith in Christ.

The only thing that we have to contribute to the whole process is our sins, for Christ has done it all. "But when the goodness and loving kindness of God our Savior appeared, he saved us, not because of works done by us in righteousness, but according to his own mercy, by the washing of regeneration and renewal of the Holy Spirit" (Titus 3:4–5). That summarizes the saving process.

Some continue to teach that works save us, whether works be in the form of faith, as a work of man, or by the sacraments, or by doing good things. But Scripture says, "For by grace you have been saved through faith. And this is not your own doing; it is the gift of God, not a result of works, so that no one may boast" (Eph. 2:8–9). There are requirements of faith and obedience, not as causes of our salvation, but as natural results of being in the covenant of grace. There is a place for good works in the life of a Christian, but not before one becomes a Christian. We might even say that faith and obedience are not simply the conditions of the covenant, but rather our obligation to it. Another way to say this is that our faith and obedience are merely our response of gratitude to God for all that he has done to save us.

The Bible also teaches that salvation is a process beginning with God's electing grace and culminating with his fulfillment of the promise when we are in the new heaven and new earth. As Christians we have only God to thank for our salvation, and in doing that we are reminded of Paul's words, "I am sure of this, that he who began a good work in you will bring it to completion at the day of Jesus Christ" (Phil. 1:6).

The Church

The fifth essential doctrine within Reformed theology is the doctrine of the church. The Westminster Confession of Faith has a good summary statement: "The catholic or universal church, which is invisible, consists of the whole number of the elect, that have been, are, or shall be gathered into one, under Christ the Head thereof; and is the spouse, the body,

the fullness of Him that filleth all in all" (25:1). The church is community. It is family, and it is the body of Christ.

In chapter 3, where we dealt with the kingdom of God and the church,
we pointed out the central role and place of the church within God's kingdom. John Calvin echoes the words of Augustine and others when he says
that whoever has God as his Father also has the church for his Mother.[13] He
thereby reminds us that Christians are part of God's church. "And the Lord
added to the church daily those who were being saved" (Acts 2:47, NKJV).

We also know that there is the church visible, and there is the church
invisible. The Westminster Confession refers to the invisible church, which
consists of all the elect. There is also the visible church, which is made up
of those who profess Christ, along with their children. Ideally the two
should be one, but we know that some in the visible church are not true
believers. Not so in the invisible church. Also, in its visible form the church
is both an organization (with officers who minister the Word and the
sacraments, with assemblies locally and beyond, with confessions and catechism, and with government functions) and an organism, a living body.

Christians are to be identified with the visible church because to that
church God has committed the preaching and teaching of the Word, the
administration of sacraments, church discipline, and the headquarters
through and from which ministry and service are to be enacted both in
the church and to the world. While the church takes on many forms today,
especially through its denominational affiliations, its styles of worship,
and diversity of ministries, Christians need to understand that there is
only one church, one universal body of Christ. The local churches are
merely that, localizations of the universal church that should reflect the
true church in all they are and do.

Christians should belong to a church, more specifically one that bears
the marks of a true church: belief in and teaching of the Bible, the requirement of a credible profession of faith in Christ, participation in the sacraments of baptism and the Lord's Supper, and clear accountability to the
spiritual overseers or leaders. The importance of church membership
should be part of any discipleship emphasis with believers. Being a mem-

ber of the visible church is not an optional matter, even though God leaves it to the individual to make the decision as to which church. Belonging is a biblical requirement. The writer of Hebrews says, "And let us consider how to stir up one another to love and good works, not neglecting to meet together, as is the habit of some, but encouraging one another, and all the more as you see the Day drawing near" (10:24–26).

God used the Protestant Reformation to remind the church that members should have access to the Bible in their own language. They need to study it on their own rather than rely solely on someone else's interpretation. However, the Reformers also reminded us, using the apostle Peter's words, that no Scripture is of private interpretation. Being a member of a church that preaches and teaches the Bible is a key to enabling Christians to know the Bible better and to experience a sense of accountability. While much damage was done in church history by keeping the Bible from the people, much damage has also been done by allowing them to read and interpret it without any accountability or checks and balances. Many of the cults, and possibly a few occult movements, have grown out of privately interpreting the Bible. The church should be a help in focusing on the Bible's message and properly interpreting it.

Last Things

The last major doctrine in Reformed theology is the doctrine of eschatology or last things. As we observed in chapter 3 on the kingdom of God, there are the present aspect of the kingdom and the not-yet or future aspect. Christians need to live in the present with an eye on the future. There is more to reality than yesterday and today. The Bible teaches that God has a future in store for us, and it will happen in a way that he has planned and in a way that will complete his plan. There is a sense that if there is no future to be gained, then our present faith and work are meaningless.

Christians need to include the doctrine of the last things in their belief system. The "end things" theme runs from Genesis to Revelation and is the thread that brings all the parts of the story together. By understanding it we will be better equipped to field some of the questions that people ask today about life, destiny, and reality as a whole.

When helping someone to understand the importance and place of the last things, we have to be careful of extremes. There is something fascinating about all the imagery and symbolism connected with this doctrine. There have been those who, like the existentialists, have tried to put everything into the present moment of time, with no past or future, and those of a more liberal orientation, who have seen God's kingdom as only for this world. On the other hand, there have been, especially today, those who are so spellbound by "end things" that everything focuses on what lies ahead. Much of modern fundamentalism is of that persuasion, often at the expense of seeing the whole metanarrative starting with creation and proceeding to the fall, redemption, and finally consummation. When the Bible refers to Christ as the first and last, or the Alpha and Omega, the beginning and the end, those references are intended to remind us of creation and consummation.

Though the Reformers believed that eschatology plays a major role in the Christian faith, they did not focus on it in their day, as they did salvation; yet they knew that without the belief in the end things, nothing really fits together. Eschatology closes the system of truth, not in a confining or limiting way, but in a way that reminds us that the best is yet to come. We are in waiting for that final day when God will make a new heaven and a new earth. Christians believe that God will finally and completely restore all things just as he originally intended them to be, and this will happen in conjunction with Jesus' last coming at the end of the age. While we can observe certain cyclical patterns within history, history is linear. It is moving toward its final destination. The Bible is one grand metanarrative that begins with creation, moves through redemption, and continues to the end, the consummation of all things. God's story has a beginning and middle, and it will also have an end. For Christians it will be a happy one.

With this doctrine, as with the others, we are dependent on God's Word to teach us the truth. If we listen and understand correctly, we will not speculate, deny, or remove it from God's system of truth. For those who suffer poverty, persecution, injustice, discrimination, and any unfairness, and for all of us who suffer the effects of sin and death, the hope of consummation is the energy that God uses to keep us going and fighting the good fight. The apostle John wrote, "Beloved, we are God's children now, and what we will be has not yet appeared; but we know that when he appears we will be like him, because we shall see him as he is. And everyone who thus hopes in him purifies himself as he is pure" (1 John 3:2–3). When Christ comes the second time, he will deliver the kingdom to God the Father.

Conclusion

While this chapter has focused on the classic doctrines of Christianity in the order adopted by theologians in Reformation times, we must realize that God would have us believe, understand, and articulate these doctrinal truths in the context of today's world, which is quite different from that of the Reformers. The doctrines do not change, but our theology, which is our way of expressing our beliefs about God, does. We must continue to communicate God's truth to today's world. As we make disciples, we desire to teach all the things that Christ has commanded with biblical soundness, great cultural sensitivity, and audience awareness, which is simply to say, we must know the Word and know the world. In the words of John Feinberg,

> Because systematic theology attempts to address itself not only to the timeless issues presented in Scripture but also to the current issues of one's day and culture, each theology will to some extent need to be redone in each generation. Biblical truth does not change from generation to generation, but the issues that confront the church do. A theology that was adequate for a different era and different culture may simply not speak to key issues in a given culture at a given time.[14]

Our role in disciple making is to help Christians understand the truth and its application to everyday life and events.

Why Reformed theology in making disciples? In making disciples we need to keep our focus on God's purpose to make us to be like Christ and to care for the things that he cares for, which requires a biblical world-and-life-view in accord with sound doctrine, taught in a way that communicates that doctrine is life and vice versa. When that occurs, we can hope to see a reversal of some of the trends that have come about through the failures and shortcomings of incorrect methods.

TOPICS FOR REFLECTION OR DISCUSSION

1. Christianity is made up of a diversity of people. This chapter suggests the importance of incorporating the Reformed faith into the disciple-making process. Why is the Reformed faith important to the process, and what is different about it as an approach?

2. There are three misperceptions that are commented on in this chapter. Discuss each one and determine if you have ever experienced any or all of those misperceptions. In what circumstance or setting, and how did you respond?

3. The chapter talks about studying doctrine within a system. What are the benefits of doing so? What are some limitations? What should we be careful to avoid with any system of theology?

4. The early pages of this chapter quote some research into the effectiveness of preaching and teaching. What do you think about the statistics, and are the suggestions in this chapter on target for addressing them? What else should be considered in the disciple-making process because of those statistics?

5. The chapter makes several references to the Protestant Reformation, the individual and the Bible, and who should study the Bible, its doctrines, and consequently theology. How do you react to the idea that each church member is equal, that everyone is a theologian, and that doctrine is life? Do those suggestions undermine the importance of gifted teachers and their roles in the church?

6. Discuss with your group the importance of the role of the Bible in the disciple-making process. What is the most effective way to use

the Bible? the most ineffective way? Who should use the Bible in this process?

7. What books or periodicals have you read recently that have emphasized the importance of doctrine and theology in the disciple-making process?

8. List several reasons why it is important to teach Christians doctrine and how to do theology. What are some cautions to consider?

Suggested Reading

Berkhof, Louis. *Manual of Christian Doctrine*. Grand Rapids: Eerdmans, 1965. A summary of the lengthier *Systematic Theology*; good outline form.

Erickson, Millard. *Does It Matter What I Believe?* Grand Rapids: Baker, 1992. A readable and helpful underscoring of the theme of this chapter. A good writer, Erickson answers his question with an absolute yes.

———. *Introducing Christian Doctrine*. Edited by L. Arnold Hustad. Grand Rapids: Baker, 2001. A good, nonsuperficial summary of the larger *Christian Theology*. While written from a Baptist perspective, the book is valuable in establishing a Christian foundation and can be supplemented on the sacrament.

Grenz, Stanley J., and Roger E. Olson. *Who Needs Theology: An Invitation to Study God*. Downers Grove, Ill.: InterVarsity, 1996. A volume underscoring that theology and doctrine are not merely for the professionals and the classroom, but for every believer.

Marsden, George M., and Mark A. Noll. *The Search for Christian America*. Westchester, Ill.: Crossway, 1983. A good study of the relationship of early America and its Christian origins. How should Christians think about early America, the American Revolution, the Great Awakening, and how they relate to America's political agenda?

Sproul, R. C. *When Worlds Collide*. Wheaton, Ill.: Crossway, 2002. A little volume demonstrating the importance not only of embracing sound doctrine but also of knowing how to use it in crisis.

Stevens, R. Paul. *The Other Six Days*. Grand Rapids: Eerdmans, 1999. An excellent book on the subject of the one body of Christ (no professional/laity dichotomony).

6

Covenant Theology

As I discussed my plans to write this book with a number of people, several whom I greatly respect encouraged me not to write separate chapters on Reformed theology and covenant theology because, in their view, the two are basically synonymous. Others suggested that if I did write two chapters, covenant theology should precede Reformed theology. Obviously, I chose to do otherwise. Reformed theology is the broader category; covenant theology is a part of it, but not synonymous with it. I believe the covenant is the glue that holds all the parts together and reminds us, as we emphasized in chapter 2, of the personal aspect of knowledge and truth.

The two chapters and their sequence within the framework of part 1, have been carefully designed to flow naturally. I did not make this choice simply because the case can be made that one can be Reformed and not necessarily covenantal or that one cannot be covenantal without being Reformed. Rather I want the chapter on Reformed theology to equip disciplers to do what Paul instructed Titus to do: "Teach what accords with sound doctrine" (Titus 2:1). As we saw in the previous chapter, Paul's words were the forerunner of Titus's training men and women in the art of discipleship, which required not only a sound doctrinal approach, but that those relationally intended truths be communicated in a relational manner to those being discipled. Thus the chapter on covenant theology.

Christians need to know, understand, and build their lives upon the basic system of doctrine taught in the Word, not as an end in itself, but as a means to deepening our relationship with God, with others, and with the world around us. Covenant theology reminds us that God deals with us and the world on the basis of covenant. We will examine the specifics as we continue, but for now the point is that the God who is above his creation is also a person very much involved in it. Unlike the pantheists who attempt to make God identical with every aspect of his creation, much as modern-day Eastern thought does, and unlike the deists who believe that there is a God but he has no day-to-day involvement with his creation, we believe that God is a personal God. He relates to those made in his image and to the rest of creation as well. He tells us that he has chosen to do this by way of covenant. Therefore, we might say that we have to understand truth, including its doctrines, covenantally. They must personally touch our lives and make a difference in how we relate to God, one another, and the world in which we live; if they do not, we do not correctly understand them.

In chapter 2 on epistemology I mentioned that while knowledge of God and reality is based on his objectively revealed truth, we cannot know his truth purely objectively because he intends that we know him and his truth personally. In fact, if we do not have that personal knowledge, we do not truly know.

In chapter 3 on the kingdom of God we saw that everything in creation belongs to him. He is the sovereign King. There is no area of life over which he has not claimed his sovereign rights. He exercises his sovereignty relationally on the basis of covenantal terms that he initiated and established. He relates to his people in a very personal and intimate way.

In chapter 4 we focused on the biblical world-and-life-view. Our belief in God must be worked out in all areas of life. As we will see, not only did he determine to relate to us by way of covenant, he was the original covenant maker. He set up this framework. He determined the conditions and made the promises connected with covenant. The title he most frequently uses to refer to himself is Lord—a covenantal title. If Christians understand the covenant concept, then we will avoid some of the "Lordship controversy" that has raised its head throughout church history. Since no area of life is exempt from his lordship, we have to learn to think and live Christianly in all areas "that in everything he might be preeminent," (Col. 1:18). Familiarity with the covenant concept will enable us to see the ramifications of this truth in all of life because covenant impacts our relation not only to the Lord God, but also to others and the world around us.

In chapter 5 on Reformed theology we argued that God has revealed to us through his Word and Spirit what he wants us to know and to do. Understanding theology from a covenantal perspective will not only help us avoid the Lordship controversy, but it will also help us understand how the law and the gospel, or law and grace, fit together rather than oppose each other. According to the Calvinistic Reformed position, both grace and law are included in the gospel of Christ.

The view of the covenant is a major difference between the first and second phases of the Protestant Reformation, that is, the Lutheran (Germany) and the Calvinistic (France and Switzerland) phases. God gave the law to his chosen people, Israel, but not as a means of entering into covenant with them. He had made it clear that only on the basis of Christ's work could that happen after the fall. The law was and is simply a written expression of his will for his people, corporately and individually. It is crucial to understand the law in the context of the covenant! Unless we do, we can easily make the mistake, as many have done, of believing that keeping the law is the means whereby we enter into the covenant relationship, and that breaking the law keeps us out of it.

The covenant concept reminds us that the law implies a prior relationship, not a legalistic system. The Lord's relation to his creation, particularly his elect, precedes all else, including the giving of the law; hence the law was never intended to establish a relationship with God, but rather to provide guidance on how that relationship is to be maintained, nur-

104

tured, and experienced. As the sovereign Lord who establishes relationship with his creation, particularly his image bearer, God describes the kind of relationship that we are to sustain with him. Those requirements are thus set in a context of grace. Never should we understand God's law as something prior to grace in respect to relationship. Before the fall, grace enabled man to be obedient; but after the fall, grace was shown in Christ's keeping the covenant for us.

I believe the Calvinistic Reformed view of the covenant is more consistently biblical because John Calvin and the second wave of the Reformation associated with him took a more holistic approach to life, an approach that is inclusive not merely in the area of soteriology, but in regard to topics such as lordship, covenant, and law. As I stated in the beginning of the book, one of the weaknesses hampering our disciple-making efforts today is the failure to take a more holistic approach to the Christian life. Robert Wuthnow asserts, for example, in the preface to his book *The Crisis in the Churches* that the church's failure to teach the biblical concept of stewardship is directly related to the failure to teach the lordship of Christ in all of life.[1]

We will look at the concept of the covenant in a summary manner, and then we will look at God's use of covenant in setting forth his relational arrangements with man. From there we will see how that covenantal perspective guided people in biblical times, and finally we will see what we can learn from covenant theology to help us understand our relationship to God, his relationship to us, and our relationships with one another. This covenant concept reminds us that we can relate to God because he is a personal God, but only on his terms, because he is the sovereign Lord. We relate to others on God's terms also. Hence the notion of covenant is not a detailed, legalistic contract established between God and man but a living relationship that required loving commitment of both parties.

The Concept of Covenant

In his book *Covenant of Grace* William Hendriksen states, "What is needed is the rekindling of interest in the doctrine of the covenant of grace. Our precious youths must be made aware of what it means to be 'children of the covenant.' "² Our children and youth do need to know about covenant, but so do adults.

As we equip, educate, and train disciples, we have not always given this topic the important place I believe God intends for it to have. Failure to incorporate it into the educational process of the Christian life is to forfeit a foundational truth that is intended to help believers understand things about God and their relation to him and to others that they will not otherwise understand. I remember my own father's testimony and excitement when, in the later years of his life, after committing to Christ, he began to study and teach the Bible and to understand something about covenant theology. I remember one of our last conversations before he went to be with the Lord, and after he had to give up teaching his Sunday school class. He said to me, there is only one thing I would like to do before I die, and that is to teach covenant theology to my Sunday school class. Covenant theology greatly enriched his life and witness.

When we refer to the covenant, we generally look at it in an individualistic way—how God relates to me and how I relate to him. Focusing on the individual fits our Western mentality; however, the idea of the covenant is much broader than this. How God relates to me and I relate to him are vitally important topics, but understanding God's covenantal way of relating to us and the world reminds us that there is more to the story than simply what happens between God and me.

While the Westminster Confession of Faith contains an outstanding chapter on "God's Covenant with Man," it tends to focus on the individual's relationship with God. Though the corporate aspect of the community is present in other places in that document, it would have been helpful for it to have underscored upfront the idea not only that covenant refers to God's relation with us individually, but that it has a family aspect as well. Of course that creed preceded the strong emphasis on the individual that has been present in our culture for the past several hundred years. For that reason, at the time of writing, the corporate nature of the covenant was not the issue that it has become for us today.

In most Presbyterian churches, including the church to which I belong, the Presbyterian Church in America, when the covenant sign of infant baptism is administered, the pastor directs several questions to the infant's parents, but the last question is asked of the congregation: "Do you as a congregation undertake the responsibility of assisting the parents in the Christian nurture of this child?" The idea of the covenant includes family but not just the immediate family. Baptism is administered to individuals, but only in the context of the believing community.

Covenant theology does not focus merely on soteriology or the study of salvation. For the Calvinistic branch of the Reformation, covenant is part of a larger framework. Many of the traditional works in systematic theology tend to bypass this larger framework. Of course there have been those such as Herman Bavinck, Geerhardus Vos, and Meredith Kline, to name a few, who have developed the broader perspective.

Geerhardus Vos gave an explanation as to why the covenant concept has been so much in the foreground of Reformed theology: "The doctrine of the covenant is taken from Scripture. . . . Because Reformed theology took hold of Scriptures in their deepest root idea, it was in a position to work through them more fully from this central point and to let each part of their content come to its own."[3] I believe the covenant must be an integral part of disciple making. It should not be neglected or overlooked in that process.

How God Reveals His Covenant

At this point we can now turn to the specifics of the covenant. God relates to man and man to God by way of covenant. Covenant is the manner in which that relationship is expressed both before and after the fall. Vos states,

> If man already stood in a covenant relation to God before the fall, then
> it is to be expected that the covenant idea will also dominate in the work

of redemption. God cannot simply let go of the ordinance which He once instituted, but much rather displays His glory in that He carries it through despite man's sin and apostasy.... The covenant of redemption is nothing other than proof for the fact that even the work of redemption, though it springs from God's sovereign will, finds its execution in free deeds performed in a covenantal way.[4]

When God made man in the beginning, he chose to add to the Creator/creature relationship and form a personal relationship by establishing a covenant with man. God revealed to Adam what we know as the covenant of works. Understanding the covenant of works is as vital to understanding relationships as is the covenant of grace.

It is at this point that the Calvinistic and Reformed understanding of the covenant is unique. Some have taught that when God created Adam and placed him in the garden, God had given him everything in its fullness. This implies that what Christ later does as the second Adam (Rom. 5:12–21) is to restore us to our original perfect and complete state. However, we believe on the basis of the promises of the covenant that there would have been much more in store for Adam and his descendants if he had obeyed God and kept the covenant. Specifically, God told Adam that the conditions of the covenant allowed him to eat of all the trees of the Garden of Eden except one. Of that tree he was not to eat. That restriction became the boundary of the covenant that man was not to transgress or ignore.

A covenant without conditions is not meaningful. In the covenant of works the condition was obedience to God's commands. Herman Bavinck comments on what the result of obedience would have been: "Although Adam was created in God's image, he was not immediately that image in the fullest sense, nor was he that image in and of himself. We do not have God's image before us in its entire richness until we consider the destiny of man involved in it both for this life and the future."[5]

Understanding this covenant concept will also reveal something of the wonder and marvel of God's willingness to bind himself to us, to humble himself, and to give man great promises on the condition of obedience to his commands. What God said to Adam, by way of paraphrase, was that "we will relate to one another on the basis of this covenant. The condition of this covenant is obedience—works. If you will obey me and keep covenant with me, I will then give you the blessings of eternal life and perfect happiness." In return for obedience, God promised Adam eternal life, meaning life in its fullness. On the other hand, God told Adam that if he broke the covenant he would surely die without realizing the fullness of the original promises.

As we read God's Word in the early chapters of Genesis and later references in both the Old and New Testaments, we see that Adam did not keep covenant with God. He violated God's conditions by eating of the tree of knowledge of good and evil. With that disobedience, Adam forfeited the promises and fulfillments of the covenant for himself and all of his descendants. "For as in Adam all die, so also in Christ shall all be made alive" (1 Cor. 15:22).

At the point of his disobedience, Adam became unable to keep the covenant God had established with him. He began to experience spiritual death. But understand that his disobedience did not nullify the covenant of works. As we saw above, God's covenant is an everlasting covenant; hence, though man is now incapable of keeping the covenant of works, God still requires perfect obedience to that covenant in order for man to be saved and have eternal life. That may be one of the reasons that sinful man still feels a compulsion to earn his salvation or to embrace a salvation by works. Obedience is still an essential part of God's plan for his people. It must be stressed in the disciple-making process.

Enter the Covenant of Grace

The Westminster Confession of Faith states,

> The first covenant made with man was a covenant of works, wherein life was promised to Adam, and in him to his posterity, upon the condition of perfect and personal obedience. Man, by his fall, having made himself incapable of life by that covenant, the Lord was pleased to make

a second, commonly called the covenant of grace; wherein he freely offereth unto sinners life and salvation by Jesus Christ, requiring of them faith in him, that they may be saved, and promising to give unto all those that are ordained unto eternal life His Holy Spirit, to make them willing, and able to believe. (7.2–3)

Christians need to understand early in their Christian lives that God still requires perfect obedience if they are to have eternal life and bliss with him; however, when Adam sinned, he and his descendants became incapable of rendering the perfect obedience required by the covenant of works. Man died spiritually. He lost his ability to keep covenant, yet God still holds him accountable for that covenant. At that point God revealed his plan to save Adam from his sin. In Genesis 3:15 we have the first unveiling of God's covenant of grace whereby Christ his Son would come and pay the penalty for our sins, in our place, thereby earning for us all the promises lost in breaking the covenant of works: "I will put enmity between you [the serpent] and the woman, and between your offspring and her offspring; he shall bruise your head, and you shall bruise his heel." That enmity would take different shapes at different times during the Old Testament period, but each of the phases of the covenant of grace would reach its fulfillment in the coming of Christ, which the Bible calls the new covenant and which would be written on our hearts.

The covenant of grace reminds us that there is one and only one way of salvation since man's fall in the opening of Genesis. Salvation can no longer be attained by man's works. However, understanding the covenant concept reminds us that God is bound to keep his word in covenant. Therefore he planned for Christ to intervene, thus suspending his judgment until the last elect comes to faith in Christ and Christ returns at the end of the age.

As the apostle Paul says, "For as in Adam all die, so also in Christ shall all be made alive" (1 Cor. 15:22). God sent his Son, the Lord Jesus, the Second Person of the Trinity, to keep the covenant on our behalf and on that basis to save us from our sins. He kept the law to its fullest.

Hence Paul could say to the Philippian jailer and to us, "Believe in the Lord Jesus, and you will be saved, you and your household" (Acts 16:31). Now, we must follow the process carefully. God established the covenant of works with all mankind. It remains his requirement; however, man the sinner is unable to fulfill that requirement; hence God made a second covenant with his elect people. He would send Jesus Christ to do for us what we cannot do for ourselves. The coming of Christ maintains the integrity and continuity of God's covenant with man. He achieves this particularly by his life of perfect obedience, along with his sacrifice on the cross by which he earned our redemption. Rather than our being saved by our own works of righteousness, we are now saved on the basis of Christ's work seen in his birth, life, death, and resurrection from the dead.

This covenant of grace is the only means now whereby we can be saved. The Westminster Confession of Faith states that even the covenant of grace has requirements and conditions; specifically, we must believe and obey the Lord. But doesn't that sound like a covenant of works agreement? Yes, except that while we are unable to meet the conditions ourselves, Jesus Christ has come and by his grace not only kept the covenant of works for us, but made us willing and able to believe and obey him. Christ earned for us what we could not earn for ourselves because of sin. As a result, by his grace we can have eternal life.

William Heyns says it like this: "The following special characteristics of the Covenant of Grace may be mentioned: that it is one-sided, unbreakable, and unconditional."[6] This simply means that the covenant of grace is one-sided in that it was made solely by Christ in establishing and meeting the conditions. It is unbreakable in that God said in Genesis 17:7 that it would be an everlasting covenant. It is an eternal covenant never to be broken, and it is an unconditional covenant. Heyns comments, "Likewise, it is to be designated as an unconditional covenant, although there are what are usually called 'conditions' of the covenant."[7] As a covenant of grace, unlike the covenant of works, it is without conditions for meriting salvation. Heyns makes a good point in saying that faith and obedience are conditions of the covenant of grace, though we might do better to refer to them as obligations of the covenant. But even as obligations, we must recognize that we are unable to meet them in our strength alone. But part of the promise of the covenant of grace is Christ's willingness to enable us to meet those obligations.

When we refer to the gospel as God's means of grace, we simply mean, "For by grace you have been saved through faith. And this is not your own doing; it is the gift of God, not a result of works, so that no one may boast" (Eph. 2:8–9). In the covenant of grace we can say that Christ imparts salvation to those for whom he died, thus restoring them to God's promised state of blessing at the beginning.

As can be seen in the suggested reading materials, God manifested this covenant in different ways throughout Old and New Testament history. In the New Testament, the new covenant that he had promised through Jeremiah (31:31–34), a covenant that would be written on our hearts, he established by Christ Jesus on our behalf. That is what the writer of Hebrews has in mind in chapter 6 when he refers to us as heirs of the covenant or heirs of the promise.

Two things need to be seen about the covenant of grace beyond what God does for us. First, he is not only our God but the God of our seed after us. His promise is to us and to our children, "For the promise is for you and for your children and for all who are far off, everyone whom the Lord our God calls to himself" (Acts 2:39). Second, God said to father Abraham to whom this promise was clearly revealed, "I will make of you a great nation"(Gen. 12:2), and "Behold, my covenant is with you, and you shall be the father of a multitude of nations" (Gen. 17:4).

The application of the covenant of grace centers not only on us but also on our children. It includes those from "every nation and tribe and language and people" (Rev. 14:6). Though the promise of the covenant is for the elect in Christ, they are found all over the world; hence the Great Commission of Jesus (Matt. 28:18–20) is a global one.

As the sovereign Lord, God establishes the conditions of the covenant and he issues the warnings and promises. At first we saw the covenant with Adam as a covenant of works whereby man could obtain eternal life and bliss with God. We also saw how man did not keep that covenant and hence experienced the reality of God's warning that death would follow disobedience. Then we saw how Christ came to keep the covenant for us and established his covenant of grace that assures us of what God promised originally in the covenant of works. Christ has merited salvation for us by his own sacrificial redemption and thus enables us to believe and obey his commands. And we have seen that the covenant promise is not only for us but for our children and those elect from all the nations of the world. God's Ten Commandments, as we know them, are still his moral guide for us today to help us make application of his will, as we obey his commands. The law was never intended as a means of our salvation.

Some Further Implications of Covenant

In a recent wedding at which I officiated, I explained that God is the covenant God who enters into relation with his people freely without coercion. We relate to him by way of covenant. Then I explained that God's Word says that we marry by covenant (Mal. 2:14 and Prov. 2:17). To understand the marriage covenant, we must understand the covenant between God and his people. In fact, Jesus uses marriage to help us understand the mystery of the covenant. I explained that God's covenant with us is God's pattern for our covenant relation with our spouse.

Also, because the covenant concept forms the setting of God's relation to us and how we relate to him, that vertical relationship also has, according to his Word, ramifications for how we are to relate to one another and the world around us. For example, in the Old Testament, "covenant" (*berith*) is used to describe the arrangements between men. Covenants in the Bible have deep religious connotations because they are meant to be reflections, horizontally, of God's vertical relationship with us. And it was a normal part of those covenants to call upon God as the witness of their establishment with the idea that breaking the covenant would result in punishment.

Gordon Spykman explains it like this:

> Covenant is the very foundation and framework for all biblical reli-
> gion. Covenantal religion defines the fundamental structures under-
> girding all human relationships and every societal calling; it embraces
> every earthly institution—marriage, schooling, labor, social service,
> science, art, even politics. Even when we in Adam betrayed our calling,
> God did not abandon the covenant. Instead, he intervened in grace to
> keep it alive. Covenant history is a story without an ending. It covers
> not only God's way with Israel, but also with the Christian community
> today and on into the future.[8]

Therefore, the Old Testament presents numerous examples of
covenants being made between individuals or families. For example,
Abimelech was not sure of Abraham's intentions toward him, so he
requested a covenant stating that Abraham would not deal falsely with
him or his children (Gen. 21:23). Both Abraham and Abimelech made
the covenant (v. 27), which is mentioned a second time (v. 32).

In Genesis 31, Laban and Jacob made a covenant to relieve tension and
suspicion between them. They used symbols of stone to signify their
covenant, and ate together as token of that agreement. Eating together
was often connected with covenant making in biblical times. In 1 Samuel
18:3 David and Jonathan make a covenant (also referred to in 23:18).
There were covenants between nations, between equals, and between ruling states and subjects. Animal sacrifices were used as symbols of ratify-
ing the covenants.

These few examples are enough to show that covenants were common
in the Bible, along with signs and seals; hence it is easy to make the connection with the signs and seals of baptism and the Lord's Supper. They
are covenant functions.

Henry Buis describes some of the noteworthy characteristics of
covenant:

> Although the covenant relationship places its stress on legal features
> which demand faithfulness as a duty, it is an agreement like the mar-

114

riage relationship, which involves a loving relationship, a continuous fellowship between the parties involved. In fact, the warm affectionate word for love used in the Old Testament (*chesed*) is a term that is so distinctively related to the covenant that some scholars specifically call it covenant-love. God is described frequently in Scripture as a God who keeps covenant (*berith*) and covenant love (*chesed*) with those who respond in faithfulness. . . .

The covenant idea in Scripture also counteracts the excessive individualism often found in the church. Living the Christian life not only involves something within the individual person, but also involves a relationship between the individual Christian and God, and relationships with Christians who are members together of the same covenant with God. The biblical covenant is never with the individual in isolation but always with the group of God's people of which the individual is a part.[9]

The idea of covenant is so pervasive in the Scriptures that S. G. DeGraaf wrote four volumes entitled *Promise and Deliverance* to assist Sunday school teachers in teaching the Bible covenantally. Convinced that every Bible story tells us something of the covenant-making God, he describes three objectives in teaching Bible stories to children:

1. To emphasize that the Bible is God's self-revelation.
2. To show God's revelation of himself in the Mediator Jesus Christ.
3. To emphasize the covenant as the only way that God comes to his people.[10]

So, when we read the Bible, we are to seek to determine what God reveals about himself, what he reveals about himself as the Mediator, and how he reveals himself in his covenant with his people.

Having a covenantal framework for understanding the things of the Lord, especially his saving grace and its implications, is vital to the discipleship process. It keeps the focus on sound doctrine as the basis for our believing and living the Christian life, while setting it within the personal relationship between God and his people. It keeps us from being imprisoned by legalism and reminds us that it is by God's grace through faith that we are saved.

TOPICS FOR REFLECTION OR DISCUSSION

1. Review and discuss how the covenant bears on our relation to God and to one another.
2. What does covenant theology provide for the discipleship process that is missing for those who do not incorporate it?
3. Discuss the relation of covenant theology to the kingdom of God, a world-and-life-view, and Reformed theology.
4. What can an early understanding of the concept of covenant do to encourage and strengthen the disciple-making process?
5. Discuss the relation and difference between the covenant of works and the covenant of grace.

SUGGESTED READING

Creator, Redeemer, Consummator: A Festschrift for Meredith G. Kline. Edited by Howard Griffeth and John R. Muether. Jackson, Miss.: Reformed Theological Seminary, 2000. In a book honoring an outstanding Old Testament scholar, twenty-two authors highlight some of Kline's greatest themes, ranging from biblical studies to ethics and theology. Some excellent chapters for expanding one's understanding of Reformed theology, particularly the covenant.

DeGraaf, S. G. *Promise and Deliverance.* 4 vols. St. Catharines, Ont.: Paideia, 1977. An unrivaled exposition of how the covenant theme runs from Genesis to Revelation.

Frame, John. *The Doctrine of God.* Phillipsburg, N.J.: P&R Publishing, 2002. A complement to the earlier volume *The Doctrine of the Knowledge of God.*

Hendriksen, William. *The Covenant of Grace.* Grand Rapids: Baker, 1932. A powerful little book that expands on the big topic of the covenant of grace. An easy-to-read gold mine.

116

Kline, Meredith G. *By Oath Consigned*. Grand Rapids: Eerdmans, 1968. Not an easy read, but no one can be well read on the covenant if this volume is slighted.

Robertson, O. Palmer. *Covenants: God's Way with His People*. Philadelphia: Great Commission, 1987. A good book for teaching the subject of the covenant.

Vos, Geerhardus. *Redemptive History and Biblical Interpretation*. Edited by Richard B. Gaffin Jr. Phillipsburg, N.J.: P&R Publishing, 1980. Demonstration of the grand narrative of the Bible that brings together all the parts. Vos shows that the theme of redemption is the key to Bible understanding.

Knowing the World: The Context of Discipleship

Part 1 was intended to construct a holistic theological and philosophical foundation for disciple making. In one sense we could say the areas covered are universal and timeless, always to be a part of the process. If they are not in place, then we will have a faulty view of making disciples and settle for less than God's holistic plan.

Part 2 begins to take those universal or timeless concepts and put them into a context or setting where we can begin to see their implications and applications. Our emphasis throughout this process is threefold: (1) We must understand the Word of God (sound doctrine). (2) We must be philosophically aware of our particular culture. (3) We must apply the truth to our specific circumstance.

We have to teach people to think biblically, and that requires more than simple Bible study. Countless people know biblical content and still are not able to think biblically about life. Part 1 was written to aid in consistent biblical thinking. However, we do not study the Word of God in a vacuum. We must understand God's revelation, particularly his inscripturated Word, in our particular circumstance to know how to apply that

Word and think biblically about life and reality. Here is where we see so much breakdown or cognitive dissonance among professing Christians. As Christians, we do not live in some ethereal thought world only. God intends for us to develop those thoughts into actions or a lifestyle. To do that properly, we must have several things in place.

We must not wish to return or advance to another time. God intends for us to live here and now, yes with "eternity in our hearts," but never failing to see the connection between his truth and our world today. Therefore, we have to be students of the world.

The words from 1 Chronicles 12:32 keep ringing in my ears. The writer refers to the men of Issachar as "men who had understanding of the times, to know what Israel ought to do." He connects knowing the world and times and what God would have us to do. That challenges us today to do the same.

As I think about this challenge, I am reminded of John Calvin's opening words in chapter 1 of *The Institutes of the Christian Religion*: To know ourselves we must know God; to know God we must know ourselves. It is hard to tell which comes first because they are so connected. I believe the same principle applies in knowing the Word and knowing the world.

I am deeply grateful to men like Abraham Kuyper, Francis Schaeffer, Cornelius Van Til, Os Guinness, Ken Myers, Carl Henry, and Millard Erickson, whose writings have challenged my thinking directly and indirectly. They have given me a desire to know both the Word and the world. Because of men like them, I am not intimidated by the world's ideologies.

In his devotional book *Resist the Powers* Charles Ringma reflects on a comment by Jacques Ellul: "The world itself once again seems to be God's instrument in forcing the church to face its conscience." What he is saying is that God has a way of allowing the world to play a part in helping the church understand its mission at a particular moment in history. Ringma concludes, "The church cannot learn from the worldliness of the world. But it can learn from the world where God's common grace is manifest."[1]

An effective disciple of Christ is one who understands the Word in the context of his or her circumstance and understands what is taking place in the world in light of God's Word. That is a powerfully effective combination. However, in challenging disciples to do that, I was recently reminded of a word of caution in that connection. Cornelius Plantinga asks, "But isn't there another side to this coin? Suppose we get close enough to secular culture to understand it, to witness to it, to try in some way to reform it. How do we keep from being seduced by it?"[2] That is a powerful reminder that we do not make disciples in isolation. We make them in the context of the church, which requires and provides accountability in thought and deed. We need to interact with other Christians to keep focused and stay the course.

What we intend to do in Part 2 is not to cover the waterfront of knowing the world, but rather to touch on several areas to underscore our purpose. James Skillen notes with approval Abraham Kuyper's overarching view of the realm of Christ:

> Kuyper put it this way in *Pro Rege*: "The Son of God is not to be excluded from anything. You cannot point to any natural realm or star or comet or even descend into the depth of the earth, but it is related to Christ, not in some unimportant tangential way, but directly. There is no force in nature, no laws that control those forces that do not have their origin in that eternal Word. Therefore, it is totally false to restrict Christ to spiritual affairs and to assert there is no point of contact between him and the natural sciences."[3]

Understanding the world is a big task, and so we will focus on two aspects: first, the philosophical developments bringing us to today's world, and second, the demographics of the people to whom we are to minister, for God expects of us what Paul said of David in Acts 13:36: "He had served the purpose of God in his own generation." Who are the members of our generation? What are they like? And in view of their underpinning philosophy and characteristics, how can we most effectively bring God's Word to bear upon them?

7

A Culture Cast in Modernity

This chapter focuses chiefly on the topic of modernity. In 1989 I attended the Lausanne Congress of World Evangelization in Manila. Os Guinness was one of the presenters. Later, I invited him to speak to a pastors' conference on the topic of modernity. In one of the lectures he said, "Modernity is both our greatest threat and our greatest opportunity today." It is a threat if we allow it to program and control our lifestyles consciously, subconsciously, or unconsciously. It is an opportunity if we understand it and its influence, and know how to use it in proper ways.

Also speaking at that congress, and working on the same track, was Ken Myers, who at the time was authoring *All God's Children and Blue Suede Shoes.* In chapter 2 of that book, Myers says:

> Modernity tends to be used in reference to sociological phenomena in industrialized secularized societies with the unintentional result of social arrangements which differ sharply from those found in traditional societies. It also applies to those changes in habits of thinking and feeling, the changes in the mood of society that often accompany social changes. . . . Modernism is that very self-conscious effort by shapers of culture to rethink and recast their own deliberate activities in the wake of modernity. The newer the better would be one way to think about it.[1]

121

Another way to look at this subject is to think of modernity as, in Peter Berger's words, "undergoing a change from the classical or traditional particularly under the influence of technology and beliefs."[2] He further says that there is an assumption that modernity refers to that which is superior to, better or more advanced than what preceded it. It is from that mind-set that we hear sentiments like "the bigger the better; out with the old and in with the new."

When I talk about "modernity" contextually, I am careful not to equate it with "modern" or "modernism" or "modernization," though they come from the same root—*modo*, "just now." In order to communicate my point and to acknowledge that many words have been used in vastly different ways, I will define several terms.

First, *premodern* basically refers to that period of time that predates the early 1600s. It was a time when the world operated on basically the same paradigm, with much emphasis on revelation, faith, and reason, probably in that order. God was very much at the center of this model. Revelation was the heart of this paradigm.

Second, *modern* refers to that period of time around the early 1600s when the paradigm of worldview changed significantly. Reason, logic, and the scientific model rearranged the premodern paradigm; consequently, revelation and faith were assigned lesser roles. God was not ruled out of the model, but man depended on his natural abilities to find God rather than on God revealing himself to man. Reason was the center of this paradigm. Thus *modernism* is the philosophy that starts with man and his ability to reason and determine truth.

Third, growing out of the modern paradigm is *modernization*, a general reference to the ideological and technological influences of the modern world.

Fourth, *modernity* is simply defined by most dictionaries as the quality of being modern; however, it is more than that. In America, it generally describes life in advanced industrial societies. It has philosophical as well as technological and sociological meaning. In America, modernity even has a moral dimension to it. But as Berger has suggested, it generally communicates the attitude that it is superior to what preceded it.

Fifth, *postmodernism* refers basically to a point in time from the early 1900s that follows modernism. It communicates an ideology that replaces both the revelation of premodernism, and the reason of modernism with the experience and feeling of postmodernism.

At the risk of oversimplification the modernization of the world develops new technologies; modernity says, "the newer, the better." It automatically espouses that thought without ever raising the questions that trouble Jacques Ellul, who wonders whether every new thing is better than what precedes it, and whether all the technological development is progress and advancement. Now there is a sense in which we could say that modernity is part of the modern period of thought, but the idea of modernity was also present in the premodern world and is in the postmodern world as well (though postmodernism reacts against modernism).

Guinness is right that modernity poses both threats and opportunities (he develops these thoughts in his book *Dining with the Devil*). The idea of modernity is very present among us. If we do not understand both the threats and opportunities it poses, it can knock the church off course and distract us from thinking critically about consequences.

For example, given the way our modern world has developed so rapidly and quickly through scientific, industrial, and other technological avenues (the modernization process), we have not always taken the time to stop, think, and evaluate what is taking place. Modernity tends to encourage or feed the idea that the past, being inferior to the present and future, need not be considered in the paradigm of life. Whatever is old, discard. "Don't fix it if it is broken; simply replace it with something newer and better." "The old" could be televisions, computers, or ideas. Richard Neuhaus in *The Naked Public Square* made a statement that is a warning to us. He referred to us modern people as "*neophiliacs*," lovers of the new. We like new things. We do not like old things. Hence we like to bring on the new and put away the old.

This is why our contemporary culture has come to value such words as "change" and "new," while showing disdain for words like "tradition" and "old." The Enlightenment philosophy that characterized the modern paradigm has put modernity into overdrive. As I read *All God's Children and Blue Suede Shoes*, I was unable to imagine a world without McDonald's or televisions or computers or Hollywood. In the name of seeking personal peace, affluence, and unlimited choices modernity has drawn us into a framework where thinking, evaluating, and assessing have not been very active.

Don't misunderstand; I am not suggesting that everything connected with modernity is bad; not at all. That would be a foolishly absurd idea. I am not opposed to modernity. In reality I am very much influenced by it. I like new things. It is often troublesome, if not impossible, to repair things. And some new things are better than old things. Every day I carry around a laptop computer capable of doing far more than our 1970s mainframe, which had to be moved from one office to another in a truck. But I also know that Christians have an enemy who is constantly stalking us and seeking to distract us or knock us off course. That is why we need to know what we believe and why. And that is why we must know how to use what we believe in order to make wise decisions about life and reality. That is part of the disciple-making process.

Modernity's Impact on Christianity

It is interesting to note that while evangelicalism in America has held steady for the past fifty years or more, the influence of evangelical Christians has been on the wane. As Christians, we seem to have less ability to influence or shape things. Maybe we have allowed ourselves to become so caught up in the drift of modernity that we have used most of our energies and efforts simply to survive; yet God calls us to do so much more than merely survive. With all the new ideas and rapid change, more Christians are feeling less capable of fighting the battles. So we do not fight; we merely go with the flow.

As Christians we cannot simply evangelize people with the good news of the gospel. We have to disciple new Christians with a biblical world-and-life-view. Someone has said, "If you win the hearts and not the minds, you may lose the hearts." He was exactly right, and it appears that Christians are being more influenced by the world around them than they are influencing the world from a Christian perspective.

This is an appropriate place to say to those who are involved at any level in the disciple-making process that I am not certain we have been called to be cultural transformationalists. In one sense God has not called us to transform culture, even though preaching the gospel and carrying out the cultural mandates will have great impact on our culture. It is a matter of objective and focus. We must seek to be like Christ, to care for the things he cares for, and to see reality as he intends for us to see it. As that happens, we will stand out in a crowd and make a difference. I believe that Ellul was right when he indicated that Christians can be and should be a fixed reference point in a changing and chaotic world. As someone on my staff said years ago, Christians need to stick out like a sore thumb.

Technology has brought the capability of doing and achieving more and more things. But is that good or not? Could it be the prelude to our destruction? And I don't simply mean the bomb or other nuclear weapons. I mean things like artificial reproduction and bioengineering. Cloning is being done with both animals and vegetables. We are told that soon cloning will be a reality with humans and certainly human body parts. What about *in vitro* fertilization? And then cryonics! At the time of this writing there was debate within a particular family as to whether the father's head could be frozen for future purposes. It is easy to see why people like Ellul suggest that not all technology is progress.

Ken Myers has said that we should do something other than denounce modernity. For modernity can enable us to clarify what we should be thinking and doing as Christians. Modernity can serve us by helping us know what God would have us know and how to serve him without compromise or without falling into a dangerously illusory trap.

A CULTURE CAST IN MODERNITY

In my seminars on modernity I have chosen ten areas that I believe are crucial to the whole topic, areas where we seem to be caving in to the influence of modernity. In *Dining with the Devil*, Os Guinness points to three dangers generated by modernity: secularization, pluralization, and privatization. These "lethal trends are at work in the principles and processes of modernity."[3] Guinness's point is that these trends are dangerous because, before we know it, they have infiltrated our lives and subtly knocked us off course. To illustrate the subtlety and danger of modernity, I will select five topics from my larger list that overlap with two of Guinness's: pluralism, privatism, individualism, relativism, and technism. We could also include secularism, materialism, spiritualism, existentialism, rationalism, as well as politics, education, power, and sex to name a few others. My comments on each of the five are not intended to be exhaustive but rather a summary explanation to make the point regarding modernity.

Pluralism. Pluralization is the channel through which pluralism enters our lives. Pluralism basically reminds us that we have more than one choice. There are many options before us in so many different areas. Simply take your pick, and if one does not work, then try another. In today's postmodern environment where authority is challenged, we make our choice, and who is to say that we could be wrong?

Pluralism encourages choice and change. Sound familiar? Those are key words in a context where terms like commitment, continuity, absolutes, and universals are so unpopular. Pluralism is why America is now called by many a mosaic or stewpot of the world's religions. There was a time when pluralism did not have a negative connotation. When America became a nation, one of the things built into our Constitution and Bill of Rights regarding religion was "chartered pluralism." The framers were committed to freedom in the area of religion in that the state would not establish, mandate, or dictate one religion for the people. In the late 1700s that sounded like a good idea, and in that context it was. Today, however, America is not the same in its moral, spiritual, and religious makeup. The once obvious Christian consensus is now an anything-goes consensus. And while America is said to have more organized religion than any other civilized nation, it is no wonder that writers like James Patterson and Peter Kim (*The Day America Told the Truth*) conclude that there is no moral consensus in America today. There are many unchallenged choices, and our culture accepts the premise that one religion is just as good as another.

In the historic sense, we obviously want to maintain a sense of pluralism. We do not want to be told what to believe or how to live. We want freedom to make those choices, but given the influence of modernity, today's pluralistic environment basically makes religion irrelevant in the marketplace of life.

Privatism. A relatively new phenomenon divides life into two areas, the public and the private. Of course there has always been the distinction between the public and private part of our lives, but today's dichotomy is different. Politics, economics, education, science, industry are delegated to the public part of our lives. Morality, religion, belief, and how we spend our leisure time and our money are in the private part of our lives.

That is not necessarily all bad because no one can tell us what to believe, what to purchase, or what religion to adopt. The effect of privatism is that we believe what we choose to believe and then leave each other alone. But not only does privatism in the culture of modernity wall us off from others who choose differently by creating smaller homogeneous groups or tribes; it also neutralizes any attempt to have a moral influence, because all morality has a religious base. In addition we cannot bring our religion into the marketplace. As someone said, we dare not mix our religion with our politics. Or as one politician said, my religion will not influence my politics.

Robert Bellah, along with his co-writers Richard Madsen, William M. Sullivan, Ann Swidler, and Steven M. Tipton, in *Habits of the Heart* (a study of two hundred average American families) concludes that Americans do not ordinarily like conflict, and because religion has the potential of creating conflict, we simply withdraw and leave our religion to our private lives. That is why, generally speaking, religion in today's courts is viewed as a private not a social or communal entity. But the reality is, as Peter Berger and others have maintained, that we need a plausibility structure where we can be encouraged and affirmed in our beliefs. We simply cannot take our religion seriously if it is only a part of our private lives; religion cannot exist that way. And if we cannot share our religious beliefs, we lose that which has the greatest potential for building relationships and community. Hence we find loneliness, isolation, and fear. Nearly half of the people interviewed by Patterson and Kim believe that nobody really knows them. We actually hide ourselves from others, especially those who are the closest to us.

If space allowed, we could explore what privatism does to evangelizing, worship, and sharing a common faith. The postmodern generation has attempted to deal with this through remedies like the electronic church, which gives the illusion of coming together while maintaining our privacy.

Individualism. According to individualism, one's own personal fulfillment, be it peace or affluence or choice, is most important. That is one of the main reasons we hear today so much emphasis on personal peace, personal freedom, and personal choice. We make ourselves the center of our world. No wonder we lack a sense of community and common good. When we put the wrong thing at the center of life and reality, bad things result. In this case, when we put the individual at the center, we tend to forget that along with individual rights we also have individual responsibilities. Unless we blend those things together, we have no hope of building community.

Patterson and Kim have further concluded that there is a new moral authority in America today. There is no moral consensus; consequently, the individual is the only source of meaning. This can also encourage the idea that individuals are a law unto themselves. As a result, we do not have to consider what the common good might be. I can be a "jerk" if I choose because it is all about me! I can make up my own rules and live as I choose. Can you see what living with self as the measure of all things has done to our culture? The notion that nothing has priority over the individual is playing havoc with our culture. I think of Ayn Rand's philosophy, "the virtue of selfishness." Ours is a selfish culture because it lacks a sense of community, commitment, and responsibility, though as we will see later, the millennial generation may be giving some signs of hope.

Relativism. Relativism is the belief that nothing is absolutely true or absolutely false. There are no universals because all things are relative. With the modern-day emphasis on cultural relativism and one culture being as valid as another, there is no standard whereby to measure whether one culture or the attributes of one's culture are more or less valid than another's.

As Francis Schaeffer often said in his lectures and writings, if there are no absolutes by which to judge society, then society itself becomes absolute. Something must determine right from wrong. By some estimates over 90 percent of Americans lie regularly, creating the illusion of control and power by redefining what is real and true. Allan Bloom made a similar observation in *The Closing of the American Mind*: students on our college campuses no longer wrestle with what is good or true, with what man is, or who God is.

Studies by George Barna, George Gallup Jr., and others chart a similar course—even the majority of professing Christians do not believe in absolute truth. Peter Berger is right in *The Homeless Mind*: modernity takes on a dynamic of its own, relativizing worldviews. I cringed several years ago when I heard about a university president receiving catcalls when he said that we need to consider intellectually and morally the well-being of students. He was challenged as to whose morality and whose moral instructions. As I remember the story, he had no answer and the meeting broke up.[4]

A CULTURE CAST IN MODERNITY

The United States is definitely one of the most culturally diverse nations. Its multicultural experience and naïve understanding of what is "politically correct" have made it impossible for anyone to maintain anything that appears to be acceptable to all, except maybe the need to be free from the fear of terrorism. (After the tragic attack on America on September 11, 2001, there was a glimmer of coming together for a common purpose. But of course there is no consensus on how to achieve freedom from terrorism.)

The problems raised by relativism are numerous. If we choose to operate on the principle of relativism, is there any hope of discerning and deciding what is right among the competing values of our culture? How can we maintain any semblance of public virtue from within a relativistic position? How can we find meaning to life, because, as the French existentialist Jean-Paul Sartre is celebrated for saying, "No finite reference point has meaning without an infinite reference point"? Because Sartre had no infinite reference point, he denied the existence of God, and his life and philosophy had no meaning.

Technism. We live in a technologically driven society. Our values, attitudes, and lifestyles are driven by modern techniques. Technism is that part of modernity that is always looking for the newer, the bigger, the better, and the faster. (Some would say we are even more fundamentally driven by technology than by information.)

Modern technology is doing and has done some awesome things. I think of the technological changes and developments just in my lifetime—television, computers, fiber optics, medicine, satellites, and transportation—even to the moon. Who can deny the astonishing things that technology has accomplished? Who can deny that technology has drastically changed our lifestyles? Look around your home. Walk through your kitchen. Go into your garage. Log on to the office network. Browse the Internet and order merchandise. Think about bioengineering and advances in curing common diseases. Yet technology can also produce Frankenstein tragedies as well.

Technology determines our lifestyle, our political choices, and our use of time. It even impacts what we learn and the skills we develop, though it may inhibit the learning and intellectual development of some. Technology also has the tendency (when it doesn't do what it was intended to do, namely, serve God's purpose of subduing the earth) to treat humankind as a commodity to be used and discarded at will. Health care has become one of our most challenging areas of life. Right now those involved in geriatrics are seeing how technology is extending our lifespan; yet they are also struggling with how to create a financially sound support system for those living longer. We also view as less valuable the very lives we are working to extend.

Pop Culture

Before concluding this chapter on modernity, we need to address the subject of pop culture. Ken Myers divides our culture into high culture, folk culture, and pop culture. High culture appeals to the intelligentsia; it focuses on the fine arts. Folk culture is the down-home, more traditional aspect of culture with its folk songs, spirituals, and home cooking. Pop culture on the other hand is entertainment, a short-order mentality where content is not essential to the experience. It is a "don't worry, be happy" culture. It is a culture that does not think about tradition or substance. Fun, entertainment, and nonsubstance characterize pop culture.

Pop culture can be found in advertisements, rock music, art, clothing styles, and the variety of choices. Its main stages are television and the movies. Its sources for morality are "Oprah" and other talk shows. It encourages individuals to do what makes them feel good without thinking of consequences. It centers on man while decentralizing God, even in worship. It feeds on instant gratification and personal happiness. It is a quick-fix approach to life.

Pop culture is an invention of and fits into the overall scheme of modernity. It encourages the compartmentalization of life and feeds the notion that if we don't like our stereo or microwave or relationship, we can change them. We have many choices. If not happy with this job or that church, then change; do not stick around. And above all, do not let your religious convictions come out into the public arena; keep them to yourself. If you do bring them up, at least make them look like the culture around you so they will blend in with the scenery.

Conclusion

How should we react to our modern world with its limitless choices? Do we withdraw from the world and isolate ourselves and do what modernity commands, namely privatize our faith? We now have "Christian" rock bands, nightclubs, advertising, and other attempts to adapt the "secular" to the religious. Or do we simply try to adapt and accommodate ourselves, including our beliefs and practices, to the culture, so as not to stand out in it? Or do we have a responsibility to make a difference? Myers writes, "Our role is not to try to sanctify the Whopper like the Lord's Supper, but rather to attempt to influence our culture to make it more fitting for human beings in the image of God."[5] Our cultural setting is not amoral, nor is it holy. But that does not mean that culture is worthless or unimportant. We need to create a culture or influence culture in a way that will enable us to serve the Lord's purpose. Our culture can either distract us or enable us to serve him better. However, if we fail in the responsibility to understand our culture and to know our world, we will not be able to be the salt and light, the pillar of truth, that God would have us be.

We have already noted that there are more of the world's ideologies in the church than the church's beliefs in the world. Thinking, reasoning, studying, and evaluating are difficult but necessary. Every day we ought to ask, *How can I live in this world, understand it, and witness to it without becoming like it? How can I enjoy life and live the way God intends rather than be programed by my environment?* The truth is that we either learn to confront the world or we will be constantly confronted by it. Disciples should neither retreat from the world nor become immersed in it.

Os Guinness has written,

We should therefore heed Origen's principle: Christians are free to plunder the Egyptians, but forbidden to set up a golden calf. By all means plunder freely the treasures of modernity, but in God's name make sure that what comes out of the fire, which will test our life's endeavors, is gold fit for the temple of God and not a late-twentieth-century image of a golden calf.[6]

(Origen was an early church father who died in the mid-third century.) Guinness then concludes, as he started, with one of my favorite statements from Peter Berger, "They that sup with the devil of modernity had better have long spoons."[7]

TOPICS FOR REFLECTION OR DISCUSSION

1. Some have said that all we need to know is that man is a sinner in need of the salvation that Christ provides. We really do not need to understand any more than that. How would you respond to such a statement?

2. Knowing about the culture can assist us in understanding the kind of issues we face, where the enemy is doing his damage. We suggested several of those issues in this chapter. What are some other areas that we really need to understand in order not only to believe and embrace Christianity, but also to communicate it better to our peers?

3. What do you understand "modernity" to be; how can it serve us in the task of understanding our world?

4. How can the understanding of modernity enable us to confront the world with the truth of the gospel more effectively?

5. Where do you see pop culture having its impact on our society?

6. What areas of life can you identify as being free from the influence of pop culture?

7. How can understanding pop culture help us communicate the gospel, as well as live as members of the kingdom of God?

134

SUGGESTED READING

Gabler, Neal. *Life the Movie.* New York: Knopf, 1998. A demonstration how the U.S. has become a dumb-down culture obsessed with the entertainment mentality.

Guinness, Os. *Dining with the Devil.* Grand Rapids: Baker, 1993. A superb, concise book on the topic of modernity.

Hibbs, Thomas S. *Shows about Nothing.* Dallas: Spence, 2001. An indictment that most television shows today are lacking in substance and geared to communicating nothing. They do not appeal to the thinking part of the brain.

Moore, T. M. *Redeeming Pop Culture.* Phillipsburg, N.J.: P&R Publishing, 2003. An easy-to-read volume on how pop culture touches all areas of our life, and how to respond.

Myers, Ken. *All God's Children and Blue Suede Shoes.* Wheaton, Ill.: Crossway, 1989). One of the best books on pop culture.

Postman, Neil. *Amusing Ourselves to Death.* New York: Viking, 1985. A treatise similar in nature to Gabler's.

Romanowski, William. *Eyes Wide Open.* Grand Rapids: Brazos, 2001. Excellent blending of sound theology and an understanding of culture.

8

The Postmodern Paradigm

"We live in a postmodern world. The culture is pluralistic, and this will not change. If, in our discomfort with the growing diversity, we make the culture the enemy, we misrepresent the Gospel and we frustrate the efforts to proclaim it. We do not represent Jesus. We represent our own fear and rigidity. Nothing more." —Mike Regele, The Death of the Church

In the previous chapter I suggested that to understand our world, we need to understand modernity and its impact on our lives and culture. I further suggested that we should not assume that everything connected with modernity is valueless or to be shunned by Christians. Rather, Christians should be able to handle modernity from a discerning Christian perspective. However, we must not assume that all is safe, just as we must not assume there is no value to culture. As disciples of Christ, we must be aware of our surroundings. It is not possible to maintain a consistent Christian walk and life by going with the flow or by living in complete reaction to everything. But as disciples, we have to bear witness to the truth of the gospel, considering the audience to whom we are called to witness.

This chapter deals with postmodernism. I will attempt to be precise without being too technical—that is, if you can be precise with Jell-O or

135

pudding. It is difficult to get a good grip on postmodernism, but there are some common threads that will help. My desire, because of postmodernism's obvious diversity, is to be neither too simplistic nor too superficial, nor to misrepresent the postmodern paradigm. I believe there are valuable things to be learned from this philosophy, but perhaps not in the way one might suspect.

Paul's words in 1 Corinthians 9:19–23 ("I have become all things to all people") are definitely appropriate for us. He is not suggesting that we have to become postmodernists for the sake of winning some to Christ, but that we do have to understand something about postmodernism to know how to communicate effectively.

The epigraph by Regele reminds us of several things, as we attempt to understand our world. First, we live in a postmodern world, and that influences how we look at reality. The paradigm of modernism has shifted and been replaced by postmodernism.

Second, Regele notes that we live in a pluralistic culture, and that will not change. Pluralism, having been around for a long time, is not an attribute of postmodernism only. But because of postmodernism's influence, pluralism has been taken to new depths. We can take our choice from a great variety of options.

Third, Regele's counsel that we must not make culture our enemy is right. For culture can assist us in understanding how to serve God's purpose in our generation. However, it can also be a deceitful foe if we do not understand, correctly evaluate, and carry out the cultural mandates from the Lord.

We saw in chapter 1 that an overarching philosophy (e.g., postmodernism) will impact us at all levels. By God's appointment (Acts 17:26) we live at a certain time and place, in a particular culture with its ideologies and experiences. The step diagram which we introduced earlier (see figure 8.1) illustrates how ideas and cultural institutions shape each other. The top step represents the prevailing philosophy that overarches the culture at a particular time. That philosophy becomes the lens through which

FIGURE 8.1. STEPS OF PHILOSOPHICAL INFLUENCE

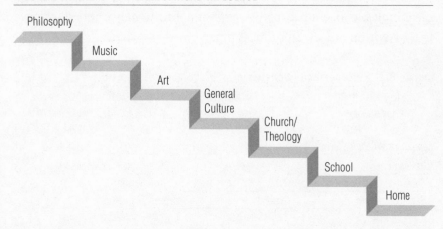

we view life and reality. Even the more critical thinkers have to be careful at this point.

As it begins to move down the steps, philosophy does not remain theoretical or abstract. It begins to influence all aspects of life: art, music, education, culture in general, even our theology, home, church, family, and the marketplace. It generally does not take long before it has infiltrated all of life, including our personal lives.

Figure 8.2 presents a time line dividing intellectual history into three periods, which were already introduced in chapter 2: premodern, modern, and postmodern. Each one represents a different paradigm for attempting to explain life and reality. The dates are somewhat arbitrary though generally on target. The change in philosophies in succeeding periods represents an attempt to offer a better explanation or understanding than the previous model.

The premodern paradigm was based on supernatural revelation and faith more than reason. Belief in a supreme being was necessary and common. Truth was not bound to the time and space of this world. The modern paradigm responded to the perceived weakness of the premodern, bringing reason and logic to the center and moving God to a lesser position. Truth, which man had to find for himself, existed within the natural order. Finally, the postmodern model arose to respond to the void left by an overemphasis on science, reason, and logic. Absolute truth is a meaningless concept because we cannot define it; hence at best we have to look within ourselves for meaning.

FIGURE 8.2. PHILOSOPHICAL SCHEMATIC OF HISTORIC DEVELOPMENT

PREMODERNISM *Age of Faith* B.C.—A.D. *1600* *Renaissance (Rebirth/Revival)*	MODERNISM *Age of Reason* *1600–1950*	POSTMODERNISM *Age of Feeling/ Experience* *1950–*
Revelation	Reason	Experience/feeling
Supernatural Religion	Natural Religion	Mysticism
Supernatural Law	Natural Law	Spiritualism
Faith	Fact (Science)	Nonreason
God-centered paradigm	**Man-centered paradigm**	**Pluralistic paradigm**
Plato	Francis Bacon	Michel Foucault
Aristotle	John Locke	Jacques Derrida
Augustine	Immanuel Kant	Richard Rorty
Anselm	David Hume	Jean-François Lyotard
	Isaac Newton	
	Rene Descartes	
"I believe in order that I might understand."	**"I understand in order that I may believe."** or **"I believe what I can understand."** or **"Cogito ergo sum."**	**"I believe whatever is meaningful to me."** or **"I believe whatever gives me the greatest experience."**

According to the postmodernists, there are no grand stories or meta-narratives to explain life and reality. A "metanarrative" is simply a grand story that becomes a final criterion for the legitimacy of all other stories or one into which all other narratives must fit. There are many explanations for understanding our universe. We have to find those which work, and they become truth for us. Building on one of its foundation stones, postmodernism tends to define truth as that which works in good pragmatic fashion, a definition from Richard Rorty, one of the four post-modernists we will discuss.

This means that if the postmodernists talk about truth, they are actually referring to truths in the plural or little truths for the individual. There is no one central or grand truth. In contrast to both premodernism and modernism, postmodernism denies the existence of a center point of reference, at least one that all can agree on. Practically, postmodernists also believe that things are what they are by chance. The artist, the musician, the literary figure, the philosopher operate on a chance or random principle because there is no fixed reference point. The suggested motto for this period is "whatever is the most meaningful to me or brings me the greatest experience is what is real." Postmodernism is an experience- or feeling-based philosophy.

While reading Millard Erickson's book *The Postmodern World: Discerning the Times and the Spirit of Our Age*, I was reminded of the phrase "Beauty is in the eye of the beholder." Without getting distracted by the object of beauty, be it a person or a landscape, let's apply each philosophical paradigm to the idea or concept of beauty.

If someone were to say, "Beauty is in the eye of the beholder," the pre-modern would think that there is a legitimate category of beauty out there that has a foundational essence, a universal idea of beauty. On the premodern model, there would be general agreement that there is a category of beauty, even though there might be disagreements as to what is beautiful.

A modernist would think there is a universal idea of beauty that can be discovered, tested, verified, and agreed on. There is an objective concept of "beauty" that can be verified because it can be defined. While there may be disagreement as to what is beautiful, some standard or criterion for such a judgment could be developed.

A postmodernist believes that beauty is a subjective idea. There is no universal category of beauty; it is something that individuals or social groups construct. "Beauty" is merely a personal term that means whatever one wants it to mean. Beauty, therefore, according to postmodernism is a feeling or emotion, an experience, or at least something quite subjectively determined. Postmodernists would appreciate the phrase "beauty is in the eye of the beholder" because it sounds so subjective and not objectively verifiable.

The same exercise could be performed with love, good, bad, right, or wrong. In a postmodern world, such notions are whatever we want them to be. Whenever we disagree, there is no standard to say whose definition is right.

Four Key Postmodernists

We will briefly look at four people whose names have been commonly associated with postmodernism. There are also others that could be considered, but I have chosen Jean-François Lyotard, Michel Foucault, Jacques Derrida, and Richard Rorty.

Jean François Lyotard may be the first to have used the term "postmodern" (though Thomas Oden in *After Modernity* claims it was Ihab Hassan in 1971 in the area of literature). Lyotard was born in France in 1924 and died in 1998. He was a professor of philosophy at the University of Paris. He also lectured at the University of California in Irvine. He believed that the metanarrative present in premodernism and in modernism is no longer capable of analyzing all that is taking place in the world, and so the philosophy of modernism has to be replaced by the philosophy of postmodernism. Lyotard sought to knock the foundationalism of modernism out of its place. The phrase "incredulity toward metanarratives" best describes his postmodern perspective. Actually, it is the collapse of the metanarrative, as a legitimizing or unifying force, that drives the nail into the coffin of modernism.

Michel Foucault is another name associated with the postmodern philosophy. He too was a Frenchman, born in 1926. Much of his emphasis focused on the relationship between power and knowledge. He too was distrustful of metanarrative or the "big story" explanations of reality. He has been described as one who developed the implications of Friedrich Nietzsche's will to power and its relation to truth. He believed that each society has its own perspective about truth. History as such has no meaning because it is not about meaning but about power.

In his book on Foucault, Paul Strathern includes an intriguing quote: "It is not as simple as that—to enjoy oneself. . . . I hope I'll die of an overdose—or pleasure of any kind. Because I think it's really difficult, and I always have the feeling that I do not feel the pleasure, the complete total pleasure and, for me, it's related to death."[1] Interestingly, Foucault died of AIDS in 1984. For him there were no absolute timeless principles or metanarratives by which we explain reality. Everything is relative to the individual and his or her circumstance. Knowledge is only a social construct, and every discourse an attempt of one person to gain or exercise power over another.

Jacques Derrida was born in 1930 in El-Biar, Algeria, into a Jewish family. His claim to fame focuses on what is called "deconstruction" or post-structuralism. There is irony in attempting to define deconstruction. A fixed definition of anything is contrary to what Derrida believes that deconstruction represents. Deconstruction means decentering. There is no center for definition or explanation. There is no fixed point that guarantees meaning. This is an anti-logocentric concept. Defining words as a center with meaning is contrary to the idea of deconstruction, which is a literary analysis based on the theory that language and usage have no fixed coherent texts. To maintain that something has a fixed meaning is to talk in mythological terms.

Derrida rose to fame in both France and America with his attempt to demonstrate that Western thought was based on the idea of a center, a fixed point, which must be deconstructed. The center must be removed. The effect of decentering a statement is to make it say either the opposite or at least something different from what was originally thought. No fixed meanings to words! It is all subjectively determined.

THE POSTMODERN PARADIGM

Richard Rorty is an American philosopher born in New York City in 1931. As professor of comparative literature at Stanford University, Rorty staked his claim in the mainstream of postmodernism by dismissing a basic premise of modernism, namely that there are certain foundational truths on which other truths can stand. He is referred to by many as a neo-pragmatist because of his appreciation for Charles Peirce, the father of pragmatic philosophy. Rorty is also a relativist because in his view there is nothing universal that holds true for everyone. Truth, according to Rorty, cannot really be defined, so why talk about it? He has admitted in interviews as well as his writings, such as *Objectivity, Relativism and Truth*, that there might be little truths but no grand truth by which to measure other possibilities. Everyone must be free to define his or her own truth.

An insightful statement from an interview summarizes Rorty's contention: "I do not think that you can define 'truth,' either as what your peers will let you get away with, or as correspondence with the intrinsic nature of reality, or as anything else. 'Truth' like the word 'good' is a primitive predicate, a transcendental term which does not lend itself to definition."[2] In the same interview Alvin Plantinga, the Christian philosopher from Notre Dame, concluded, "I guess what strikes me most forcibly about Dick Rorty's work is that he seems to move from the failure of classical foundationalism and the quest for Cartesian certainty to the idea that there really isn't any such thing as truth."[3]

Key Terms

Postmodernism is a somewhat complex paradigm with many different subthemes running in a variety of directions. This is because it simultaneously grew out of numerous disciplines, for example, literary criticism, art and architecture, humanities and philosophy, and modernity. However, it does have a definite central motif that is more than just individualism.

At this point it is necessary to define several technical terms that will be useful in understanding postmodernism: *foundationalism*, *pragmatism*, *relativism*, and *structuralism* (and *deconstructionism*).

Foundationalism

In order to understand the postmodern paradigm and how it differs from the premodern and modern, we have to understand the problem that it has with modernism: foundationalism. The common thread running through the diversity of avenues of postmodernism is a reaction to foundationalism's emphasis on the certainty of knowledge, at least the seventeenth-century version of knowledge.

Foundationalism refers to the belief that there are different levels or ranges of beliefs and knowledge, but for any to be true, there must be a basic support for everything, a support that is indisputable, without the least doubt. For Descartes, David Hume, or John Locke, in order for something to be indubitably true, we must know it through our sense experience or rational capabilities. God is not foundational in this respect because we cannot know him through our sense experience or rationally. Therefore, we cannot build our beliefs and knowledge on God, but rather, according to Descartes, we become the foundational standard. As Stephen Davis explains, the final appeal for the seventeenth-century foundationalists had to be "the mind's own experience of certainty."[4]

The basic philosophy of modernism operated on the premise of René Descartes's "*Cogito ergo sum*"—"I think, therefore I am." Descartes struggled for something that he could believe with absolute certainty. His motto gave him the ultimate foundation upon which all other beliefs and knowledge could be built. From that statement he had finally removed all doubt, an achievement which he had not been able to accomplish with any other. His conclusion was the ultimate guarantor of itself.

Men like John Locke and Thomas Reid stood on that same foundation. Basically, foundationalism says that there are certain givens or certainties that can be discovered, and as a result, we can be sure that what we know and believe is true.

144

Locke, Hume, and Descartes disagreed as to whether the basis of cer-
titude was the mind of man or his sense experience, but either one makes
man the center of the paradigm. As we saw in the time-line diagram, the
shift from the premodern philosophy to the modern meant a move away
from the supernatural, revelation, and faith to the natural, logic, reason,
and man's own sensory experience.

The Age of Reason, resting on classical foundationalism, maintained
that there is an objective world of truth that man can discover. He does
not need to depend on the supernatural God or his revelation. The postmodernists reacted against the idea of an objective realm that we can
know objectively, though ironically, they agree with the modernists that
man is the center of knowing and controlling. As the step diagram illustrates, a particular overarching philosophy eventually influences theology and the church. Many classical theologians, not realizing that Reid's
version of foundationalism derived from Descartes and Locke, bought
into it, paving the way for postmodernism's rejection of Christianity
along with classical foundationalism. For some postmodernists, Christianity was just another rational attempt to do what cannot be done. For
the postmodernist, the only certainty is that there is no certainty, no central objective reference point upon which everything else can stand.

Obviously, postmodernism is a reaction to the natural, logical, rational,
scientific approach to reality. In that sense we can say that it is antimod-
ern, because modernism's emphasis on the observable and objective does
not connect with the importance of the individual and the subjective in
the postmodern scheme of things. Postmodernism attempts to exchange
the foundations of belief and knowledge for a web of beliefs and knowledge entertained by the individual and his community. In other words,
belief and knowledge are really social constructs, not universal givens.
Rather than standing on certain foundational truths and drawing conclusions, postmodernists believe that their task is to simply keep the conversation in motion.

In the time-line diagram a statement or motto was given to characterize each period. Each of the four words defined in this section will be

accompanied by a statement or phrase to help in understanding the concept. Foundationalism's catchphrase is, "It's true because I said so, and I cannot be doubted."

Pragmatism

A second term necessary for understanding postmodernism is "pragmatism." That term may be familiar because it represents what some have called the only genuinely American philosophy. It is a term associated with Charles Sanders Peirce, William James, and John Dewey. Richard Rorty's postmodernism is closely tied to this philosophy. Rorty's works reveal a genuine friendliness toward pragmatism. Stanley Grenz says that if Foucault is Nietzsche's disciple and Derrida is Heidegger's, "then Richard Rorty is unabashedly the protégé of John Dewey."[5]

Rorty has played a key role in the renewed focus on pragmatism. The pragmatists' understanding of truth and Rorty's understanding, though he questions the legitimacy of discussing truth, are quite similar. Grenz is right when he says that Rorty is not simply restating Peirce's and James's pragmatism, he is giving it a new twist that we know as postmodernism. We can illustrate this point regarding truth, which would hold for both the pragmatists and Rorty's postmodernism: a glass of tea may or may not be sweet; we have to taste it to know. The pragmatist, especially Peirce, would say that if it works, it is true; or if it is true, it works. The postmodernist would say that if it is real to us and if we experience it, it is real; otherwise it is not.

William James represented this position when he seemed to say that if a religious belief provides some benefit, one is justified in holding it—for example, a bereaved mother finding comfort in believing that her child is in heaven. From what has already been said about postmodernism it can be seen how pragmatism is one of its foundation stones both in its timing in history and in its method. All knowledge must be practical. What we know is connected to what we do. Charles Peirce was famous for emphasizing that knowing is doing or knowing is activity. Things have meaning only if they have practical application and effects.

The catchphrase for pragmatism is, "If it works, it's true."

Relativism

The third and possibly the most familiar of the key terms to help us understand postmodernism is "relativism." Like foundationalism and pragmatism, the term "relativism" was not developed by postmodernists but adapted by them. Richard Rorty champions a type of relativism in his postmodern philosophy. He says that "objective truth" is no more or less than the best idea we currently have about how to explain what is going on. Put in its simplest form, relativism basically suggests that there are no universals or absolute truths for everyone.

There are several forms of relativism that exist today. There are cognitive relativism, ethical relativism, and cultural relativism to name a few. Cognitive relativism simply means that there are no universal truths, only different ways of approaching and explaining things. This is the view that was espoused by the early Greek philosopher Protagoras with his much quoted "Man is the measure of all things; of things that are that they are, and of things that are not that they are not."

Ethical relativism is self-explanatory. There are no absolutes or universal standards of right and wrong, good and bad. They vary from society to society. What is acceptable in one society may not be accepted in another—hence the third form, cultural relativism. It all depends on the culture. We can say, "This is the way we do it in our culture, and it is just as right and good as the way you do it in your culture; therefore we cannot pass judgment on either approach. It is all relative." This contrasts with the cultural and ethical absolutists who insist that their way or their group's way is the right way, and every other way is wrong.

It is easy to see how relativism is an important building block for postmodernism. No standards, no center or point of reference. It depends on who and where we are and what the circumstance dictates.

The catchword for relativism is, "whatever."

Structuralism (and Deconstructionism)

The antithetis of structuralism, "deconstructionism," may be the better fourth choice of key words. We cannot understand one without the other. This fourth term may be the least known and understood, but is equally important in that Jacques Derrida is one of the key postmodernists. "Structuralism" may also be the newest of the four terms. Norman F. Cantor has stated, "Structuralism may be the most important intellectual movement of the last forty years."[6] He suggests that without structuralism there would have been no deconstruction, because deconstruction was developed as a response to and critique of structuralism.

One of structuralism's pioneers, Claude Lévi-Strauss, attempted to correct the lack of structure and system in existential philosophy in his time. Existentialism centered everything on man in a nonsystematic way. Lévi-Strauss sought to develop a system where structure brought meaning and authenticity to the system and replaced the individual as the center. He placed much emphasis on the existence of universal structures.

As we indicated earlier, Derrida believed that there is no structure and as a result there is no fixed meaning or reference point, no canon, nor tradition. Everything has a multiplicity of meanings. When I say that something is white, I am giving you my opinion, and that is all that I am doing. The same thing may be black or gray to you. Texts and words cannot be tied to a single message or definition. All is relative. While structuralism's appeal came from its objectivity and certainty, deconstructionism's appeal was for the opposite reason—no objectivity and no certainty. Deconstruction emphasizes decentering, removing the center from things.

Practically, this means that words or texts can mean whatever we want them to mean. To suggest that they have only one meaning and message runs counter to postmodern philosophy. It works like this: if I maintain that a word or a text means one thing and you maintain something else, and if I can then manipulate and gain control with my definition, I have marginalized you. I have put you down and repressed your meaning and definition.

The catchphrase for deconstructionism is, "That's the way you see it, but I see it differently."

Evaluating Postmodernism

I have been asked on several occasions, "Is postmodernism a reaction to modernism?" to which I have cautiously responded, it is either a reaction to it or the fulfillment of it. Postmodernism is a philosophy that has replaced God and his authority with man. While modernism has had much to commend to Christians in its methodology, postmodernism helps us to see some things to which modernism and to a lesser extent premodernism have blinded us.

Having said that, I do not encourage a return to a previous point in time. That needs to be said because several evangelical scholars and writers have given the impression that such a move would be the right course of action. However, God put us here to serve his purpose to this generation; and going back in time in an attempt to re-create the past or living too futuristically is not the answer. We need to take the timeless truths from each era and relate them to today.

I have selected three areas to evaluate: first, God, truth, and authority; second, community and relationships; and third life- or experience-orientation.

The first helpful thing that has come from postmodernism relates to the area of God, truth, and authority. Modernism so emphasized objectivity, it gave the impression that man can be totally objective or unbiased, that is, that he can objectively know true truth (to use Schaeffer's phrase). We dealt more fully with this point in chapter 2, but basically modernism emphasized that we can know things without any personal bias, that objective knowledge is obtainable. Postmodernists know the fallacy of that position.

Modernism did encourage the idea that a word or text has only one meaning for all times and places, and it can be logically or rationally demonstrated. We must never forget that there is an objective realm where God, truth, and authority exist, somewhere outside ourselves, a cosmic reference point so to speak. However, since we are subjectively involved in the knowing process, we cannot know things, including God, with total objectivity.

This means that we have to be aware that our knowledge of God along with our understanding of texts and words is influenced by our place and time in history. Postmodernists in this sense have done us a favor by reminding us that we need to exercise caution in defining and claiming that we know certain words and texts. On the other hand, we have to be extremely careful not to go the full route of the postmodernists in maintaining that objectivity is merely an illusion. Both are traps into which many unaware of the danger have fallen.

The late Lesslie Newbigin, theologian and missiologist, has written effectively in this area. The reader might have also heard of scientist-philosopher Michael Polanyi, who left the field of science and moved into philosophy over this very point—the inability to be totally objective even in the scientific realm.

This brings us to a second positive emphasis that we can appreciate from postmodernism. The postmodern philosophy emphasizes the importance of community, relationships, and social groups. Whereas modernism focused on rugged individualism, postmodernism focuses on the tension between the individual and community. Again, it goes too far by overemphasizing the role of community, particularly in determining truth, but we cannot overlook the importance of community.

Those of us who have been immersed in our Western culture's philosophy, which has been extremely devoted to modernism, need to know that we cannot function well alone. We cannot understand things in a vacuum, nor can we be the final interpreter of truth and reality. We need accountability, encouragement, and belonging.

The idea that man is master of his life is not valid. God made us with the need for community. We are social beings; "it is not good that the man should be alone" (Gen. 2:18). While postmodernists tend to be anti-institutional, even with organized religions, they value interdependency. And they are right to do so. Community is essential to our well-being and survival. The church is the community of believers with each person mutually dependent on the others of the community, just as we are dependent on Christ the head. We need one another!

It would play well in our Christian witness to postmoderns to demonstrate our high value on personal relationships. Our belief in and practice of the "communion and fellowship of the saints" are a major part of our bearing witness to the postmodern age. A relational apologetic will be more persuasive than the rationalism of the modern approach. Peter advised that we should always be "prepared to make a defense to anyone who asks you for a reason for the hope that is in you" (1 Peter 3:15). Why would others ask for a reason for our hope in Christ? Because they see something different and hopefully genuine about our lives. We cannot win postmodern people by argument but rather by example and building relationships that will give validity and credence to what we say.

This underscores a third postmodern emphasis we can appreciate—what we believe must be life-oriented, an integral part of our lives impacting our thinking and actions. What we believe must be intentionally more relational, experiential, and authentic, demonstrating a more caring lifestyle. In chapters 4 and 5 we talked about doctrine being integrated into our everyday experience by living what we believe. We must become more skilled at communicating the truth of the gospel in the language of the people to whom we witness, and one of the key ways we do that is by showing them the reality of what we profess to believe and know.

Conclusion

The philosophy of postmodernism falls short of the gospel truth and reality in that it offers no real hope. God, if there is a God, is whatever we want him or her to be, and that kind of God can make no real difference in our lives. While postmodernism does emphasize relationships and community, and they are vitally important, we cannot have good solid relationships by leaving God out. Sociologists have confirmed what we have known all along. Religion is vital for building strong community life. We understand that because our God is the "super-glue" that holds people and things together, as the apostle Paul said to the Colossians. We are reconciled to God and to one another by Christ's atoning work, and that reconciliation process has horizontal, as well as vertical, implications.

While postmodernism has correctly reminded us that how we see and interpret things is influenced by culture, we must work carefully to understand the Word of truth, which ultimately transcends any culture, including ours. Part of that process requires that we, intentionally and with God's help, integrate what we know with our daily lives.

We cannot reject the concept of foundationalism, only the Enlightenment, Cartesian version of it. Our faith in God, his truth, and authority is foundational to all else. While we cannot totally embrace the philosophy of pragmatism, we agree that if our faith in God is real, it will produce results. It will be a faith that works. While we cannot embrace the philosophy of relativism, we do understand the importance of our circumstance both in understanding and in applying God's truth. In addition, admitting as D. A. Carson has reminded us in both *The Gagging of God* and *Exegetical Fallacies*, that all topics are culturally laden and driven, we must demonstrate extreme care in interpreting texts.

Finally, while we must not be guilty of believing that everything has to satisfy our understanding of what is logical and rational to be true—because our supernatural God can and does often transcend our reason and logic—and while we must willingly admit that the Christian faith does have mystery, in that "we walk by faith, not by sight" (2 Cor. 5:7), we must not go to the opposite extreme and believe that God is whatever we create or define. He is our self-contained and redeeming God who reveals himself to us in his Word and world.

The Triune God—Father, Son, and Holy Spirit—is the center point of reference that makes things knowable for all peoples at all places and times. While our knowledge of him may be applied differently according to the circumstances, his existence as the center is real. As Christians, we believe the center of everything is God, his Word, and authority, not in some deconstructed way, but as he reveals himself. Words and texts are important, and if properly understood and defined, they are the ground upon which we stand in order to understand truth and reality.

There is a grand narrative or a metanarrative that is the gospel. Everything must relate to the gospel story, or else it is ultimately meaningless.

Postmodernism has caused us to realize the shortcomings of modernism's paradigm and has sensitized us to a number of key points. As a philosophy, however, it is antithetical to the Christian faith. Disciples of Christ need to develop a Christian philosophy of life that begins at the top step and flows down through all life—it will become the grid through which we see life in all of its fullness.

A Christian disciple, responsible to know his or her world, needs to understand the overarching philosophy of that world; and today, at least in the West, that philosophy is postmodernism.

TOPICS FOR REFLECTION OR DISCUSSION

1. As you read chapter 8 on postmodernism, were you able to see the correlation between that topic and what you see throughout our world today?
2. Using the model of the step diagram, adapted from Francis Schaeffer, are you able to see how postmodernism has invaded the areas of life suggested by the steps, particularly our churches and homes?
3. Why is it important to understand the historical development illustrated in the philosophical schematic and time line?
4. How would you explain what postmodernism is and how it affects us today?
5. Would we be accurate in saying that each paradigm shift was a reaction to the prior paradigm? If so, why? and how was postmodernism a reaction to modernism?

SUGGESTED READING

Carson, D. A. *The Gagging of God.* Grand Rapids: Zondervan, 1996. A study of our pluralistic society and how to witness to the postmodern mind; a reminder that Christianity is losing ground.

Erickson, Millard. *The Postmodern World: Discerning the Times and the Spirit of Our Age.* Wheaton, Ill.: Crossway, 2002. Lectures to college students and churches on the philosophy of postmodernism. Erickson demonstrates how this philosophy has permeated American life. A good read!

Greer, Robert C. *Mapping Postmodernism.* Downers Grove, Ill.: InterVarsity, 2003. Full of good history, a very helpful explication of the main points of this hard-to-group philosophy.

Guinnes, Os. *Time for Truth.* Grand Rapids: Baker, 2000. A good brief analysis of how postmodernism grew out of the deficiencies of modernism.

Veith, Gene. *Postmodern Times.* Wheaton, Ill.: Crossway, 1994. A helpful critique of the ideologies, lifestyles, and values of postmodernists.

9

The Generational Context

Why include a chapter on generations in a book on kingdom disciple-making? This is a valid question that deserves a clear answer. Disciples need to know the Lord and know themselves. They also need to understand the world in which they live. We must know the Lord, ourselves, and our world because our responsibility is to bring the word of the gospel to this world in a way that it can be grasped, related to, and applied to individual lives. This is not intended to suggest that we can do the work of the Holy Spirit in making spiritual truth real to the people we work with in the disciple-making process. Rather, the Bible is full of models of God's truth being presented in such a way that the audience can more readily relate to and identify with it. (We will observe this in the next three chapters as we look at three Scripture passages.) Jesus was a master at this, but so was the apostle Paul.

In the previous two chapters we suggested that modernity and postmodernism represent different perspectives and conclusions. Beginning with the twentieth century and particularly post–World War II, the idea of generations became more prominent and significant in our culture. In trying to relate to the different generations, we must remember that one generation's seeing things a certain way does not mean the other gen-

156

erations will do the same. This is clearly demonstrated by what we have come to know as youth culture, adolescents and young adults. Those twentieth-century categories are important in understanding the diversity among the different generations. In *Lifetrends: The Future of Baby Boomers and Other Aging Americans*, Jerry Gerber, Janet Wolff, Walter Klores, and Gene Brown make the point that "when the experience of one generation differs greatly from that of the preceding generations, social change becomes the norm. Much common sense about life can't be passed on because it no longer contains accurate information and useful advice."[1]

In the chapter on postmodernism, one aim was to suggest the need to understand the undergirding philosophical ideology that determines the thinking and actions of people at their particular moments in history. Today that ideology is postmodern. But we also need to understand the people because, after all, they are what disciple making is all about. I also attempted to demonstrate in earlier chapters that the disciple-making process, which aims at life transformation, often breaks down because a person who professes to believe in Christ does not always understand how that belief makes any difference on a day-to-day basis.

Interestingly enough, many of the younger generations react negatively to the church and Christianity because they have not seen Christianity making a difference in people's lives. One reason is the Western influence upon our concept of religion. We must show the younger generations that Christianity is a life-system. We need to help them see the results of transformation, as we demonstrate Christianity in its biblical setting being transferred to our circumstance.

Similarly, Muslims are perplexed by the difference between the Western view of religion and the Eastern view. Islam is a system that touches every aspect of a Muslim's life. It is a world-and-life-view system. Western religion generally demonstrates a dichotomy between religion and the rest of life. There is a place for religion, but not in the marketplace. That perplexes an Easterner, but it also bewilders those of us Westerners who understand that Christianity is actually an Eastern religion, and it too is a system or a way of life. As we saw in the early chapters on the kingdom of God and the world-and-life-view, there is no area that is not under Christ's lordship.

Generational Differences

The word "generation" has several different meanings. Commonly a generation refers broadly to the people that are alive at a particular time in history. But it also has a more specific usage upon which we focus in this chapter: the different age groups that are alive at a particular time in history.

In their foundational book entitled *Generations: The History of America's Future, 1584 to 2069*, William Strauss and Neil Howe define generation as "a cohort group (all persons born in a limited span of consecutive years) whose length approximates the span of a phase of life and whose boundaries are fixed by peer personality."[2] This definition is helpful in a couple of ways. First, it reminds us of what a generation is. Second, it also reminds us that we cannot automatically say that on a particular calendar day one generation begins and another generation ends. There will be some overlap in years and ideas among the generations.

I remember preaching one Sunday to a congregation of several hundred and being struck with the fact that there were children, young people, young adults, middle-aged people, and senior citizens present. They represented at least five different generations. I was preaching on the topic "Developing a Christian Mind." I realized the challenge I faced because I had to speak to the group as a whole. I also realized that each generation would hear me a little differently from the others. How could I hope to make any sense to the audience?

I knew that each of the age groups, representing a particular generation, while having some things in common with the others, also had their own particular perspective or "glasses" through which they filtered what I said. God reassured me, in my moment of anxiety, that all these different age groups needed his truth, real and authentic relationships, contacts with one another at more than a superficial level. I saw my chal-

158

lenge as developing a Christian mind within them. My objective was to communicate to all members of the group. I knew that I was totally dependent on the Holy Spirit to speak to the different generations at the same time. I wanted so much to understand them and for them to embrace the truth. That could not be done without the Holy Spirit's work. Only time will tell whether anything positive happened that morning.

Every disciple maker faces the challenge that I faced that morning. Know your world! Know your audience! By God's grace, present his truth to our audience with sensitivity to where they are coming from because that affects how they hear what you say.

I have come to realize more and more that a kingdom approach to making disciples has to demonstrate an awareness of several things. For example, we have to realize what we have in common, such as being made in God's image and being sinners needing salvation. And we need to understand the differences that exist between us. We also need to show sensitivity and a desire to communicate the truth and hope of the gospel in the most meaningful way.

It is simplistic to believe that differences among the generations are insignificant or nonexistent. In my seminars on cultural awareness I have heard people ask, "Why do we need to do this? We just need to present the gospel because we are all the same." Actually, we are different in many ways. Each generation reflects clear differences in strengths, weaknesses, in outlooks and aspirations.

I continue to be amazed at the church's slowness or reticence to learn this. I read demographic trends regularly, and I have noted that marketers are much more aware of this topic and use that knowledge to influence buying patterns. I am convinced that there is much to learn as we study people. In the process we will learn how to communicate the gospel in the most meaningful way to each person.

I reviewed a book several years ago entitled *Generations at Work: Managing the Clash of Veterans, Boomers, Xers, and Nexters in Your Workplace*, by Ron Zemke, Claire Raines, and Bob Filipczak. The thrust of that book was how to manage the different generations within an organization.

This causes an untold amount of headaches and costs much money to the organizations as their managers try to "mold a hodgepodge of ages, faces, values, and views into a productive collaborative group." The bottom line of the book was that each generation must be managed a little differently. As the authors expressed it, "The generational diversity, and the tension and challenge, opportunity, and promise it presents are the focus of this book. There is a growing realization that the gulf of misunderstanding and resentment between older, not so old, and younger employees in the workplace is growing and problematic."[3]

There are four primary generations, according to some sociologists. And if the last generation, the millennials, is dated from around 1980 to 2000, then a new fifth generation is now coming along. We will have to wait and see, because a generation is characterized not only by age, but by ideas also. I will briefly describe each generation and then draw some conclusions that connect with our kingdom model of making disciples.

The Traditionalist (Pre–WWII) Generation

Strauss and Howe speak of the silent generation. It is also referred to as the veterans' generation, the graying generation, the builders' generation. We will use "traditionalist generation" to refer to those people who were born before the Second World War.

Who are the traditionalists, and what distinguishes them from the other generations? Tom Brokaw has called them the greatest generation. As their label indicates, they represent tradition. These loyalists stick with relationships and are the least likely to divorce (with the possible exception of the millennials, who are only now old enough to marry). They are extremely patriotic, civic-minded, and have great respect for authority and chain of command. Their focus has tended to be more on community, group, and organization as a whole rather than on the individualism that characterized the preceding generation. They embrace (and are the primary financial support for) traditional institutions such as home, church, school, and mission organizations. They have had the most money to spend, at least until now. According to some sources, they hold three quarters of all the financial assets in the United States with a total net worth of over 7 trillion dollars.[4] Among their more celebrated representatives are former presidents John Kennedy, Jimmy Carter, Ronald Reagan, and George H. W. Bush, as well as Billy Graham, Carl F. H. Henry, Bob Hope, Glenn Miller, and Benny Goodman.

This generation lived in the golden age of radio, television not having appeared with any significance until the late 1940s. Since almost every home had a radio, it was commonplace to hear "The Green Hornet," "The Lone Ranger," "Amos and Andy," and the big bands night after night. Traditionalists remember rationing, air raids, and blackouts during World War II. They predated the pill, credit cards, electric typewriters, frozen foods, and air conditioning. They survived the bitter Depression of the 1930s, worked hard and saved, often for their children. Debt was something that they abhorred and did everything possible to avoid. They never would have considered burning the flag or draft cards or doing anything to reflect negatively on their country. Their characteristic commitment to hard work and long hours and their respect for authority have caused them frustration as they watch the younger generations. They have been conditioned to an autocratic style of leadership; hence being told what to do and telling others what to do are normal for these builders. They have a harder time dialoguing and collaborating. Their work ethic and core moral values also differ from later generations. They view the family as a mom, dad, and two or three children.

In Betweeners (1940–45)

Some sociologists tend not to refer to the In Between as a distinct generation, but adjust the dating to put them in one of the other categories. Even though this is the smallest of the five generations in terms of years (most generations are fifteen to twenty years long), I believe they need to be considered a separate generation. They were the transition generation. Some refer to them as the Eisenhower or the swing generation. Among them can be found a synthesis of the builder or traditionalist generation and the baby boomers to follow, though many move closer to the boomer side of the equation. As Susan Mitchell has written, "Some members of the swing generation identify with the values and lifestyles of the older World War II generation. Others identify with the rebellious and youthful baby-boom generation. Marketers must account for these attitudes and lifestyle differences when targeting swing consumers."[5] They are a significant group in that they represent some 11 percent of the population or over 30 million people.

The baby boomers are often referred to as the older brothers and sisters of the busters. The In Between or swing generation, as some refer to it, are the older brothers and sisters of the baby boomers or the post–WWII babies. As a member of this generation, I like to say that we have a foot in two generations. We are the sandwich generation that has great respect for the values of the traditionalists but openness to the changes coming from the boomers.

Baby Boomers (1945–64)

This is the generation of which Jerry Rubin said, "We ain't ever gonna grow up. We're gonna be adolescents forever, and we don't trust anyone over 30."[6] There are an estimated 76 million boomers, which makes them, at the present time, the largest of all the generations. They were the post–WWII babies. With the exception of the youngest of the boomers, the pill had not been introduced, but once it was, we entered into the sexual revolution. Morality took a drastic turn and not for the better. This was often referred to as the Dr. Spock generation, the pediatrician who helped make this the most pampered and permissive of all the generations.

There was a major change in the core values of this generation from those of their parents. Commitment, loyalty, continuity, and doing the greatest good for the largest number changed to "what's in it for me," broken relationships, a high divorce rate, church dropouts, and a philosophy of living for the moment. This was the first television generation. While the traditionalists were the first automobile generation, the boomers were the first to sit behind the wheel as young teenagers with their own car, a factor which further separated them from their parents' oversight and control.

What their parents would have referred to as licentious and tasteless, they saw as being more open and honest about things. They claimed to be demonstrating a new standard of truthfulness in contrast to what they called the old standard of faithfulness. They definitely charted a course of greater personal freedom, particularly from the more traditional doctrines and religion. That course drew them to value materialism as a way of life. This too created a major shift from their parents, who made a sharp distinction between spirituality and materialism. Not so for the boomers!

Also unlike their parents, baby boomers dared to ask, Must I stay in a relationship that does not meet my needs, whether it be marriage, church, work, or any other relationship? "Recreation," "fun," "experience," "opportunity," and "individuality" became watchwords for this generation. Relationships were more open, more sexually active. More liberty and personal freedom resulted in a more illusory concept of relationships. Family was not dismissed from the paradigm, but it did not have the high level of importance it had with their parents. Career and education were generally given higher priority than family. With the introduction of the pill, child bearing was more of a choice.

The boomer generation rejected the authority structure, bureaucratic mentality, and the telling (or dictated) approach to life in favor of the selling (or participative) approach. They wanted more involvement in decision making and did not respond well to being told what to do or to believe. The boomers became the dialogue generation. They had disdain for monologue in any area of life, including church. They were less receptive to information and expected it to be cast in more of an entertainment mode. They were more relational and less task-oriented than their parents.

Landon Jones, author of *Great Expectations*, one of the earliest books dealing with the boomer generation, said that they believe in themselves and can do the impossible. They are hugely ambitious and have great expectations. But he also said that they are not motivated by guilt or institutional loyalty. They insist on having input and respond well to the idea of partnership. The phrase "felt needs" became associated with this generation. And as we know, that concept began to move into all areas of life: marriage, church, workplace, and relationships in general; and that changed the paradigm for each of those areas.

The boomer generation does not value belonging as highly as did the previous generations. They have demonstrated an anti-institutional orientation. They have adopted pragmatism as long as it works for them. Innovation and ignoring the past also characterize them. They are experience-oriented and are the first generation of modern time to openly advocate women in leadership positions. Until the millennial generation began to emerge, the boomers tended to stand out more than previous generations. Whereas the concept of marketing really went into full swing with America's emphasis on consumerism, for the first time we began to hear about marketing things like the church to this generation; after all, marketing works well with them and their "what's in it for me" attitude. It remains to be seen what this will mean for those ministries and institutions that depend on the traditionalists for financial support as the boomers replace the traditionalists on the time line.

Generation X (1965–79)

Generation X is probably the most complex of all. They are also called gen-Xers, baby busters, the busted generation, the nowhere generation, the thirteenth generation (i.e., since the settling of America), the boomlets, or the echo booms. However, they do not like labels, particularly labels referring to them. They represent some 42–45 million Americans.

The most common name is generation X, which was coined by Douglas Coupland. In his *Life after God*, Coupland, a gen-Xer himself, makes a revealing statement that is very descriptive of this generation:

> Now—here is my secret. I tell it to you with an openness of heart that I doubt I shall ever achieve again, so I pray that you are in a quiet room

as you hear these words. My secret is that I need God—that I am sick and can no longer make it alone. I need God to help me give, because I no longer seem to be capable of giving; to help me be kind, as I no longer seem capable of kindness; to help me love, as I seem beyond being able to love.[7]

This generation is deeply concerned with survival. They watched America fight a war only to lose for the first time. They saw a very popular president resign in the disgrace of Watergate. Being the first of the genuine postmodern generations, they did not have a good view of the past, nor a hope for the future. The economic outlook did not encourage them, and they realized that they were not going to earn the salaries and achieve the lifestyle of their parents. They actually have lived out the philosophy "I work to live" and not "I live to work." This was also the first generation that did not have any heroes.

They married later in life, if they married at all. And if they did marry, both spouses had to work in order to maintain the lifestyle that they had grown up with; it took two incomes to make that happen. They became very self-reliant because they did not feel they could trust anyone to care for and look out for them. Informality is a valued commodity for this generation. Skepticism, pessimism, doubt, fear, and anxiety characterize the X-ers. AIDS and HIV were introduced to them early on. Money was not their prime motivating factor, especially in the workplace: they would not work just for money, but insisted on being happy as well. Therefore in order to hire talented people, employers had to meet some unusual demands such as allowing them to bring their pets to work. As a result of this mentality, they were called slackers, though not because they were lazy. They were motivated only by their own internal values.

Generation X is characterized by both a hunger for relationships and a fear of getting too involved because they have not seen relationships working very well. To avoid the pain of breaking up, they often do not commit to marriage, nor do they look to their sexual practices to supply them with any lasting intimacy. They are so fearful that they have popularized living together and trying out a relationship before any commitment is made.

This is the first virtual community or virtual relationally oriented generation. They develop relationships via the Internet and create the illusion of coming together, if for no other reason than that it is safer and less demanding. Hence as Strauss and Howe say, "13ers have built a powerful survival instinct, wrapped around an ethos of personal determinism, though they have been taught to blame all their woes on themselves."[8] Why should I vote, they ask? It would not make any difference.

Baby busters do not see themselves as trendsetters but as responders to whatever comes down to them. But what can we expect from this most aborted generation in all of history, given that dissatisfaction with family and divorce have invaded their lives more than any other generation? So it is no surprise to learn that their generation has a higher percentage of suicides than any other. They are cynical, fearful, but desperately hope for something better.

Strauss and Howe sum up their description, "So 13ers were deliberately encouraged to react to life as you would hack through a jungle: Keep your eyes open, expect the worst, and handle it on your own."[9] Further, this "streetwise generation does indeed bring a bag of savvy tricks their elders lack—skills that may come in handy the next time America gets into real trouble. . . . Take note, Beaver Cleaver, Thirteeners may never have glimpsed Nirvana, but they know how to win."[10]

The Millennials (1980–2000)

Somewhere between 1978 and 1980, we see the entrance of what appears to be the most unusual of the five generations. They are called the millennials. Some refer to them as generation Y. Thom Rainer's book *The Bridger Generation*, a must read on this generation, refers to this group as the bridgers into the twenty-first century.

At present this generation is the second largest of the five, though there could be some further change (through immigration, for example). There are approximately 73 million millennials. They are the most academically educated of all the generations; and unlike their older brothers and sisters, the gen-Xers, they are not pessimistic even though they share the same realities with them about relationships, economics, politics, and especially organized religion.

As the second postmodern generation, the millennials are experience-oriented. Unlike the individualism demonstrated by their boomer parents and older brothers and sisters, the busters, they are interested in community because they admittedly want relationships. They express openly a desire for relationship with their parents, grandparents, and other older people, but are afraid to take the initiative. They may not be as interested in being in a large group as were the two previous generations; they want meaningful relationships with close friends.

The millennials describe the older generations as inauthentic, lacking integrity, and superficial. They see them dumbing down almost every area of their lives; witness their worship, education, and the entire pop culture movement. In some ways the millennials are much more like their traditionalist grandparents than the other generations with the exception that they may not express themselves or look the same way their grandparents did. But being extremely perceptive, they want to see some of the things that are missing from their world brought back into place. I have suggested to a number of churches searching for pastors and schools looking for teachers that they not forget those over sixty. That's what the young people really want. Confirming my statements, George Gallup Jr.'s *Next American Spirituality* says basically the same things. He further states that older people are a key to reaching this younger generation.

The millennials are the most spiritually minded of all the generations; 39 percent, according to Gallup and Lindsay, say that they are going to be more religious than their parents, though for them religion and organized religion are not synonymous. They are also the most biblically illiterate. Many of them may attend church, but once they reach their fifteenth birthday, dropouts rise dramatically. They want to know, before making any commitment, what it will do for them and their world. Will it make any difference in my life and the lives of those around me? Those are not bad questions, if channeled properly.

Millennials appear to be conservative, optimistic, and committed to making a difference even if it requires sacrifice. George Barna writes:

> Whether we acknowledge it or not, we leave a lasting impression on the minds and hearts of teenagers. They are not beyond influence. But making a difference in the life of a teenager is radically different from influencing a younger child or adult peer. Taking the time to have a positive impact is more than just "worth the effort"; it is a vital responsibility of every adult and a contribution to the future of our own existence.[11]

Further, "These young people represent perhaps our most significant legacy to the world. And for their development we will answer to God some day, having been allowed to be stewards of their development. The values, perspectives, beliefs and skills we help to implant in them today will largely determine the future of the world."[12]

Not only are the millennials highly educated, but they have excelled in being street-smart as well. This young digital generation is growing up with the highest level of computer and technology savvy. Many a teenager will design his parents' Web page because they know nothing about the process. This is the Internet generation unlike any who have gone before. It is second nature to them. They are not intimidated by technology.

Millennials are also growing up in a world of terror and danger. Events such as September 11, 2001; the shootings at Littleton, Colorado, and Conyers, Georgia; and passing through metal detectors on school campuses have been a standard part of their lives. As Zemke, Raines, and Filipczak have noted in *Generations at Work*, this is also the most tolerant of all the generations, a generally positive characteristic. What has to be factored into the mix is that much of that attitude is the result of having grown up without absolutes and expecting more than one answer to everything.

When it comes to the disciple-making process, it is as though God has given us an open door to bring together the generations in authentic spiritually driven interconnections that will create community, healthy relationships, and opportunities to study and teach the truth. This is vital because Thom Rainer states that given present trends, only 4 percent, or 2.5 million millennials, will be Christians. That does not have to materialize, but God help us if it does. "Millennials resemble a fully charged rocket—or to use Ortega y Gasset's classic definition of a generation, 'a species of biological missile hurled into space at a given instant, with a certain velocity and direction,'"[13]

Strauss and Howe quote *San Francisco Examiner* columnist David Sarasohn: "'The scariest thing about kids today is how adults feel about them.' There are, to be sure, many reasons why adults speak ill of kids— and why so much that is positive about today's young millennials remains half hidden behind the clouds of elder doubt and suspicion."[14] The authors also refer to those who are "fulfilling" adult lifestyles that exclude children. What a tragedy to leave children and youth out of our lives. They write about a youth power that the adult generations have yet to see. Indeed, Gallup calls the millennials the most revered and feared of all the generations. We can ill afford to neglect them in the disciple-making process.

Conclusion

We must study people with much prayer and wisdom while seeking to build the kind of relationships that will survive the greatest demands of life. We need all the generations coming together to produce the kind of covenant family that will survive the pressures, dangers, and consequences of today's often degenerate and demoralizing world.

The generation chart (figure 9.1) is included as a review and a checklist from which to ask how we can communicate with and encourage one another in the things of the Lord. God is the author of diversity, so we do not all have to be at the same age level or have the same experiences to relate to one another. We will not know the world without knowing

FIGURE 9.1. A COMPARISON OF GENERATIONS

	BUILDERS	BOOMERS	BUSTERS/XERS	BRIDGERS/MILLENNIALS
Population	46 million	76 million	42 million	73 million
Born	Pre-1940	1945–64	1965–79	1980–2000
Worldview	Modern	"Modern" (in transition)	Postmodern	Postmodern
View of marriage	High	Low	Higher than boomers	Higher still
View of family	High	Low	Pessimistic	More optimistic
Rate of divorce	Low	High	Less high	Less than previous two
Leadership	Above average	Below average	Below average	Above average
Self-confidence	Above average	Below average	Below average	Above average
Family life	Desired	Less desired	Fearfully desired	More desired
Place of TV	None	TV generation (3 -4 channels)	MTV (40–100 channels)	Dawson's Creek (100- plus channels)
Audial or visual	Audial (radio)	Both (TV)	More visual (cable/video)	Highly visual (Internet)
Orientation	Task	Individual	People	Community
Sermons	What to	How to	Why?	So what?
Participation	Unnecessary	Higher	Some participation	High participation
Tasks	Completed	Partially done	Undone	Relationships vs. tasks
Outlook	Irrelevant	Indifferent	Pessimistic	Optimistic
Worship style	Traditional	Moderate traditional	Nontraditional	Neo-traditional
Worship music	Hymns	Praise choruses	Variety	Eclectic
Other music	Orchestra	Rock-'n'-roll	Variety (jazz)	Pop/rap
Religious emphasis	Loyalty, program-oriented, duty	Personal satisfaction People vs. programs	Causes, issues, community	Community, relationships

© Christian Education and Publications 1999

people. Relating to one another will be more successful if we have some understanding of and appreciation for where others are coming from and why they believe and behave as they do.

And we must remember that while there are things that all generations share, among which is the need for the gospel and God's truth, each generation has its own unique way of searching for those things. If we do not answer the questions they are asking or help them to clarify their questions, we may miss tremendous opportunities to make disciples. Let us allow one another the freedom to be what we are generationally, even where those differences intrude into our comfort zones. There is too much at stake to let music and worship styles, clothing styles, and other incidentals build walls around us instead of bridges into one another's lives.

TOPICS FOR REFLECTION OR DISCUSSION

1. Why is it important to include something about the generations in the kingdom model of making disciples?
2. Can you see how the different generations today are alike and how they are different in their outlook on life?
3. How have you experienced, in your family, your church, your workplace, and the marketplace in general, the differences between the generations?
4. The older generation has been charged with being inauthentic, lacking in integrity, and superficial. Is that a fair judgment? Why or why not?
5. How can the topic of this chapter be effectively incorporated in discipleship study?

SUGGESTED READING

Gallup, George, Jr., and Timothy Jones. *The Next American Spirituality.* Elgin, Ill.: Cook, 2000. A volume highlighting the rising millennial generation as one of the three most important groups to know about.

Gerber, Jerry, Janet Wolff, Walter Klores, and Gene Brown. *Lifetrends: The Future of Baby Boomers and Other Aging Americans.* New York: Macmillan, 1989. A very helpful book for expanding our understanding of the different generations.

Hicks, Rick, and Kathy Hicks. *Boomers, Xers, and Other Strangers.* Wheaton, Ill.: Tyndale, 1999. A good, readable book on this topic. It examines the differences in the lifestyles, values, and opinions of the different generations, and why they differ. It also helps us know more about ourselves and why we think the way we do.

Howe, Neil, and William Strauss. *Millennials Rising: The Next Generation.* New York: Vintage, 2000. A challenging volume focusing on the millennial generation.

McIntosh, Gary L. *One Church, Four Generations.* Grand Rapids: Baker, 2002. Recommended for anyone interested in or attempting to understand the different generations.

Mitchell, Susan. *The American Generations: Who They Are, How They Live, What They Think.* Ithaca, N.Y.: New Strategists, 2003. Helpful data on the different generations; written from a marketing perspective.

Rainer, Thom S. *The Bridger Generation.* Nashville: Broadman and Holman, 1997. In-depth insights on the rising millennial generation.

Strauss, William, and Neil Howe. *Generations: The History of America's Future, 1584 to 2069.* New York: William Morrow, 1991. In-depth book on the history of generations in America; full of valuable information and insights.

Zemke, Ron, Claire Raines, and Bob Filipczak. *Generations at Work: Managing the Clash of Veterans, Boomers, Xers, and Nexters in Your Workplace.* New York: AMACOM, 1999. A clear expression of the different perspectives of the different generations on issues like work, ethics, and values; written from a management setting and with good information on the topic of generations.

Biblical Models for Applying the Word to the World

Part 3 of this book focuses on three different biblical paradigms or models that develop the ideas of Parts 1 and 2. The first biblical model is Paul's ministry at Athens, and particularly the way he framed his presentation of the gospel to connect with his audience. He clearly reflected knowledge of the culture and world around him, as well as the message of the gospel. Spiritual truth is spiritually discerned, but how we express or frame that truth should reflect an identification with our audience. Words and concepts mean different things (or nothing) to different people, and if we forget or ignore that, we may assume that we have communicated when actually we have not connected at all. Paul demonstrates in Acts 17 how to communicate the gospel and the truth of God to a people with no background understanding of God, much less a biblical world-and-life-view.

The second biblical model is an overview of Ecclesiastes, which contrasts and compares two different worldviews, the Christian and a non-Christian view. We noted in Part 1 that the Christian faith is a system, a worldview that impacts all of life. We either look at life through a correct biblical lens or, as Ecclesiastes reminds us, we live with only an earthly human worldview.

174

Our third and last biblical model will be a situation in the life of Abraham. The historical narrative in Genesis 13 demonstrates how important it is to understand covenant theology and especially how to read and understand the Scriptures from a covenantal perspective.

PART THREE

10

Paul's Example in Acts 17

Ａnd he made from one man every nation of mankind to live on all the face of the earth, having determined allotted periods and the boundaries of their dwelling place" (Acts 17:26). This verse is a clue to the larger passage we will be looking at, verses 16–34. Paul is pointing to God's providential control of his creation. Not only did God create us and all other parts of creation as well, but Paul explains to the Greeks that God also rules over his creation in many ways, particularly in determining the boundaries where nations and people are to live. The location of people groups is part of God's overall plan for his creation.

In an earlier passage in Acts, Paul makes a specific reference to King David, which could be a clue as to why God's plan determines where we are located: "For David, after he had served the purpose of God in his own generation, fell asleep and was laid with his fathers and saw corruption, but he whom God raised up did not see corruption" (Acts 13:36–37). God places us where he wants us to be so we may serve his purpose for our lives.

Serving God's Purpose in This Generation

In the Old Testament, there is also an interesting reference relevant to what Paul says in Acts 17: "Of Isaachar, men who had understanding of

175

the times, and to know what Israel ought to do" (1 Chron. 12:32). As David was gathering his men together for battle, they were coming from many different places. As the writer names them, he gives a distinguishing characteristic of each group. The men of Isaachar were known for their understanding of the times and what God would have them to do.

That is a basic concept that all followers of Christ ought to understand. They need to know that they are here to serve the Lord, which requires, among other things, knowing the times or the situation or circumstance in which they live. That becomes a key in both understanding the Word of God and determining his mission for our lives.

However, in seeking to know those things, it is easy to become so overwhelmed that we do not know what to do or where to start serving the Lord. Often we end up doing nothing. But God offers a reminder that spurs us on to serve his purpose. Jehoshaphat exclaimed, "O our God, will you not execute judgment on them? For we are powerless against this great horde that is coming against us. We do not know what to do, but our eyes are on you" (2 Chron. 20:12).

There is no more challenging and exciting time for us to live than now. One of the reasons God does not immediately call us to heaven when we are converted is that he has enlisted us in his army. We are on a co-mission with him. The Great Commission recorded in Matthew 28:18–20 teaches us that. There is no other substantive explanation for our presence here and now. You and I fit into God's scheme of ministering to this generation, just as Paul said to the Athenians and underscored to the Antiochians in reference to King David. We can ignore that purpose and mission, or we can commit ourselves to carrying it out. Of course the latter is the right choice; but having made it, we can also choose to be mediocre and average, or we can be gung ho and like U.S. marines go forward and establish the beachhead in the face of the enemy.

The apostle gives us a pattern of doing ministry or carrying out a mission that will enable us to live and witness in a way that will gain an audience and persuade people to listen to what we have to say. I don't believe that we can expect people today, especially the young generations, to automatically want to hear what we have to say about God, truth, and reality. Yet, as Peter said, one must always be "prepared to make a defense to anyone who asks you for a reason for the hope that is in you" (1 Peter 3:15).

One key to gaining an opportunity to give the reason for our hope is living a consistently godly and holy life that is different from those around us. A second key is knowing how to bridge into the lives of the people we are seeking to win over, through persuasion, to the gospel of Christ. This requires becoming more and more expert in understanding our audience. Communicators have talked for years about the importance of being audience-aware. It may have been a luxury in the past, but today it is absolutely necessary if we are to gain a hearing. Since the fall, communication has been a problem for mankind, but it is especially complicated in today's postmodern world.

Simon Kistemaker in his commentary on Acts reminds us of how "skillfully Paul addresses his audience. . . . Paul needs a point of contact from which he gradually can lead his audience to a knowledge of eternal values in Christ."[1] Likewise, Ben Witherington III in *The Acts of the Apostles* says, "What we see here [in Athens] is not an attempt to meet pagans halfway, but rather a use of points of contact, familiar ideas and terms, in order to make a proclamation of monotheism in its Christian form."[2] He further writes, "Familiar ideas are used to make contact with the audience, but they are used for evangelistic purposes to bolster arguments that are essentially Jewish and Christian in character."[3] Witherington then states that Paul was not interested in adding something to what these pagans already knew, but in converting them to a new, Christian worldview. At this Paul was a master communicator.

One of the biggest mistakes we often make is to assume that the way we communicate the gospel is not important, that only the content is important. In reality both are extremely important. Paul's pattern in Acts 17 is relevant to us because that Athenian context permeated by Greek philosophy parallels today's world in many ways.

For example, Athens was a non-Christian culture. The people of Athens did not know the Bible, much less anything about church history. While

178

there was some Jewish influence there which Paul did not overlook, he focused on the Greeks because they were steeped in all the latest ideas (at least from their perspective); in addition they were never satisfied that they knew everything they needed to know. The Jewish presence probably reflected a very small group of people among the multitudes. Athens was a pagan environment with all the attributes of a pagan society, much like our neopagan, barbaric society today in America.

To zoom in on Paul's ministry: he believed that he was in Athens on a mission to preach the gospel. He prudently realized that how he did that in Athens had to be different from how he did it in other places such as Antioch, where the people knew the Old Testament Scriptures, or in Corinth, where there was a mixture of Hebrew and Greek culture. Remember what he wrote in 1 Corinthians that energized him wherever he went!

> If even lifeless instruments, such as the flute or the harp, do not give distinct notes, how will anyone know what is played? And if the bugle gives an indistinct sound, who will get ready for battle? So with yourselves, if with your tongue you utter speech that is not intelligible, how will anyone know what is said? For you will be speaking into the air. There are doubtless many different languages in the world, and none is without meaning, but if I do not know the meaning of the language, I will be a foreigner to the speaker and the speaker a foreigner to me. (1 Cor. 14:7–11)

If we are to serve God's purpose to this generation, then we must know how to speak in an intelligible way to the audience. The words we use should reflect an understanding of our message and a sensitivity to the people we address. We must know where they are if we are to be effective. If we do not know how to speak meaningfully in the context where the people are, we will never utter a clear and sensible sound to their ears. I am aware that only God can open a person's mind and heart to the truth of the gospel, but I am also aware that he uses us in that process. That's what serving his purpose involves.

Being culturally sensitive can be a slippery slope. It is easy, as we have seen in many mainline churches this past century, to begin accommodating the message, changing it, adding to, or subtracting from it for the audience's sake. But being "politically correct" by today's definition in order not to offend the audience is dangerous. We are called to proclaim the message of Christ (which is exclusive) without adding offense through our manner or attitude, and in a way that shows a love for and identification with our audience.

We cannot win today's war if we are still fighting yesterday's battles. Desert Storm in the early 1990s is a reminder that the old ways of doing battle will not work in today's technological environment. That's why Paul's model or example is so important. It shows us we must maintain the truth without compromise while framing that truth in a way that persuades people where they are.

I study trends and culture, especially youth culture. The questions youth are asking are not necessarily the same as those the older generations ask. Unless we listen carefully, we will answer the questions of the older generations and miss those of the younger generation. If we fail to start where they are, we will fail to bring them to where Christ would have them to be. This means that for the sake of winning some to Christ we must be able to look beyond the music, the hair, the clothing, the body piercing. Whether one is speaking with relevance is not determined by the speaker but rather by the hearers. They will either understand what we are saying, or they will not. We must speak for their sake, not for ourselves, unless we simply like to talk to ourselves.

As we examine Paul's method in Acts 17 three things will stand out: first, Paul's general knowledge, his biblical worldview; second, Paul's immediate knowledge of the situation or circumstance; and third, Paul's methodology growing out of this general and specific knowledge.

Paul's General Knowledge (Worldview)

Paul operated with a general knowledge or biblical worldview. No matter where he went on his missionary journeys or no matter to whom he ministered, he operated on the basis of certain fixed truths that never changed. Paul's fixed truths are different from the foundations of the modern philosophers, such as René Descartes. Descartes and those of the Enlightenment period sought to find a fixed point in man upon which all other truths could stand. With Paul those truths were not found in himself or any other than God. Paul operated on those truths in his entire ministry in the New Testament. On these fixed points he never equivocated. He was always clear. No compromise!

Whether he was in Athens, Thessalonica, Philippi, or wherever he happened to be, Paul knew first that there is a living and true Creator God, the Judge of creation. Second, he knew that man is a finite creature made in God's image and likeness. Those were always Paul's foundational or starting points. Third, he knew that man is inescapably a religious being who already knows God because of God's general revelation. Though man may suppress this knowledge or in sin try to deny it, nonetheless, it is indelibly stamped on his life. Man is God's image. Fourth, Paul knew and reflected in his teaching and preaching that there are two classes of people on earth, those who worship and serve the Creator God, and those who worship and serve the creature. For Paul there was no middle ground on that point. Fifth, he also knew that those who genuinely worship God the Creator are saved, and those who do not are lost. And finally, as reflected in Acts 17, Paul believed that earth's history has a climax. History is not an endless cyclical pattern. Certainly there are recognizable cycles in history, but history is moving in a certain direction toward a final destination. Paul reflected that knowledge and belief no matter to whom he ministered. They comprised Paul's worldview through which he saw all of life. To Paul those were the universals, the absolute truths for all times and peoples.

Paul's Specific Knowledge of Context

Paul's immediate knowledge of the culture or context demonstrated his awareness of the need to speak those truths to his particular audience in the most meaningful way. In the case of the Athenians, he knew something about them. He was familiar with their culture. He knew for example that they were monists, that is, they did not distinguish between the creature and the Creator. All is one and one is all! Does that sound familiar?

Paul further knew that the Athenians believed that the universe was mysterious and unknowable because their concept was that something was out there that was so completely "other" or different that they could not know whatever it was. Yet on the basis of his worldview described above, Paul was very aware that he was not starting in a vacuum with these Athenians: he knew that the Greeks had already received God's self-revelation. They already knew that God is the all-powerful and everlasting God. Therefore, knowing that God had already revealed that truth to all men everywhere, he didn't have to argue with them to convince them of God's existence. They already knew that.

Paul also knew that his audience was not satisfied with their system of learning and their approach to knowledge, because in reality it led to ignorance. They did not have a grasp on full knowledge. That was also why they were always eager to listen to new ideas and the latest teachings. That was even why they were willing to listen to Paul. Their altar to the unknown god and their willingness to hear new ideas confirmed Paul's understanding of them. He further knew that they were without the gospel. That was the reason he was there, to take Christianity to Athens, the center of learning in the ancient world. Paul knew another thing about the Athenians. They did not recognize absolute authority; hence, they were willing to listen to the likes of Paul himself though he was a Christian missionary. And finally, he knew that the Greeks respected personal authority based on knowledge and special experiences; therefore the ability to persuade was an important element in his ministry.

Paul's Methodology

Using both his general and immediate knowledge, Paul developed his method of communicating the gospel truth to the Athenians. Here is what he did that underscores why his methodology is so appropriate and necessary and helpful for us today: Paul met those people where they were without necessarily agreeing with them. Notice as the method unfolds that he did not accommodate his message to them in the sense of altering it. Instead, here, where the people had no background in the Scriptures, he intentionally constructed a biblical world-and-life-view that appeared philosophical but was actually the same as what he preached in all the other places that he visited. This is an important point because many have missed what Paul was doing here and have been critical of his method.

Paul was masterful in knowing how to speak in both the marketplace and the Areopagus. He identified the point of contact that served as a bridge into the Athenians' lives. He did not start by building a wall, but rather a bridge, and in so doing he gained an audience. In the tradition of Socrates the Greek philosopher, Paul likely employed the Socratic question-and-answer method in framing his message. He would have known the Athenians were familiar with that approach.

He started with God and his revelation to all men by showing an awareness of the Athenians' religious expressions and their motive for being religious (though he knew he would in the end challenge their religious commitment). Paul said to them, "I perceive that you are a very religious people. I see the signs of your religion everywhere I go. I see your idols, even the one of the unknown God." He didn't alienate them up front by being hostile. They were pagans and in a sense heathens, but Paul would not bludgeon them with that. Instead, he said, "I observe that you are not only a religious people, but that you are superstitious in that your belief in the mystical leaves you uncertain."

"Actually," Paul might have said, "that which you call knowledge is really ignorance." Then he explained what he meant. Having built the bridge and now broken the ice, he proceeded to preach Christ and him crucified. But notice as you read the passage that his approach was different from what he had done in other places. For example, he didn't mention the name of Jesus Christ. Instead he referred to the man God had appointed Judge of the world. Simon J. Kistemaker comments:

But the Athenians might ask whether this man, who remains name-less, possesses divine authority to judge the world. What proof can this man furnish that God has conferred on him the power to judge? Paul states affirmatively that God himself provides proof to all men, because he raised this man from the dead.[4]

While the Greeks were having trouble connecting the dots, Paul declared clearly that who this man is and what he has done have everything to do with reality. Presently, you worship your idols, but now you must stop and worship the living and true God. At that point some sneered but some believed the gospel.

Clearly Paul practiced true tolerance of the Athenian beliefs, not the fake tolerance of today's world that seeks to neutralize truth. Having done that, he then challenged them and called them to faith and repentance.

Paul's approach here becomes our model today in our postmodern, post-Christian culture. Let's review: (1) We must be certain about the basics of our Christian faith—no wavering, faltering, or capitulating to the enemy. We must not compromise the truth. (2) Then we must be students of our culture in order to frame our message in the most meaningful way for our audience.

Though Gallup's surveys seem to indicate the opposite, I will assume that we do know the truth and embrace it as absolute for us and all peoples, that is, that our general knowledge or worldview is in place. From there we must pick up the second element of Paul's method: understanding our immediate context. Our world is changing. Things are far different now from even one hundred years ago. There are so many factors related to modernity and modernism that make our world different from that of the Athenians. Yet there are similar patterns or norms that help us understand more about the kingdom model of making disciples.

To apply Paul's model we must draw on two major components of our study thus far that will help us to understand our world and establish a clear line of communication with our audience. First, remember the philosophical shifts in worldview paradigms that occurred in history to create the current cultural climate: from the God-centered, faith-and-

184

revelation-based premodern period, through the man-centered, reason-and-empiricism-based modern period to the pluralistic, experience-and-feeling-based postmodern period. (See chapters 2, 7, and 8 to review this in detail.)

Second, remember the distinguishing characteristics of the four primary generations presently alive. The traditional, task-oriented builders respect authority and institutions, respond to information and instructions, and value hard work and delayed gratification. The affluent and self-centered boomers question authority, ask "What's in it for me?," value collaboration, and drop relationships and commitments that don't satisfy them. The pessimistic busters, the first postmodern generation, desire relationships but fear commitment, expect a lower standard of living than that of their parents, and have no heroes. The experience-oriented bridgers are highly educated but biblically illiterate, search for community, value spirituality but doubt organized religion, and see diversity as the norm. (Review chapter 9 for more detail.)

Just as the Westminster Confession of Faith reminds us that the Word of God written is to be translated into the everyday language of the people in order for them to read, study, and understand, so must we learn how to frame our message and witness in the language of the people to whom we are reaching out. Some communicators make a distinction, and I believe rightfully so, between actual relevance and functional relevance. Actual relevance deals with what the message really has to do with our lives, and functional relevance refers to whether or not we see the actual relevance for our lives. The Bible has actual relevance. It contains exactly what this generation needs. There must be no doubt about that. God has given us in his Word everything we need for salvation and life; however, if we do not see its relevance, then we will not get to the actual connection between the message and our lives. I believe that is part of our problem and why the younger generation is not impressed with Christianity and the church.

If we are to apply Paul's methods to our twenty-first-century world, we must understand that as we present the truth of God in the gospel, we must be more relational and more oriented to explaining the personal implications ("so what") of our message. The real point of contact with the postmodern generation is how the truth can touch their lives in the most meaningful way and in a way that links them together with other likeminded people. Just as Paul did in Athens, we too are going to have to become more adept at helping people to know how to ask the right questions and find the right answers. As George Barna has reminded us in his surveys, we cannot win the younger generation or bridge into their lives simply by preaching to them in a way that dispenses content without living illustrations and good applications. It has to be more reality-oriented than that for them. They have to see a connection with their lives.

Topics for Reflection or Discussion

1. In light of the comments regarding Paul's strategy at Athens, read Acts 13:13–43; compare and contrast Paul's approach at Antioch with his approach at Athens.

2. Discuss the challenges and opportunities to make ourselves more audience aware as we seek to communicate the gospel, but also the danger of changing the message in the process. John R. Stott, an outstanding communicator of the gospel, wrote about that tension in his book *Between Two Worlds*. Paul demonstrated Stott's point that in communicating the gospel we are not to be technique-driven but rather content-driven in our presentation or conversation. On the other hand, certain techniques such as understanding the culture and language and being socially sensitive can be helpful if properly used. The apostle Paul meets Stott's challenge to know how to communicate to the audience in a language they can understand without sacrificing the theological content of what is being said.

3. As you think about Paul's preaching at Athens, consider how he appeared to take a more "apologetic" or world-and-life-view approach in setting forth the gospel and why that was necessary in that context.

4. Discuss some modern-day circumstances where this approach will be particularly important, especially in light of the postmodern culture around us.

5. Consider whether in his sermon and ministry at Athens Paul altered the message in order to communicate to the audience.

6. As an exercise, any reader who leads a Bible study, teaches a Sunday school class, or preaches to a congregation should take time to write out an audience analysis—age, educational level, social characteristics, political and philosophical orientation, etc. How can that help lead to more meaningful communication?

SUGGESTED READING

Barrs, Jerram. *The Heart of Evangelism*. Wheaton, Ill.: Crossway, 2001. Advice on how to communicate the gospel to today's world. An excellent chapter expands on Acts 17.

Kistemaker, Simon J. *Acts*. Grand Rapids: Baker, 1990. A valuable reference for understanding the Book of Acts, particularly chapter 17.

Johnston, Graham. *Preaching to a Postmodern World: A Guide to Reaching Twenty-First-Century Believers*. Grand Rapids: Baker, 2001. Very useful book for anyone interested in communicating the gospel in the postmodern world.

Stott, John R. W. *Between Two Worlds*. Grand Rapids: Eerdmans, 1982. An excellent book focusing on preaching and communicating in a truly biblical sense that relates to the context in which it is done. How truth is communicated is the passion of this book.

———. *The Spirit, the Church, and the World: The Message of Acts*. Downers Grove, Ill.: InterVarsity, 1990. John Stott understands how to combine good exegetical work with homiletical flare. This commentary demonstrates that ability by providing helpful insight for teaching and preaching from the Book of Acts.

11

Ecclesiastes: A Study in Worldviews

In chapter 4 we dealt with the subject of a Christian world-and-life-view. In this chapter, as with the previous chapter, we will deal with that topic from a biblical paradigm. I encourage the reader to refer back to chapter 4 before or while reading this chapter.

Ecclesiastes is one of the best scriptural examples of setting forth a Christian world-and-life-view and contrasting it with a nonbiblical world-and-life-view. For many, Ecclesiastes has been a confusing and perplexing book. Actually, many Jews believed that it did not belong in the Scriptures. Rabbis held widely different opinions about what to do with it. We believe it is a very important and legitimate part of the Word of God and has a rightful place in the canon of Scripture.

When I was in public high school (and this will date me), we had Friday chapel meetings, each of which began with a Scripture reading. My friend Ernie often read the Scripture, and he frequently chose Ecclesiastes 3:1–8. I was not a Christian at the time, though I did attend church. What I did not realize at the time was that Ernie's explanation of the passage was the opposite of what the writer had in mind. This illustration serves to show how our worldview, or the glasses through which we see and interpret life, plays out in our conclusions.

Contrasting Christian and Non-Christian Worldviews

While I hope to write from a faithful exegetical position and preserve the purpose of this Old Testament book, I do not want this chapter to be an exegetical commentary on Ecclesiastes. (Many commentaries debate authorship. Was it Solomon, David's son, the king of Israel? Or was the book written by any one of several other possible authors? There are references to *Qoheleth*, a teacher and the main speaker in the book. *Qoheleth* is someone who gathers people for the purpose of teaching them. Tremper Longman in his commentary suggests that *Qoheleth* is an occupational designation rather than a proper name. I follow that position; and, while I see more problems with Solomonic authorship, we will not spend time on that issue. It is also hard to determine the exact genre of this book. It is similar in some ways to Job and in other ways to Proverbs. This contributes to the difficulty of interpreting and understanding *Qoheleth*'s message.)

I believe that Ecclesiastes is much like Acts 17 and the Book of Job, which makes it a most relevant book with a contemporary message for today's postmodern world. There are places in Ecclesiastes that defy logic or at least remind us that human logic will not always match up with God's. As the prophet Isaiah has reminded us, "My thoughts are not your thoughts, . . . declares the LORD" (Isa. 55:8). For the Teacher, life does appear to be full of contradictions, paradoxes, and antinomies. Words often take on a meaning of their own, depending on and often determined by their context.

Ecclesiastes is important in the disciple-making process because it shows a stark contrast between the Christian and a non-Christian worldview. Also, it shows that people are willing to try many different avenues to make sense out of life and reality only to come up short of what they are hoping to find in the process. The Teacher does not hesitate to say, in building his case, that life from a non-Christian perspective is meaningless because it goes nowhere.

Qoheleth uses the metaphor of living (thinking) above the sun to refer to a Christian worldview, and living beneath or under the sun to refer to a non-Christian worldview. As soon as one realizes that those are his only two choices, to live either above the sun or under the sun, the more strongly the challenge to think Christianly begins to develop. However, one of the things that we have to understand about Ecclesiastes is that the Teacher, while setting forth the two choices of world-and-life-view, also realizes the tension and struggle that develop from having a foot in both places. For example, as a Christian consciously thinks and acts from above the sun, he remembers that life's meaning is not ultimately tied to this world but is understood only in light of eternity. But because Christians are not yet fully sanctified, we often search for meaning in things of this world.

What I really appreciate about Ecclesiastes and why I believe it to be such an important ingredient in the disciple-making process is that it clearly points to the importance of beginning with God. Unless we begin with God in our understanding and interpretation of life, we cannot expect to end up with God at the center. God must be our center point of reference and interpretation of reality. The only way that we can experience and understand our significance is to begin with God. Our life has meaning and significance only if we know the Lord and know we are made in his image. If we start with any reference point other than God, we will believe that this life is all there is to reality; however, if we start with God, we will understand that this life has meaning and significance in the light of eternity. The grave is not the end; there is more to come! That is why throughout Ecclesiastes the Teacher makes frequent reference not only to the meaninglessness of life, but also to the hope for those who have God and eternity in their frame of reference.

One reason that Christians have such a struggle with the Christian life and make so little difference in the world around them is that, though they are converted to Christ, their worldview has not really changed. We dealt with that issue in chapter 4. Our Western world emphasizes the idea that we can be religious in a certain part of our life and nonreligious in others. However, we must see the totality of life. We pay a price when we do not.

ECCLESIASTES: A STUDY IN WORLDVIEWS

We are seeing a resurgence of the Islamic religion in today's world. The tragedy of September 11, 2001, brought it to the foreground. If we intend to understand and witness to Muslims, we must know how to think from the paradigm that life is a total system. We cannot be nonreligious in anything. Muslims see religion much more holistically than do Westerners, even Western Christians. Some of my friends involved in ministry to the Muslim community understand that in sharing the gospel they must know how to deal with systems, because Muslims think of their religion as a way of life. The way Westerners isolate their religious faith from the rest of life is a perplexing stumbling block to Muslims.

In Bernard Lewis's book *The Crisis of Islam,* he has a chapter containing criticism of America, the church, and the moral and spiritual degeneracy stemming from being partly religious. He is reflecting some of the thoughts of Sayyid Qutb, an Egyptian who is a leading ideologue of Muslim fundamentalism and an active member of the Muslim Brotherhood. We have to take that criticism seriously because we have not been consistent within the Christian community (though Qutb may be guilty of equating the church with America). Ecclesiastes helps us to see the importance of a systematic or holistic approach.

When Johnny and his family attend church and Sunday school, they need to be challenged with the truth that the Christian faith is a total life-system. From the very earliest in a person's discipleship pilgrimage, he or she needs to see that Christianity touches every area of life. The church plays a key role in helping the family understand the world-and-life-view position. What Johnny is taught at home will be supported and strengthened by what he learns at church. It is vital that Johnny and his entire family understand from the earliest that Christians have two great commissions, one to make disciples and the other to carry out the cultural mandates both to subdue all things and to do all things to the glory of God.

The contrast presented in Ecclesiastes shows that our worldview makes a difference in how we perceive and experience the Christian life. One motif in Ecclesiastes that is often interpreted wrongly is, "There is nothing new under the sun." Given the "under the sun" paradigm, we are left with the idea that life is the same day in and day out. The "same old same old"! God is placed in a box, and life is regimented by a closed-universe theory that says that life comes around and goes around. Nothing new is added! However, *Qoheleth's* intention is to show that in a Christian world-and-life-view we do not live in a closed universe. We cannot put God in a box, nor can we be put in a closed box because we are made in the image of God. We can be creative and make new things.

As we disciple God's covenant children, youth, and adults, we want them to see early on that we have the choice of either "chasing after the wind," which leads to meaninglessness, or starting with God and seeking to see things through his eyes, having a Christian philosophy of life in place to help us make sense out of the otherwise meaninglessness of life. Ecclesiastes is a book of hope set against the backdrop of meaninglessness and hopelessness.

Jay Adams comments in the introduction of *Life under the Sun/Son*:

> Ecclesiastes is eminently valuable to counselors who regularly (in our day especially) encounter persons whose difficulties stem from their focus on this world and what it has to offer. People are confused about this neglected book because they do not understand it, and therefore, do not know how to integrate it into Christian living. Your task (and opportunity) is to introduce them to the meat of this important work, showing them that there is a philosophy of history not to be found in this depth elsewhere in the Bible.[1]

One other thought that keeps coming to the surface in Ecclesiastes is a phrase my friend Steve reminds me of over and over: "It's not about us or me, it is about God."

Specific Topics Reflecting Worldviews

From the general backdrop of the two philosophies of life, "above the sun," and "under the sun," *Qoheleth* deals with a number of topics such as life, money, pleasure, happiness, wisdom, work, possessions, man, and eternity. All of these specifics actually point to who God is. Either he is the sovereign Lord over all things and ruler of his creation, or he is not. Those are our two choices. If we choose to believe the latter, then Ecclesiastes graphically describes the consequences. Unless we learn to see the specific categories of life from the "above the sun" philosophy, we will not develop a biblical Reformed world-and-life-view.

Using Ecclesiastes as our manual, let us take a look at each of these topics. I will give a general summary of *Qoheleth's* emphasis and encourage a more detailed study of each. None of the topics in the list (see figure 11.1) is exclusive because each part of life and reality touches all the other parts.

Figure 11.1. Contrasting Worldviews

	Non-Christian Worldview (under the sun)	Christian Worldview (above the sun)
Life	Meaningless/hopeless	Hopeful/purposeful
Pleasure	Vainly sought after	Real but not our aim
Happiness	Circumstantial/fleeting	A result and gift
Wisdom	Increases misery	Right perspectives
Work	Self-oriented	God-ordained
Possessions	Mine/never enough	We are only stewards
Man	No clear identity	Image bearer of God
Eternity	Life ends at grave (death)	Fullness and more beyond grave (everlasting life)

Life

As *Qoheleth* speaks from the non-Christian worldview, life under the sun is meaningless. The opening chapter of Ecclesiastes sets the stage for him to show in the rest of the book how this plays out. The first chapter leads to the realization that a non-Christian philosophy doesn't give any meaning to life. Life simply comes and goes and is full of weariness (1:8). Life is merely a striving after the wind in that we reach for it and try to hold it in our hand only to find it is nothing. The "under the sun" view leads to the conclusion that it is better not to be born than to live this miserable life (4:3). According to chapter 3, life under the sun is monotonous at best. The conclusion within that worldview is that life is vain and empty of meaning, and it is better to be dead than to live (4:2). However, when *Qoheleth* speaks from the Christian worldview, he realizes that there are worse things than death and that he is meant to enjoy life (9:9). Also, because God is the Creator of all things, life does not have to be empty, monotonous, or meaningless. Man can actually live this life to its fullest and enjoy the process. The key is keeping God at the center and seeing life from his perspective.

Recently, a middle-aged pastor died after battling a prolonged illness. I was told that on the day of his death, his family gathered around his hospital bed and sang hymns with him participating as he could. Knowing what life is all about and what was in store for him after death made it possible for him and his family to celebrate, even as the tears of separation came. They had things in perspective.

Pleasure

Personal pleasure or hedonism as a way of life is not unique to our contemporary world. It has been around since the beginning. How one understands pleasure and whether or not it serves a good purpose are determined by one's worldview. For example, a person living with the "under the sun," non-Christian worldview who strives after pleasure or makes that the aim in life will find it is empty of meaning and satisfaction. "I said in my heart, 'Come now, I will test you with pleasure; enjoy yourself.' But behold, this also was vanity" (2:1). *Qoheleth* said that he tried to fill his life with everything that was pleasurable. He denied himself nothing, and yet his heart found no pleasure in those things. They were merely a "striving after wind" (2:10–11). He tried one pleasure after another, and with each one he felt an emptiness that did not satisfy his desires. Going to parties did not give his life meaning and purpose. He ate, drank, and tried to find pleasure in his work, but to no end (2:24; 7:1–6).

After beginning to grasp the significance of a biblical worldview, however, *Qoheleth* realized there was a place for pleasure that was not simply a striving after the wind. He could find pleasure in his work (5:18). He could eat, drink, and enjoy life and experience pleasure and satisfaction at a good party. The difference between the two philosophies was pronounced. When we make anything except God our center point and seek after things other than God, nothing satisfies. However, with God in his rightful position things will fall into place and bring a measure of satisfaction. I say "measure" because *Qoheleth* realized that nothing in this life is complete. That is why we must learn to live each day with eternity in our hearts. Being a Christian does not deprive us of pleasure and joy, but when we make those things our objective and adopt a hedonistic approach to them, they fall far short and actually produce a "striving after wind."

No doubt many of us in childhood may have tried to catch or see the wind. Neither was possible, no matter how hard we might have tried. Trying to find pleasure in life without the Lord at the center is equally impossible. That's *Qoheleth*'s message. That's what we are to teach and model for the next generation.

Happiness

Closely related to pleasure is happiness. Reading through Ecclesiastes gives the distinct impression that even happiness is empty and void of meaning with a non-Christian worldview. In a sense we learn early on in 2:1–2 that striving after happiness is madness, and seeking it is vain and meaningless. Yet man with an "under the sun" worldview often attempts to make his *summum bonum*, his highest good, things like happiness, joy, and pleasure, only to be deeply disappointed in his quest. We can look around us and see the foolishness of those who make that mistake. Do this and that, or purchase this or that, consume this product or that product, and it will bring you much happiness, so the advertisers tell us. We easily take the bait, and before we know it, we are caught in the whirlpool of unhappiness and dissatisfaction.

Qoheleth reminds us that happiness can bring meaninglessness and the opposite of what it promises. I remember learning a brief saying as a young Christian: "I sought the Lord, the dove of peace came; I sought the dove of peace, and the Lord left." Happiness as an end in itself will produce the opposite of what we seek after. If happiness becomes our goal or aim, then whether or not we possess it is completely determined by our circumstance.

But as with other qualities, if we have the right worldview, happiness can be very much a part of our life. *Qoheleth* states, "To the man who pleases him, God gives wisdom, knowledge and happiness" (2:26, NIV). He also says in 3:12, "I know that there is nothing better for men than to be happy and do good while they live" (NIV). But in 5:19 he reminds us of the "above the sun" or Christian worldview that is required: "Moreover, when God gives any man wealth and possessions, and enables him to enjoy them, to accept his lot and be happy in his work—this is a gift of God" (NIV). He also counsels us to be happy when times are good (7:14). Further, he states that while we are young we are to be happy (11:9).

A reading through Ecclesiastes makes it clear that happiness is not something necessarily tied to wisdom, knowledge, and wealth in the sense that one who does not have those things cannot be happy. Happiness is really the gift of God that comes to those who have their priorities straight and understand that God is the center of all things. And this is a good place to point out that a Christian philosophy of life is freeing; for instance *Qoheleth* suggests in 9:7 that we can eat and drink with a merry heart. As Jacques Ellul states in his provocative book on Ecclesiastes, *Reason for Being*: "In the midst of all this vanity, it becomes possible to rejoice and be happy. Everything moves on and disappears, but that in no way changes the pronouncement God makes on our life. This is the meaning and the limit placed on happiness. Any other meaning given to it falls within the circle of vanity."[2]

Wisdom

Next we look at wisdom, another quality that people seek. Everyone would like to be known as wise; however, once again we have to listen to the Teacher and realize that wisdom's value is determined by one's worldview. There are at least fifty verses in Ecclesiastes that refer to wisdom or the wise. One might think on the surface of things that any philosophy of life that has wisdom as its aim would be honorable. But that depends on our starting point and our objective. *Qoheleth* says in 7:16, "Be not overly righteous, and do not make yourself too wise. Why should you destroy yourself?" As Tremper Longman says, "*Qoheleth's* observation leads him to offer some shocking advice."[3] Why would *Qoheleth* say that? In 1:16–17 he prepared us for the shock by reminding us up front that seeking after wisdom is "striving after wind." And then in 1:18 he further reminded us that there are trouble, and distress, and vexation in much wisdom, and having it can only increase our sorrow.

We know from the outset, as Jacques Ellul reminds us,[4] that *Qoheleth* is referring not to the wisdom of God ("above the sun" wisdom), but to human wisdom, which is limited, finite, and sinful. The second part of the first chapter establishes the point that wisdom is meaningless. Longman comments, "Proverbs emphasizes that wisdom brings joy and life. *Qoheleth* begs to differ, complaining that it brings frustration and pain."[5] He goes on to explain that *Qoheleth*, unlike Proverbs, is concerned about the mental anguish that wisdom brings. I like James Crenshaw's summary, that wisdom and reason alone do not satisfy. Actually, they can have the opposite results, which Crenshaw describes as "burdensome."[6] I believe the point being made is similar to what we found reflected in the Acts 17 passage in the previous chapter. The Greeks were never completely satisfied with their understanding and knowledge base. They felt there was something more that needed to be learned, so they were always seeking after new ideas and thoughts. That is the point of Ecclesiastes and its worldview focus. When we live with a Christian philosophy, we realize that only God is all-wise; and while human wisdom has its merits, it can be overextended and become a negative force that destroys us.

Having a Christian worldview helps us with this concept, as Ellul reminds us, in that it keeps before us the reality that philosophy and wisdom, just like everything else, are subject to vanity and meaninglessness. So Ellul concludes with *Qoheleth* that wisdom is an enigma in the end. It is actually a riddle. But this conclusion is a "below the sun" view of wisdom that is quite different from the "above the sun" perspective. Beneath the sun, we tend to make wisdom our goal; but above the sun, with God at the center of our lives, we know that wisdom can be good and helpful. We also know that we should not confuse wisdom and knowledge; they are related, but not synonymous.

How then do we interpret and apply verses such as 8:1: "Who is like the wise? And who knows the interpretation of a thing? A man's wisdom makes his face shine, and the hardness of his face is changed"? The answer is that no one can do it in himself. It has to begin with God. He is the interpreter of things. He is the one who changes man and causes him to be compassionate toward others. Again, the emphasis is on focusing on or having God as the center point of life and reality.

Work

We know from other Scripture passages that work is to be a part of a Christian's life. God means for us to be both "be-ers" and "doers." We are to do the things that he tells us to do, and part of those instructions includes work. Most people are given to work. Idleness is not valued in today's busy life. Most of what we do is work-oriented, but what is our motive? What is work? Are we working for the right reasons? Again, our work ethic and practice all depend on our worldview. *Qoheleth* says in 2:4–11:

> I made great works. I built houses and planted vineyards for myself. I made myself gardens and parks, and planted in them all kinds of fruit trees. I made myself pools from which to water the forest of growing trees. I bought male and female slaves, and had slaves who were born in my house. I had also great possessions of herds and flocks, more than any who had been before me in Jerusalem. . . . Whatever my eyes desired I did not keep from them. . . . And behold, all was vanity and a striving after wind.

Were those things wrong for him to do? Actually, they were good things, if done from the right perspective, but the text tells us he did them for himself. That is an "under the sun" approach to work. With that view of work, it becomes bitter toil and a real drudgery. It is full of sorrow and vexation (2:23).

Qoheleth also warns that a wrong worldview can cause a person to become what we would call a "workaholic," a condition often stemming from trying to have more than our neighbor (4:4). Sadly, we never seem to be satisfied with what we have. The more we have, the more we want, and the more we want, the less we are satisfied with what we have. "For whom am I toiling and depriving myself of pleasure?" (4:8). The answer is not for my family, or to help the needy, but for myself. "This also is vanity and an unhappy business" (v. 8).

If we have a wrong worldview as a result of failing to start with God, then our understanding of work is going to be off base. Whether we work or not, we will not be satisfied. Work is hard and can require much labor, but with the right perspective, we can receive much pleasure in our work. "Also that everyone should eat and drink and take pleasure in all his toil—this is God's gift to man" (3:13). Being able to work is a great gift from God. Those who want to work and are not able for various reasons find it difficult to handle. God brings joy in our work, and therefore we should find enjoyment in it (5:18, 20). "So I saw that there is nothing better than that a man should rejoice in his work, for that is his lot" (3:22).

Possessions

It is extremely important for Christians to understand the biblical view of possessions. Robert Wuthnow has written quite effectively about the church's failure to address this issue and teach the biblical idea of stewardship.[7] He sets forth statistics to show the financial crisis that churches are facing because the people see no connection between their possessions and their Christian life. Hence there is a real need to teach people how the Scriptures address this issue, which is a clear reflection of our failure in the disciple-making process.

I will never forget Bill, a faithful member of a church I pastored years ago. Bill struggled with this teaching about work and possessions. He was a "committed" Christian, but he could not understand why the teaching about work and possessions had to be included in his Christian life. When I realized that this was a problem for him, I intentionally spent personal time with him, talking, studying, and reinforcing the concepts. Not only did Bill come around to what I called the right Christian perspective on these matters, he became the chairman of our board of deacons. He taught and modeled the Christian perspective in his life, and God gave him an effective ministry in the church.

What *Qoheleth* wants us to know is that as we live with a non-Christian worldview, we tend to hoard and keep for ourselves things that are really a gift of God. And when we operate on the premise that our possessions are really ours, we risk disobeying God's instruction. We also find ourselves squandering our possessions despite the needs around us. If we are disciples of Christ, but living in his kingdom with a non-Christian philosophy of possessions, we can never be satisfied with what we have.

Qoheleth says that we may work to obtain possessions and wealth for our family, or if we have no family, we may work to acquire more for ourselves, only to say, "I hated all my toil in which I toil under the sun, seeing that I must leave it to the man who will come after me, and who knows whether he will be wise or a fool?" (2:18–19). Also, "Again, I saw vanity under the sun: one person who has no other, either son or brother, yet there is no end to all his toil, and his eyes are never satisfied with riches, so that he never asks, 'For whom am I toiling and depriving myself of pleasure?' This also is vanity and an unhappy business" (4:7–8).

According to *Qoheleth*, what this means is that wealth and possessions are vain if we use them for ourselves (5:8–17). Whoever loves money will never be satisfied with what he has, and hoarding backfires because we do not know what tomorrow may bring. We cannot take our possessions with us into eternity. So with an "under the sun" philosophy or worldview we will not have a proper view of wealth and possessions. It is even stated in 6:2 that though God gives us our possessions, we cannot enjoy them if we use them in a non-Christian manner.

The flip side is that if we live with a Christian worldview, we will know where possessions and wealth actually fit into our lives, and we will know it is better to be poor and wise than to be wealthy with many possessions (4:13). We understand from a Christian perspective that our wealth and possessions should help us live from day to day. Yet because we are not sure about tomorrow, we must give to the needs of others as the Lord teaches us to do. What we do with what we have today is more important than our personal benefit in the future, as far as wealth and possessions are concerned. If we have the right perspective on these things, then we can follow the Teacher's advice to be joyful in prosperity (7:14). We will even look for ways to "squander" our wealth, according to *Qoheleth*. Of course he is not talking about wasting our possessions but about not holding them too tightly.

The message in chapter 11 is clear. God would have us give and share and not be a "Scrooge" with what we have. After all, we know that what we have belongs to the Lord in that he gave it to us, even though we may have earned it. It is of his grace that we have what we have.

As we demonstrate a Christian worldview, we will reflect God's image in us in that we will have a giving spirit just as he did in creation and redemption. We will be a giving people and will not lay up treasures on earth.

Man

Qoheleth gives the clear and distinct impression that man living with a non-Christian worldview sees himself or herself as made only for this life. We are born, we live, and then we die, and that is all there is to life. We work and increase our wealth primarily because we envy our neighbors, yet we fail to realize what will happen when the end comes. We lose it all! The grave becomes the final place for those born to woman. A non-Christian worldview focuses all the attention on the here and now and fails to consider eternity. No matter whether one parties or increases his wealth by working hard, his life has no real meaning or purpose; therefore he sees himself as a victim living in a fallen world with no hope for anything else.

As *Qoheleth* contrasts the man under the sun with the man above the sun, he starts with God, who is the key to understanding man. To have a proper and right understanding of who we are, we must have a right knowledge and faith about God. "Remember also your Creator in the days of your youth . . ." (12:1). We live at God's pleasure, because he is our Creator. He made us in his image and likeness, and though we know that we must go to the grave, a Christian worldview enables us to live with the certainty of eternity in our hearts. We know that we are pilgrims and strangers here; and while we do not know what tomorrow holds for us as far as our earthly life is concerned, we know that we were made for eternity. While we are unable to find real satisfaction in our pleasure, our toil, or our possessions and wealth, we live with the anticipation of eternity, which reminds us that we are "not nothing." We are God's handiwork. And besides, says Qoheleth in 8:14–17, man cannot know truth and reality on his own. But he can know those things because God shows them to him. "Then I saw all the work of God, that man cannot find out the work that is done under the sun. However much man may toil in seeking, he will not find it out."

Most important of all, as man lives with eternity in his heart and mind, he is aware that his life is in God's hand, that God determines his days upon earth; and he can find meaning in that knowledge. He can live above the fear that his death may be meaningless and his life over in an instant. A Christian worldview opens the door to a satisfying experience with this life as we anticipate the life to come.

Eternity

One last example, closely related to man, is eternity. Nowhere is the contrast between the two worldviews more apparent than over the issue of life, death, and eternity.

The non-Christian mind-set presented throughout the book lacks a self-conscious notion of eternity. The non-Christian worldview ultimately sees this life as all there is. When it's over, it's over. There is hope only for today because we have no certainty about tomorrow; therefore,

202

as in existentialism, "now" is all that there is. Though the Bible teaches that "it is appointed for man to die once, and after that comes judgment" (Heb. 9:27), the person operating from a non-Christian perspective sees only the present moment. Though his Creator God put eternity in his heart and he cannot ultimately deny the afterlife, he has to focus on this life. It is all about self and not about God. Today's younger generations have been so oriented to the present that many decisions and choices are being made without long-range considerations. We even see institutions make short-range decisions with long-range consequences.

However, *Qoheleth* demonstrates throughout the book that an awareness of eternity enables us to hope for better things to come. It opens the possibilities of greater joy and pleasure in this life while removing fear and hopelessness. He helps us to see that clearly in passages such as 3:9–13. The contrast between the two worldviews as they relate to life, death, and eternity is evident throughout the book.

Several years ago when my dad died, I had the honor of conducting his memorial service, as he had requested. Though he thought of himself merely as a humble small businessman, he loved the Lord and taught God's Word faithfully for many of his latter years. His Sunday school class served as honorary pallbearers. He told me many times, as his health was failing, and especially after having to give up his teaching, that he was ready to be with the Lord in heaven. He modeled for me a man that had eternity in his heart. Though I still long for opportunities to talk with him, knowing that he is with the Lord, and that that was his hope and assurance, made it much easier for me and my family to accept God's timing and plan for his life.

To embrace a Christian worldview requires that we live daily with both the knowledge of and hope for better things to come. It will also encourage us to do what *Qoheleth* says at the end of the book: "The end of the matter; all has been heard. Fear God and keep his commandments, for this is the whole duty of man. For God will bring every deed into judgment, with every secret thing, whether good or evil" (12:13–14). That really summarizes the importance of developing a Christian mind that operates from a distinctively biblical approach to life.

My hope in making disciples is that Christians come to see the importance of thinking, making decisions and choices, and living from an eternal perspective. Things just simply look different or take on a different meaning when they are placed in the perspective of eternity.

A Christian Worldview and Legalism

Somewhere in the disciple-making process, Christians must come to understand that Christianity is no legalistic straitjacket of rules and regulations. One of the things that Jesus and the apostles had to deal with early on was the tendency of some to make religion into a list of dos and don'ts. In showing the contrast between the two ultimate worldviews, *Qoheleth* makes it clear that Christians have liberties that enable us to participate in and even enjoy things like a good party, eating and drinking (not drunkenness), and working and making money. There is so much for Christians to enjoy in this life; we don't have to live in fear of so offending God that God will turn away from us. We simply have to operate from a Christian perspective.

While *Qoheleth* was quick to point out that work, money, possessions, food, beverages, marriage, and a host of other things can be detrimental without a proper biblical perspective, he also wants the reader to see that from a biblically Reformed outlook these things can be enjoyed as part of God's good plan for his children. It is obvious in studying Ecclesiastes that there are many things that we can participate in and enjoy doing that some legalists would call taboo. But the main thing that we are reminded of is that we cannot win God's favor nor can we earn his grace. "I perceived that whatever God does endures forever; nothing can be added to it, nor anything taken from it. God has done it, so that people fear before him" (3:14).

Conclusion

Ecclesiastes is an important part of the kingdom model for making disciples because it underscores so clearly the need for Christians to operate from a biblically based position in regard to all of life. Choices and decisions grow out of one's worldview. The challenge to "think God's thoughts after him" is key to developing one's worldview, and we learn from Ecclesiastes that genuine conversion and its fruits result in developing a Christian world-and-life-view. New Christians should understand this early on. We must learn to think differently about things, to see things from Christ's perspective as he has revealed them in the Scripture. He has given us his Holy Spirit to enable us to do that.

The Westminster Shorter Catechism asks, "What is the chief end of man?" The answer: "To glorify God and to enjoy him forever." Ecclesiastes shows us how to do that more intentionally.

God's model and method for making disciples is all-inclusive. It requires developing a Christian mind and heart for the things of God with an ability to operate on a day-to-day basis from a Christian world-and-life-view perspective. That's where we begin to see the transformation taking place, because it will affect every area of our lives and touch every area of our culture as we live our faith.

TOPICS FOR REFLECTION OR DISCUSSION

1. As you have worked through this chapter (and chapter 4), how do you respond to the statistics indicating that many if not most Christians do not have a self-conscious world-and-life-view?
2. At what period in your Christian growth did you first understand that being a Christian involves more than a mere profession of faith and more than going to church and Sunday school?
3. Give some specific examples of how you have applied your Christian world-and-life-view to situations and circumstances that you

have encountered and how you made better choices and decisions as a result.

4. There are many other specifics that could have been included in this chapter on Ecclesiastes: power, the good, friendship, family, and even God. Try working through the book to see how the contrasting worldviews speak to those issues.

5. Which part of the book or passage in the book did you find to be the most challenging and helpful in thinking about a biblical world-and-life-view?

SUGGESTED READING

Adams, Jay E. *Life under the Sun/Son: Counsel from the Book of Ecclesiastes.* n.p.: Timeless Texts, 1999. A practical and helpful little book packed full of ministry materials.

Ferguson, Sinclair. *The Pundit's Folly.* Carlisle, Pa.: Banner of Truth, 1995. A great little easy-to-read commentary; helpful, practical, and theologically excellent.

Longman, Tremper, III. *The Book of Ecclesiastes.* New International Commentary on the Old Testament. Grand Rapids: Eerdmans, 1998. By far the best commentary on Ecclesiastes.

————, and Dan Allendar. *Bold Purpose.* Wheaton, Ill.: Tyndale, 1998. The Book of Ecclesiastes in narrative form; an excellent way to teach Ecclesiastes.

Provan, Iain. *Ecclesiastes; Song of Songs.* NIV Application Commentary. Grand Rapids: Zondervan, 2001. A user-friendly, thought-provoking commentary; good ideas on moving from the original setting of the text to today's context.

12

A Covenantal Reading of Scripture:
Genesis 13

In chapter 10 we looked at Acts 17 as a biblical model for how to take the Christian faith and frame it in such a way that listeners will understand or relate to what the speaker is saying. Athens was a pagan culture, much like ours today. Paul tried to present the gospel to the people in a bridge-building fashion without altering the content of the message. Chapter 11 surveyed how the writer of Ecclesiastes set forth a Christian worldview by contrasting it with a non-Christian worldview. In this chapter we will use Genesis 13 to demonstrate how to read, study, understand, and apply the Scriptures from a covenant framework. (We have already dealt with the covenant in chapter 6.)

Within the kingdom approach of making disciples it is important to know the Bible as a book of the covenant. This chapter will show the importance of reading the Scriptures from a covenantal perspective and will contrast that approach with two others (legalism and moralism). This chapter will also underscore the point made in chapter 2 that knowledge is personal knowledge built on God's revelation of himself in his Word.

Biblical theology is covenant theology and vice versa. The concept of covenant is neglected in most disciple making. Its absence, I believe, contributes to a weak understanding of Christianity as a total way of life, as well as a personal relationship with God and others. Understanding the Scriptures from a covenant perspective will bring several benefits.

First, covenant puts us in the context of a community. I agree with Calvin that when a child of the covenant is publicly identified as such by the sign of baptism, the administration of that sign actually begins the educational or disciple-making process in the life of that child. Christianity is not merely an individualistic religion. It is family.

Recently I had the privilege of baptizing my grandson. I told him (young as he was) and reminded the congregation that this sign gives him a sense of belonging to God, to a Christian family, and to a Christian church. The vows taken at a baptismal ceremony by parents and congregation remind us that Christianity is a family-oriented religion that is based on the covenant concept that God has established.

Christianity is a religion of truth fleshed out in relationships vertically and horizontally. A relationship with the Lord God implies and even requires relationships with one another. Though there may be different types of relationships, all of them are part of my Christian life. For example, I have a certain kind of covenant relationship with my wife. It differs from that which I have with my children, parents, and Christian sisters and brothers. Yet we are all family, related to God and to each other.

Western culture is guilty of being individualistic, emphasizing "self," "me," and "I" so much that we often forget the importance of "us." We do not always understand where others fit into our lives, particularly when it comes to religion. In chapter 7 we talked about how the sinful part of modernity has attempted to convince us that religion is a private matter, between only us and God (if we believe in God). Therefore, we can use religion only in certain areas of our lives, not in all areas, particularly not in our connections with other people. In other words, no marketplace religion for our culture! The concept of the covenant reminds us how wrong that view is. Our religion, our faith in God, touches every area of our lives and therefore the lives of others as well. We will see this in the Genesis story.

Second, as we understand the covenant concept in the disciple-making process, we will be able to see that there is really a grand story, a meta-narrative in history. Postmodernism tries to convince us that there is no grand theme or story of life, but the scriptural idea of the covenant is proof that there is such a story, and it is about God's relationship with his world and people. The Scriptures show that history is his story threaded together by the unfolding of his covenant with his people. Understanding the covenant not only reminds us that there is a unifying theme for life, it helps us to see that it is not primarily about us but rather about God and his plan and will. Things make sense only as we see them in light of God's plan and purpose. We will see this played out in Genesis 13.

Third, an understanding of the covenant reminds us that it all begins with God's initiating grace. He is the covenant-making as well as the covenant-keeping God. He has chosen to relate to his creation by way of covenant. His plan involves the covenant framework. Though his covenant is about him and his plan, he tells us that we are included in that plan; therefore our relation to him is a covenantal relation. It did not come about because of merit on our part or doing good to earn God's favor.

Most of us want things spelled out in black and white with rules for this and regulations for that. We see that down through history, though Christians have had the freedom to walk by faith and not by sight, many have neither appreciated nor appropriated that freedom. Many Christians are not comfortable with gray areas; hence our natural tendency is to develop rules and standards of behavior that say, do this and you will live. We have also seen how this plays out within religious groups.

Christianity has been bothered with both legalism and moralism since the beginning. A legalist is someone who bases his life on his ability to keep rules, often man-made and imposed on others. If he does not have enough rules, he writes more. A moralist is what we might call a do-gooder. Some people, not reading or understanding the Scriptures covenantally, trivialize God's plan. I recall a chapter in R. J. Rushdoony's book *Intellectual Schizophrenia* that was entitled "The Menace of the Sunday School." Rushdoony's point was that most Sunday schools are guilty of teaching moralism: be good, please God, earn his favor, and you will be all right. Even with the best intentions, such an approach demeans grace and misunderstands God's covenantal love; yet many Christians operate from a moralistic framework rather than a grace principle. This suggests that it is not first about God, but about us. However, as we will see in Genesis 13, when the focus is first on us, we reverse God's intended order and right things do not happen. From that perspective we mistakenly believe that salvation is a matter of earning God's favor or attempting to manipulate God to do certain things in ways that we choose. This is how some have attempted to interpret Genesis 13.

Fourth, understanding the covenant will enable us to learn about God and his will in a life-changing way and to see life from God's perspective. He is the ultimate reference point for all of life and reality. If we do not understand how he has chosen to relate to us by way of the covenant, we will not have things in the right perspective.

In chapter 6 I referred to *Promise and Deliverance* by S. G. DeGraaf. One of the real blessings in my Christian growth was discovering that four-volume set of books. It focuses on learning, studying, and teaching the Bible from a covenant framework. I underscored a statement in the translator's introduction (from Dutch to English) that has stuck in my mind and heart:

> Useful as such studies may be, in the final analysis they make little sense to minds that have not yet grasped the divinely established order of things and the basic covenant relationship to God in terms of which this order is to be understood.... That covenant embraces all possible earthly relationships—family, marriage, education, economic life (work), politics, arts, communications, worship.[1]

DeGraaf explains how to read, study, understand, and apply the Scriptures from within the covenant framework. He suggests that three questions should be asked about each text:

1. What does it teach us about God, or what is God's revelation of himself here?
2. What does it teach us about Christ the Mediator of the covenant?
3. What does God teach about himself in his covenant with his people, including the privileges and responsibilities related to the covenant?

Those questions became the grid for DeGraaf's hermeneutical principle of understanding the Scripture. This grid is a good way to keep things in perspective and to keep our focus on God and what he requires of us. That is the heart of discipleship: knowing about God in a way that transforms our lives by making us more like him, loving and caring for what he loves and cares for. This covenantal method contrasts with simply studying the Bible or looking at life from our own perspective.

Fifth, in chapter 2 I made the point that all true knowledge requires two things: objective reality and subjective experience. In other words, we can know the content of our faith only as we believe it. Remember the slogan, "I believe in order that I might understand" à la Augustine. Understanding the Scriptures requires a faith and commitment on our part, and covenant theology is that thread that underscores the reality of a personal relationship with God and his people. In one sense we could even say that it is covenant theology that provides us with the path to knowing what and whom we believe and the implications which that brings to our lives. Knowledge from a Christian perspective requires a relationship between the knower on one hand and who and what are known on the other. Thus making disciples within the kingdom model requires vertical and horizontal relationships based on truth.

Background for Genesis 13

The grand narrative reflected in the covenant did not begin in Genesis 13. Actually, it had its beginning with the creation of Adam and Eve. God entered into a covenant with this first pair of people on earth that gave them certain privileges and responsibilities. That covenant (the covenant of works) stated, Do this and you will live and share the benefits of paradise. However, by sinning Adam not only broke that covenant but rendered himself powerless to repair the breach or ever keep that covenant again.

In Genesis we see that God, who had every right to destroy Adam as he said he would do if man broke the covenant, intervened, suspended his judgment, and interjected what we now know as the covenant of grace. Basically, he was saying to Adam in his state of sin, "What you did in your disobedience and what you cannot remedy by your efforts, I will remedy for you. I will send my Son to undo your sinful work." From Genesis 3:15 on, the story begins to reveal the multifaceted developments of the covenant of grace. That new covenant finally reached fulfillment in Jesus Christ, who came as the new Adam to keep the covenant for us and enable us to live in covenant relation with God.

The covenant of grace unfolds itself in different epochs throughout the Old Testament. As each part of the story develops, more knowledge about that covenant is revealed, not changing the original promise but revealing more of its richness. What God said to Adam, he reaffirmed to Noah after the flood. Then as we read further in Genesis, we come to the next part of the story and the person of Abraham. In Genesis 11 we have a record of who he was and where he was. God's special call came to him. He was to be a key person in the covenant story. At the time of God's call, Abraham was living with his father and brothers in Ur of the Chaldeans (see Acts 7:2–4). Genesis tells us that he was married to a woman named Sarah.

It was while there that Abraham heard God's word to leave his country, kindred, and father's house and follow the Lord to a land yet to be revealed (Gen. 12). God wanted Abraham to understand that his plan in separating him from his surroundings was to make of him a great nation and to use him to bless all the nations of the earth. It is important that we see in this part of the narrative that God was already beginning to unveil more about the seed promised in Genesis 3:15, who would be none other than Jesus Christ, God's Son. Abraham, as the father of the new community, clearly foreshadowed Christ. He too had to separate himself from all human ties. As we read the rest of the story, we begin to understand from Christ's fulfillment of the covenant why certain things had to happen in Abraham's life.

God called, and Abraham responded positively; along with his wife Sarah and his nephew Lot (son of his deceased brother Haran), he left his homeland. Abraham was seventy-five years old and Sarah was sixty-five. They had no children. When he arrived in Canaan, he stopped at Shechem, where the Lord said, "Through you I will give this land to your offspring." The closest thing Abraham had to a child was Lot. Was he to be that offspring? Abraham built an altar and worshiped the Lord.

Abraham traveled to Negeb to live there, but a famine arose in the land; therefore, he sought refuge in Egypt. Still childless and yet remembering God's word about offspring, Abraham thought, *My wife Sarah is a beautiful woman. I fear that in Egypt I will be killed, and Sarah will be taken by the Pharaoh for his wife. What would that do to God's promise?* We can imagine Abraham saying to himself, *I have to devise a plan that will protect Sarah and keep me alive at the same time.* He told Sarah his plan. "I will tell Pharaoh that you are my sister and that way he will keep us safe." Pharaoh did spare Abraham and even gave him many possessions. However, when Pharaoh approached Sarah, God visited Pharaoh's household with great plagues that led him to discover that Sarah was actually Abraham's wife. He rebuked Abraham for not having told him the truth. Instead of killing both of them, Pharaoh added to Abraham's possessions and allowed them to leave Egypt physically unharmed.

The Situation with Lot

On the exodus from Egypt, Abraham, Sarah, and Lot took their possessions, and returned to Negeb. They went back to an altar built earlier between Bethel and Ai and worshiped the Lord. Genesis 13 states that by this time Lot had also accumulated numerous possessions, including livestock. Tension arose between Abraham's herdsmen and Lot's. Abraham loved and treated Lot as a son, but circumstances were straining their

relationship. Abraham saw a need to separate from Lot in order to preserve both their relationship and their witness to the people.

They agreed, and Abraham gave Lot first choice of the land. Lot chose
what appeared to be the better part of the land, the Jordan Valley, which
led him to settle near Sodom, a wicked city. That choice having been
made, God visited Abraham once again and reaffirmed his earlier promise about his fathering a great nation. We now find Abraham settling by
the oaks of Mamre at Hebron (Gen. 13:18). He built an altar at that place
to worship the Lord.

Let's leave the account there and examine a covenantal approach to
this passage before finishing the story. As we follow the kingdom approach
to making disciples, it is vital to lay a foundation that will enable believers to correctly understand the apostle Paul's words: "For by grace you
have been saved through faith. And this is not your own doing; it is the
gift of God, not a result of works, so that no one may boast" (Eph. 2: 8–9).
It is disappointing that many misunderstand redemption from sin. I
selected Genesis 13 for our kingdom model of making disciples to underscore the right and wrong ways to understand redemption. We will review
two wrong ways to interpret and apply this passage, and then the covenantal approach.

I divided a class that I taught in Kingston, Jamaica, into three groups.
I assigned each group to a specific position. We had some interesting and
varied interpretations of Genesis 13. Here are two:

First, it is easy and tempting for legalists to believe that we have to earn
God's favor. If we are good and live a certain lifestyle, we will merit God's
special favor and be saved. If we do not follow the correct pattern, we will
not be saved. That is the simplest example of what salvation by works or
by one's own effort means. At first Abraham had trouble believing God's
word about redemption. Hence he tried to work out his own plans and
make God's promise a reality. We see this clearly in his lie to Pharaoh
about his relation to Sarah in the twelfth chapter. His lack of faith betrayed
a failure to correctly understand the covenant promise.

Second, moralists would say this story gives us models to follow. For example, God blessed and protected Abraham and Sarah because Sarah obeyed and submitted herself to her husband, even though they lied. If we do the "morally right" thing, though our action questions God's Word and his ability to fulfill it, he will bless us as he blessed Abraham and Sarah. Or, pertaining to Abraham and Lot's separation: Abraham, though the older leader, humbled himself and put Lot first. As Abraham was willing to share his wealth with his nephew, we should be willing to share what we have with others. God's blessings were contingent on Abraham's humility, giving Lot first choice of the land. We can excuse Abraham and say that all he was trying to do was to help the fulfillment of God's promise along, as though God could not do what he said.

The legalistic (salvation by works) and the moralistic approach miss the point; they misunderstand God's promise. As a result, they miss the blessing of God's promise and the hope of its fulfillment.

There are several truths to be observed in Genesis 13 and those events that built up to it. One is that when God makes a promise or gives his word, he does not depend on us to bring that word to fruition. He speaks and it is done, as we observed in the creation account. When God made a promise to Abraham, though all the details were not revealed, Abraham should have believed God completely. He did not have to assist God in the task. For example, he did not have to lie to Pharaoh. God had said that Abraham would be the father of many nations and through his offspring all the nations of the earth would be blessed. That should have been enough for Abraham. The fact is that God protected Abraham and Sarah not because Sarah was obedient to Abraham, but because God had made a promise and his word does not return to him void, as the prophet Isaiah reminds us. He does what he says he will do. This is a basic truth about God that disciples need to understand. Though he usually works through his children to accomplish his purpose, he will complete what he has begun and keep his promise.

I do not mean to convey that Abraham and Lot are insignificant players in this story. Obviously, they are significant or God would not have included them in this biblical account. If we were doing an in-depth exegesis of this passage, we could and should say many things about Abraham and even Lot. We could talk about their relationship and the tensions that developed. There are also things we could learn from Lot's choice of the Jordan Valley. However, we want to emphasize in relation to the kingdom approach to making disciples the importance of focusing on first things first, namely, God. Start with God, get things in perspective, and then other aspects will fall into place. They will also make more sense. We can make sense out of the incidents with these people only if we begin with God as the primary focus of the story.

As we make disciples and help them to become better students of the Word, we want them to see the grand narrative of redemption. In one sense we can say that as the tapestry of the story of redemption unfolds, the covenant is the thread that holds it together. If we understand that perspective, then the Bible is seen as more than multitudes of stories and episodes that do not cohere. It is one grand story of God's design and plan for his covenant people.

As we apply our covenantal hermeneutic, how are we to understand Genesis 13? First, we ask, what does Genesis 13 teach us about God? The lesson is simple. When God makes a promise, he keeps it, even if we cannot understand how it will be fulfilled, or even if it involves great risk on our part. God is sovereign and will do what he says he will do, and that is not dependent on us.

Second we ask, what does God teach us about himself as the Mediator? Abraham, in his separation from family and friends and then finally from his nephew Lot, was to be the father of many nations. (Some have suggested that Abraham was not obedient to God's call to leave family because he took his nephew along, but the text doesn't support that.) In his role he was a type or foreshadowing of Jesus Christ, the only one who could fulfill the law's demands and bring eternal life. As a type of Christ with the covenant family, Abraham had to experience complete separation, as the Lot incident in Genesis 13 indicates. Though the seed promised to Abraham later found immediate fulfillment in his son Isaac, the seed was none other than Jesus Christ, who would undo everything that Adam and Eve had unleashed upon their posterity.

When we finally see Abraham and Lot going their separate ways, we are reminded of God's redemptive promises made initially in Genesis 3:15. We are reminded that the promise was to be progressively revealed. Through each significant episode in the Old Testament, we see the promise opening up like a blossoming flower, until it is finally realized in all of its fullness with the coming of Christ. What Abraham had to learn was that it was not about Abraham; it was really about God. Or maybe we could say it like this: God's covenant promises focus primarily on God, not Abraham.

However, we see clearly from the early events in Abraham's life that the focus on God does not excuse man from his responsibilities, nor does it negate his privileges as a covenant person. And so DeGraaf's third hermeneutical question must be answered: What does the passage teach about God in covenant with his people, including the responsibilities and privileges of the covenant? We must believe and obey; when we do not, there are consequences. What we hope for when we read the Scriptures from a covenantal position is that we will focus totally on God and his sovereign grace. As a consequence, we will eagerly respond to him in loving and constant obedience. When we fail, as we are sure to do, we will immediately repent and seek his forgiveness.

When Isaiah saw the beatific vision of the Lord, all he could do was cry out, "Holy, holy, holy is the LORD of hosts; the whole earth is full of his glory!" (Isa. 6:3). Similarly, when we see God through his gracious plan of redemption, what can we do but build our altars, worship, and adore him? Seeing through the covenant grid or perspective will enable us to do that more and more. It is first and primarily about God before we ever ask, What about me?

So many Bible study methods would have us read a passage from the Bible and quickly ask, What does this mean to me? The covenantal approach reminds us that it is not first about us, but rather about God. Only after we have that in place can we then ask, What about me? What

218

does this passage mean to me? Reading the Scriptures from a legalistic orientation or a moralistic framework reverses that process by starting with man. We see only part of the picture and even that is not in its proper place. That is one reason why we find that the kingdom concept in discipleship is so difficult.

While we must focus on God as the primary object of our understanding his Word, we cannot leave out the incidentals. We have to see Abraham, not only as the obedient servant, but also as a sinner in need of God's grace and mercy. He sinned, he lied, and he thought more about himself than God. How could he be the one through whom God would bless the nations? If we focus on Abraham, that is a legitimate question, but if we start with God, the story takes on an entirely different perspective. Think about how many human covenants have been broken because the emphasis was upon self. Marriage covenants have been broken by not starting with God. Business partnerships have been damaged or severed because they did not focus on God. Churches have split and splintered because God was not the primary object, and so it goes. The real issue with Abraham and Lot was not the property. The promise was about Jesus Christ, of whom Abraham was a type. The seed promised to Abraham depended completely on God and his timing. And we learn later in the story that God acted at the right time and place with the birth of Isaac.

Life takes on a different meaning when we realize that it is not primarily about us. We are here at God's bidding to serve him. We are here to love people as God loves them and care for the things God cares for. If our lives are not transformed by that love, and if it does not transform us more and more into his likeness, then life has no real meaning and purpose. Starting with self is a dead-end street.

Abraham had to learn that God's promise was not dependent on Abraham's understanding or Abraham's efforts or works. "We believe in order that we might understand" should be our motto. We would then begin to understand more and more the significance of the "seed born of a woman." The psalmist said that in God's light we see light. When we first see God's light, then things take on a new slant and meaning. Teaching others to see things in God's light is what discipling is about.

As we grow in grace, we will fall from time to time and even displease the Lord by our lack of faith and obedience. But when we do, God does not break his covenant with us. He does not turn us away or cast us out. He is the God of grace who promises forgiveness and restoration to those who love him with all their heart, mind, body, and soul.

I have counseled some people who came to believe that God had abandoned them because of their sinfulness. How could he love them given the things they had or had not done? "Can I be forgiven?" they ask. The answer is simply that his love is not based on what we do or do not do. He determines whom he loves and how he will deal with each one. But no matter what that may look like in everyday life, he will never leave us nor forsake us. When God makes a promise to us, he will follow through because all of his promises are Yes and Amen in Christ Jesus. God has not told us to first take care of "number one" or to look out for our own interests, but to trust, believe, and love him.

Christians must be clear that salvation from sin is not by man's efforts, but rather by God's grace. Christian growth will not take place unless this truth is firmly fixed in a person's mind and heart.

It has been a real thrill in my ministry to see people come to grips with this truth. I remember from my own Christian life when I finally, though embryonically, understood the truth about God's grace and unconditional love. When I learned that God would keep his covenant and complete what he had begun in my life, I took a giant step forward in spiritual development. But that did not lead me to believe that it did not matter how I lived; rather, it made me want even more to live for the Lord. And that's what a disciple, transformed by God's grace, is passionate to do.

Conclusion

I have attempted to demonstrate from Genesis 13 the difference the covenantal approach to the Scriptures makes. The crux of the story in Genesis 11–13 is not Abraham's lying to Pharaoh about his wife Sarah.

220

Nor is it Abraham's sharing the land with his nephew Lot, thereby illus-
trating how Christians must be willing to share with others, true as that
may be. Those were important parts of the story, but the main or primary purpose was to help us focus our attention on God as he reveals
himself in this Scripture. Seeing the whole redemptive narrative is the
key to understanding the parts.

Unless we begin with the basic questions suggested by DeGraaf, we
will not end up with the message that God intends for us to receive. I
believe this is one of the major breakdowns in the modern-day methods
of making disciples. It is one reason we do not see total life-
transformation. The covenant story is about God who gives and keeps
his word. It was on that basis that the prophet Isaiah could remind the
people of his day, as well as ours, "So shall my word be that goes out from
my mouth; it shall not return to me empty, but it shall accomplish that
which I purpose, and shall succeed in the thing for which I sent it" (Isa.
55:11). Or as God said to the Virgin Mary regarding the birth of Jesus,
"For nothing will be impossible with God" (Luke 1:37; lit., "for no word
of God shall be void of power").

Several years ago we lost a grandson. He did not survive a heart trans-
plant. But our comfort and that of his parents was that he was a child of
the covenant. Because we believe that God keeps his word of promise,
we could mourn with hope that Jake was with the Lord. Jesus' death and
resurrection were the crowning fulfillment of God's promise in Genesis
3:15. He was that seed born of a woman who would redeem his people
from their sins. Soon he will return from his throne to renew his entire
creation. That is the grand narrative of the story of redemption threaded
together by the truth of God's covenant with us.

Now for the "rest of the story." After Lot made his choice of land, God
said to Abraham, "Lift up your eyes and look from the place where you
are, northward and southward and eastward and westward, for all the
land that you see I will give to you and to your offspring forever. I will
make your offspring as the dust of the earth, so that if one can count the
dust of the earth, your offspring also can be counted" (Gen. 13:14–16).

God stated it like this in Genesis 17:7: "And I will establish my covenant between me and you and your offspring after you throughout their generations for an everlasting covenant." In other words, "I will be your God and the God of your children." God kept his covenant with Abraham. And he also keeps his covenant with us in Christ.

I believe the postmodernists will give us a better hearing if we can show them that Christianity is a religion of truth fleshed out in vertical and horizontal relationships. Christianity touches lives at their deepest level, and from that relationships and community develop.

At our church we sing the following hymn with each administration of the covenant sign of baptism to children. Sung to the tune of "Beneath the Cross of Jesus," it is a powerful testimony to the continuance of God's covenant love:

Beneath the blood-stained lintel I with my children stand;
A Messenger of evil is passing through the land.
There is no other refuge from the destroyer's face;
Beneath the blood-stained lintel shall be our hiding-place.

The Lamb of God has suffered; our sins and grief he bore;
By faith the blood is sprinkled above our dwelling's door.
The foe who seeks to enter doth fear that sacred sign;
Tonight the blood-stained lintel shall shelter me and mine.

My Savior, for my dear ones I claim thy promise true;
The Lamb is "for the household"—the children's Savior too.
On earth the little children once felt thy touch divine;
Beneath the blood-stained lintel thy blessings give to mine.

O thou who gav'st them, guard them—those wayward little feet;
The wilderness before them, the ills of life to meet.
My mother-love is helpless; I trust them to thy care!
Beneath the blood-stained lintel, oh, keep me ever there!

The faith I rest upon thee, thou wilt not disappoint;
With wisdom, Lord, to train them my shrinking heart anoint.

A COVENANTAL READING OF SCRIPTURE: GENESIS 13

Without my children, Father, I cannot see thy face;
I plead the blood-stained lintel, thy covenant of grace.

O wonderful Redeemer, who suffered for our sake,
When o'er the guilty nations the judgment-storm shall break,
With joy from that safe shelter may we then meet thine eye,
Beneath the blood-stained lintel, my children, Lord, and I.[2]

TOPICS FOR REFLECTION OR DISCUSSION

1. This chapter suggests a number of benefits that come from studying the Scriptures from a covenant perspective. Can you think of others?
2. Does it really make a difference which of the two following approaches to Bible study we choose?
   a. Model One: What does the passage say? What does the passage mean? What does it mean to me?
   b. Model Two: What does the passage teach about God? What does the passage teach about God as Mediator? What does the passage teach about covenant privileges and responsibilities?
3. Use Model One to study a passage from the Old Testament, reading from either a moralistic or a legalistic framework. Then use Model Two to study the passage from a covenant approach. Compare the results.
4. The Book of Hebrews is a good place to read further in the Scriptures about the covenant. Using a concordance, find the relevant passages and study them in light of what we have suggested in this chapter.

SUGGESTED READING

DeGraaf, S. G. *Promise and Deliverance*. 4 vols. St. Catharines, Ont.: Paideia, 1977. An unrivaled exposition of how the covenant theme runs from Genesis to Revelation; see especially volume 1.

Hunt, Susan. *Heirs of the Covenant*. Wheaton, Ill.: Crossway, 1998. A practical discussion of the covenant.

Jocz, Jacob. *The Covenant: A Theory of Human Destiny*. Grand Rapids: Eerdmans, 1968. An extremely valuable resource on the covenant.

Moore, T. M. *I Will Be Your God*. Phillipsburg, N.J.: P&R Publishing, 2002. A very readable study of the covenant for both groups and individuals.

Robertson, O. Palmer. *Covenants: God's Way with His People*. Philadelphia: Great Commission, 1987. A good book for teaching the subject of the covenant.

Epilogue

These twelve chapters have been written with the hope that they will contribute to the making of disciples from a "kingdom of God" perspective. I have not intended to discourage anyone who wants to be involved in making disciples. As a matter of fact, my desire has been to encourage more pastors, teachers, leaders, and Christians in general to think about being and making disciples.

This volume has suggested some reasons why the present methods have not succeeded in carrying out hopes. We did not deal with the obvious because we assumed that those interested in this topic are already cognizant of several requisite for success: Bible reading and study, personal evangelism, sharing the Christian faith with others, and prayer. Nothing will be effective without prayer and witnessing; however, looking at the whole we suggested other areas that are often overlooked or neglected.

In Part 1 we focused on those foundational philosophical, theological, and doctrinal areas that are not usually included in disciple making, at least not until somewhere down the line. I suggested, however, that they are basic to the process and should be incorporated. Having told Titus, "But as for you, teach what accords with sound doctrine" (Titus 2:1), Paul then went on to instruct older men and women what to do in the discipleship process. I believe he was bringing those basics back into the very beginning of disciple making.

There are three possibilities: (1) to not be a Christian and not think like one; (2) to be a Christian yet not to think like one; and (3) to be a

Christian and think like one. The third position has been the aim of all that has been written in this volume. The concerns of those who are frustrated over disciple making, as well as the statistics highlighting the failure of present approaches, show that we need a more holistic or a kingdom approach, as we have called it. I am convinced, by God's grace, that it will offset some of the disheartening trends we see today. I believe Christians need to see the Christian faith and their relation with the Triune God as touching every area of their lives. I also believe that if that were to happen, there would be more Christian influence in our world.

In Part 1 we evaluated the foundational elements needed—a good assessment and an understanding of the all-inclusiveness of the kingdom of God. Our thesis was that this will in turn produce a unique world-and-life-view from which we will develop a clearer spiritual perspective. The Reformed faith gives us a doctrinal system that easily translates into life, as all truth must do. Clearly, theology is life and life is theology. The covenant was included as the thread that binds the life-system together. Our slogan was "the need to understand the Word."

Part 2 centered on the need to know the world. We do not live in a vacuum. Understanding our world and culture is vital in disciple making for two reasons: (1) It keeps us from falling into the mold of the world, being swept along without realizing it; and (2) It helps us to know how to think, to make decisions and choices that are not merely reactions or fleeting whims.

We chose three topics that we believe are crucial to understanding our world. The first was modernity, because it has shaped the framework of present-day life with all the developments in technology, which cause things to happen at such a rapid speed that we have no time to think through their implications. We then chose postmodernism as the present philosophical paradigm of our culture, because it influences every part of our lives. We also suggested that postmodernism is not all bad. It is not void of value, and it does influence our thoughts, choices, and lifestyles. Therefore, we need to know and be able to assess it. Finally, the chapter on generations was an attempt to fine-tune our understanding of the people in our culture with whom we as disciples of Christ need to be able to interact. Knowing something about people is key to knowing how to relate to, witness to, communicate with, and appreciate them.

In Part 3 we showed how to combine the foundations in Part 1 with the cultural sensitivity in Part 2, as we study and apply the Scriptures to our lives. For example, Paul's approach to ministry in Athens (Acts 17) provides us with a good overall model of the kingdom framework for making disciples, and is very applicable to our culture and time. Ecclesiastes enables us to see that there are ultimately two world-and-life-views, one Christian and the other not. Christians have to make the choice between the two. One might think that Christians would automatically think like Christians, but such is not the case, as Ecclesiastes teaches. Finally, with the Abraham and Lot narrative in Genesis 13, we tried to demonstrate the importance of reading the Bible covenantally. A kingdom disciple learns to see God as the reference point of all things. Neither creation nor redemption nor the Christian life makes sense unless we start with God and see from that perspective.

My prayer is that God will use this book in some way to encourage you in your own personal life and development, as well as in training those who are members of your ministry team. I will be grateful if that prayer is answered in some way. It has been a privilege and challenge to communicate these thoughts to you, not knowing you. Aristotle once said that we learn best from our friends. I would like to think of us as friends, and maybe we will have the opportunity to become better acquainted.

Thank you for taking the time to read and study this book. God bless you. To him be all the honor, praise, and glory.

1

The Role of Baptism and the Church in Disciple Making

As we deal with the topic of the kingdom approach to making disciples, we should not forget that the essence of the Great Commission, Jesus' last instructions before the ascension, was to make disciples. That was a command from our Lord himself. Not only did he give the command to make disciples, but he explained how to do it.

Since the days of early revivalism in the tradition of the Second Great Awakening and Charles Finney's emphasis on individual conversion, we have added to the mix a method of evangelism removed from the corporate body. Actually, Jesus' words connect disciple making with baptism and Christian nurture. Brett P. Webb-Mitchell points out in good Reformed fashion that "baptism is the unofficial beginning of our education in the performance of Christly gestures. It is a sacrament and thereby a gestured ritual that announces to all in the present world and to the communion of the saints that we are God's possession and thus have been given a new name—child of God."[1] He further directs attention to John Calvin's reference to "understanding of our baptism," implying that discipleship is actually learning the full significance of our baptism.

If we are correct, whether one is baptized as an infant on the basis of God's covenant promises, or is baptized as an adult as a later-in-life convert, baptism really does mark the beginning of one's educational process. And because the sacrament of baptism belongs to the church, the church has the responsibility to be actively and intentionally engaged in disciple making. It cannot assign that responsibility and privilege to any other.

To paraphrase John Calvin regarding the church's responsibility in this process, the church's role is to nourish and train those who are God's children. In reality, the ideal is for a child of God to never know a time when he or she was not trusting in Christ for salvation and growing spiritually as a result of that trust and faith and then to live every moment of every day to the glory of God.

2

A Comment on Robert E. Webber's
Ancient-Future Evangelism

As I was completing this book, I received a copy of Robert E. Webber's *Ancient-Future Evangelism: Making Your Church a Faith-Forming Community* (Grand Rapids: Baker, 2003). It is a sequel to his *Ancient-Future Faith*. I could have simply listed the new volume in the bibliography; but because of its focus and particularly its beginning, I wish to comment on it.

Webber discusses the September 1999 International Consultation on Discipleship, a conference of 450 church leaders in Eastbourne, England. He quotes several of the participants, including some well-known evangelicals. For example, John R. W. Stott said, "Evangelicals have experienced enormous statistical growth . . . without corresponding growth in discipleship." Tokunboh Adeyemo from Africa lamented, "The church is one mile long but only one inch deep." The conference manifesto declared, "The Great Commission is not only to evangelize but to make disciples." Discipleship is "a process that takes place over a period of time for the purpose of bringing believers to spiritual maturity in Christ." David Neff, an editor of *Christianity Today*, responded, "Now that the consultation has placed disciple-making higher on the global evangelical agenda, it is vital that our biblical scholars, theologians, and spiritual guides develop for us a full-orbed vision of the life of the disciple." That challenge, which I had not heard from others before commencing my writing, well expresses the motivation behind *Making Kingdom Disciples*.

Webber goes on to state the major concern of the consultation: "the failure of the church to disciple new converts. . . . Discipleship is a life-long process, and the church must attend to keeping and forming disciples throughout life."

Though Webber's approach is a bit different from mine, I believe we are moving in the same direction. While I would be flattered if everyone adopted my scheme and terminology, I am more concerned that we clearly define the need and then move in a generally concerted effort to do what Jesus commanded. We both agree that in our postmodern world we cannot simply continue to use methods intended for the modern world. In that world things like logic, reason, arguments, and evidence had a far more powerful influence. I am not saying that we need to discard those things, but that we must intentionally use them in a more relational manner. By contrast, in a postmodern environment, the approach is more everyday and relational, less rational, logical, demanding of evidences. The culture does make a difference in how we speak and even what we do. We have to learn to express the biblical content of the Christian faith in much more of a relational and experiential manner than in previous periods.

I appreciate Webber's emphasis that the place to begin discipleship is in the church. I also applaud him for including items like worship, teaching, prayer, fellowship, mercy, ministry, and community in his approach. His book is well worth reading in its entirety.

Notes

Chapter 1: An Overview of the Kingdom Model

1. George Barna, *The Second Coming of the Church* (Nashville: Word, 1998), 23.

2. George Gallup Jr. and D. Michael Lindsey, *Surveying the Religious Landscape: Trends in U.S. Beliefs* (Harrisburg, Pa.: Morehouse, 1999), 4.

3. Barna, *Second Coming*, 8.

4. David Williamson, *Group Power* (Englewood Cliffs, N.J.: Prentice-Hall, 1982), 5.

5. Robert Wuthnow, *I Come Away Stronger* (Grand Rapids: Eerdmans, 1994), 6.

6. Abraham Kuyper, *Souvereiniteit in Eigen Kring. Rede ter Inwijding van de Vrije Universiteit* (Kampen: Kok, 1930), 32.

7. Norman De Jong, *Education in the Truth* (Lansing, Ill.: Redeemer, 1989), 118.

8. Ibid.

9. J. P. Moreland and William Lane Craig, *Philosophical Foundations for a Christian Worldview* (Downers Grove, Ill.: InterVarsity, 2003), 5.

Chapter 2: Epistemology: What and How We Know

1. Francis Schaeffer, *The Francis Schaeffer Trilogy* (Westchester, Ill.: 1990), 303.

2. W. Jay Wood, *Epistemology: Becoming Intellectually Virtuous* (Downers Grove, Ill.: InterVarsity, 1998), 17.

3. N. T. Wright, *The New Testament and the People of God* (Minneapolis: Fortress, 1992), 45.

4. Robert Reymond, *A New Systematic Theology of the Christian Faith* (Nashville: Nelson, 1998), 96–97.

5. J. Richard Middleton and Brian A. Walsh, *Truth Is Stranger Than It Used to Be* (Downers Grove, Ill.: InterVarsity, 1995), 165.

6. Cornelius Van Til, "A Christian Theistic Theory of Knowledge," *The Banner*, 6 November 1931.

7. Cornelius Van Til, *Defense of the Faith* (Philadelphia: Presbyterian and Reformed, 1955), 152–53.

8. Henry Meeter, *The Basic Ideas of Calvinism* (Grand Rapids: Zondervan, 1939), 76.

Chapter 3: The Kingdom of God

1. Cornelius Plantinga, *Engaging God's World* (Grand Rapids: Eerdmans, 2002), 107.

2. Meredith Kline, *The Structure of Biblical Authority*, 2nd ed. (Eugene, Ore.: Wipf & Stock, 1997).

3. Douglas Bannerman, *The Scripture Doctrine of the Church* (Grand Rapids: Eerdmans, 1955), 249–50.

4. Raymond O. Zorn, *Church and Kingdom* (Philadelphia: Presbyterian and Reformed, 1962), 9.

5. Ibid., 13.

6. Herman Ridderbos, *The Coming of the Kingdom* (Philadelphia: Presbyterian and Reformed, 1962), 354.

7. Edmund P. Clowney, *The Church* (Downers Grove, Ill.: InterVarsity, 1995), 199ff.

8. George Eldon Ladd, *A Theology of the New Testament* (Grand Rapids: Eerdmans, 1974), 111.

9. Jacques Ellul, *The Presence of the Kingdom* (Colorado Springs: Helmers and Howard, 1989), 11–13.

Chapter 4: A Christian World-and-Life-View

1. James Sire, *The Universe Next Door: A Basic Worldview Catalog* (Downers Grove, Ill.: InterVarsity, 1988), 17.

2. Ibid., 18.

3. Albert M. Wolters, *Creation Regained: Biblical Basics for a Reformational Worldview* (Grand Rapids: Eerdmans, 1985), 2.

4. Arthur Holmes, *Contours of a World View* (Downers Grove, Ill.: InterVarsity, 1983), 5.

5. Paul Hiebert, *Anthropological Insights for Missionaries* (Grand Rapids: Baker, 1983), 48.

6. Wolters, *Creation Regained*, 73–74.

7. Ibid., 97–98.

8. David Naugle, *Worldview: The History of a Concept* (Grand Rapids: Eerdmans, 2002), 336.

Chapter 5: The Reformed Faith

1. Stanley Grenz, *Created for Community: Connecting Christian Belief with Christian Living* (Grand Rapids: Baker, 1998), 18–19.

2. Frances Schaeffer, *A Christian Manifesto* (Westchester, Ill.: Crossway, 1981), 17.

3. George Barna, *The Second Coming of the Church* (Nashville: Word, 1998), 62.

4. Cornelius Plantinga, *Engaging God's World* (Grand Rapids: Eerdmans, 2002), ix.

5. George Gallup Jr. and D. Michael Lindsay. *Surveying the Religious Landscape: Trends in U.S. Beliefs* (Harrisburg, Pa.: Morehouse, 1999), 5.

6. George Barna and Mark Hatch, *The Boiling Point: It Only Takes One Degree* (Ventura, Calif.: Regal, 2001), 242–43.

7. Grenz, *Created for Community*, 9.

8. John M. Frame, *The Doctrine of God* (Phillipsburg, N.J.: P&R Publishing, 2002), 5.

9. Ibid.

10. Grenz, *Created for Community*, 18–19.

11. Millard Erickson, *Does It Matter What I Believe?* (Grand Rapids: Baker, 1992), 67.

12. Louis Berkhof, *Manual of Christian Doctrine* (Grand Rapids: Eerdmans, 1965), 161.

13. *Institutes of the Christian Religion*, 4.1.1.

14. John S. Feinberg, *No One Like Him: The Doctrine of God* (Wheaton, Ill.: Crossway, 2001), xxii.

Chapter 6: Covenant Theology

1. Robert Wuthnow, *The Crisis in the Churches: Spiritual Malaise, Fiscal Woe* (New York: Oxford University Press, 1997).

2. William Hendriksen, *The Covenant of Grace* (Grand Rapids: Baker, 1932), 9.

3. Geerhardus Vos, *Redemptive History and Biblical Interpretation*, ed. Richard B. Gaffin Jr. (Phillipsburg, N.J.: Presbyterian and Reformed, 1980), 241.

4. Ibid., 245.

5. Herman Bavinck, in *Creator, Redeemer, Consummator: A Festschrift for Meredith G. Kline*, ed. Howard Griffeth and John R. Muether (Jackson, Miss: Reformed Theological Seminary, 2000), 169.

6. William Heyns, *Manual of Reformed Doctrine* (Grand Rapids: Eerdmans, 1926), 127.

7. Ibid., 131.

8. Gordon Spykman, *Reformational Theology: A New Paradigm for Doing Dogmatics* (Grand Rapids: Eerdmans, 1992), 359.

9. Henry Buis, "Biblical Covenants," in *Encyclopedia of Christianity*, ed. Philip E. Hughes (Marshalltown, Del.: National Foundation for Christian Education, 1972), 3:219f.

10. S. G. DeGraaf, *Promise and Deliverance*, 4 vols. (St. Catharines, Ont.: Paideia, 1977), 1:17–26.

Part 2: Knowing the World: The Context of Discipleship

1. Charles Ringma, *Resist the Powers* (Colorado Springs: Pinon, 2000), May 21 reading.

2. Cornelius Plantinga Jr., *Engaging God's World: A Christian Vision of Faith, Learning, and Living* (Grand Rapids: Eerdmans, 2002), 150.

3. James Skillen, "Why Kuyper Now?" in Luis Lugo, ed., *Religion, Pluralism, and Public Life: Abraham Kuyper's Legacy for the Twenty-First Century* (Grand Rapids: Eerdmans, 2000), 370.

Chapter 7: A Culture Cast in Modernity

1. Ken Myers, *All God's Children and Blue Suede Shoes* (Wheaton, Ill.: Crossway, 1989), 58.

2. Peter Berger, *The Homeless Mind* (New York: Random House, 1973), 4.

3. Os Guinness, *Dining with the Devil* (Grand Rapids: Baker, 1993), 48.

4. See Carl F. H. Henry, *The Twilight of a Great Civilization: The Drift towards Neo-Paganism* (Wheaton, Ill.: Crossway, 1988), 170.

5. Myers, *All God's Children*, 52.

6. Guinness, *Dining with the Devil*, 90.

7. Ibid.

Chapter 8: The Postmodern Paradigm

1. Paul Strathern, *Foucault in 90 Minutes* (Chicago: Ivan R. Dee, 2000), 81.

2. Richard Rorty, "On Religion—A Discussion with Richard Rorty, Alvin Plantinga, and Nicholas Wolterstorff," interview by Stephen Louthan, *Christian Scholar's Review* 26.2 (Winter 1996): 180.

3. Alvin Plantinga, "On Religion," interview by Stephen Louthan, 183.

4. Stephen Davis, *God, Reason and Theistic Proofs* (Edinburgh: Edinburgh University Press, 1997), 90ff.

5. Stanley Grenz, *A Primer on Postmodernism* (Grand Rapids: Eerdmans, 1996), 108.

6. Norman F. Cantor, *The American Century: Varieties of Culture in Modern Times* (New York: Harper Collins, 1997), 435.

Chapter 9: The Generational Context

1. Jerry Gerber et al., *Lifetrends: The Future of Baby Boomers and Other Aging Americans* (New York: Macmillan, 1989), 7.

2. William Strauss and Neil Howe, *Generations: The History of America's Future, 1584 to 2069* (New York: William Morrow, 1991), 35.

3. Ron Zemke, Claire Raines, and Bob Filipczak, *Generations at Work: Managing the Clash of Veterans, Boomers, Xers, and Nexters in Your Workplace* (New York: AMACOM, 1999), 1.

4. Ibid., 30.

5. Susan Mitchell, *The American Generations: Who They Are, How They Live, What They Think* (Ithaca, N.Y.: New Strategies, 2003), 23.

6. Quoted in Gerber et al., *Lifetrends*, 1.

7. Douglas Coupland, *Life after God* (New York: Pocket, 1994), 359.

8. Strauss and Howe, *Generations*, 322.

9. Ibid., 329.

10. Ibid., 334.

11. George Barna, *Generation Next* (Ventura, Calif.: Regal, 1995), 11.

12. Ibid., 128.

13. Neil Howe and William Strauss, *Millennials Rising: The Next Generation* (New York: Vintage, 2000), 28.

14. Ibid., 24.

Chapter 10: Paul's Example in Acts 17

1. Simon Kistemaker, *Acts* (Grand Rapids: Baker, 1991), 630.

2. Ben Witherington III, *The Acts of the Apostles: A Socio-Rhetorical Commentary* (Grand Rapids: Eerdmans, 1998), 518.

3. Ibid., 524.

4. Kistemaker, *Acts*, 639.

Chapter 11: Ecclesiastes: A Study in Worldviews

1. Jay E. Adams, *Life under the Sun/Son: Counsel from the Book of Ecclesiastes* (n.p.: Timeless Texts, 1999), v.

2. Jacques Ellul, *Reason for Being* (Grand Rapids: Eerdmans, 1990), 112.

3. Tremper Longman III, *The Book of Ecclesiastes*, New International Commentary on the Old Testament (Grand Rapids: Eerdmans, 1998), 195.

4. Ellul, *Reason for Being*, 133ff.

5. Longman, *Ecclesiastes*, 85.

6. James Crenshaw, *Ecclesiastes: A Commentary* (Philadelphia: Westminster, 1987), 73ff.

7. Robert Wuthnow, *The Crisis in the Churches: Spiritual Malaise, Fiscal Woe* (New York: Oxford University Press, 1997).

Chapter 12: A Covenantal Reading of Scripture: Genesis 13

1. H. Evan Runner, introduction to *Promise and Deliverance*, *Promise and Deliverance*, by S. G. DeGraaf, 4 vols. (St. Catharines, Ont.: Paideia, 1977), 1:13–14.

2. H. A. Ironside, "Beneath the Blood-stained Lintel," in *The Continual Burnt Offering: Daily Meditations on the Word of God,* 3rd ed. (Neptune, N.J.: Loizeaux Brothers, 1995). Used by permission from Loizeaux Brothers.

Appendix 1: The Role of Baptism and the Church in Disciple Making

1. Brett P. Webb-Mitchell, *Christly Gestures: Learning to Be Members of the Body of Christ* (Grand Rapids: Eerdmans, 2003), 245.

Glossary

Apologetics. The branch of theology having to do with offensively and defensively setting forth the Christian faith over against non-Christian religions or philosophies.

Assumption. That which we presuppose before we reason or do anything else, or that which we believe to be logically or causally necessary.

Covenant. An interpersonal bond or contract-like arrangement according to which God relates to creatures, especially man (his image bearer). God's covenant with us has strong implications for how we relate to him, our surroundings, and other people.

Culture. Our environment comprising the values, beliefs, and behavior that determine our lifestyle.

Enlightenment. That period at the beginning of the eighteenth century when man presumably came of age and began to think, reason, and know things on his own. Man became a free thinker; that is, he believed that he no longer needed to start with God in order to know things.

Epistemology. The study relating to how we know or the theory of knowledge, especially as it relates to what we know and believe and why.

Foundationalism. A view concerned with that upon which we base our early beliefs and knowledge. For Descartes, it was man's ability to doubt. For Christians, it is God's revelation. The first is not good, while the second is. Postmodernism, while rejecting both concepts, is mainly reacting to Descartes's concept.

Ideology. The system of ideas or doctrines that guide people into certain understandings and behaviors.

Infotainment. A combination of the words "information" and "entertainment" that refers to today's propensity to make information, often confused with knowledge, entertaining.

Kingdom of God. A phrase used interchangeably with "kingdom of heaven" to refer to the rule and reign of Jesus Christ the King.

Logic. The science of correct thinking or valid inference; the study of the formal principles of reasoning.

Modernism. An ideological outgrowth of Enlightenment philosophy that claims that the Christian faith should be altered to fit naturalistic assumptions. It is a paradigm shift that replaces God as the central reference point with man at the center.

Modernity. In most definitions, simply "the quality of being modern." It is more than that. In Western thought it generally describes life in advanced industrial societies. It has both philosophical and sociological meaning. It is also a term with moral dimensions. It refers to ideologies of the modern world, especially in the context of the advanced industrial societies.

Modernization. The ideological influences of the modern world sociologically, economically, technologically, and philosophically.

Monism. The belief that all is one and one is all.

New Age movement. An attempt to bring Eastern philosophy and religion into a Western framework, creating a belief that God is everything and everything is God. Man is ultimately god and the creator of his own reality.

Nihilism. The belief that nothing is really knowable, including life, man, and God. All is basically nothing, hence senseless and useless.

Pop culture. In our context, an intellectually dumbed-down focus on entertainment, fun, and the lighter, more current trends of life rather than on substantive and traditional matters.

Postmodernism. A philosophical paradigm that either negates or fulfills the philosophy of modernism. It places truth and reality, if in fact it uses those terms, within man's determining framework. It highlights egalitarianism, subjectivity, feelings, and mysticism in place of authority, objectivity, reason, and the scientific model.

Pragmaticism. The view that truth is determined by the practical, experiential consequences of a belief.

Presupposition. See Assumption.

Rational. Having to do with thought and reason.

Rationalism. The belief that man has the intellectual faculties to discover truth by intuition unaided by outside sources. This is in fact a misuse of God's gift of reason because it implies that we can arrive at truth through logical means apart from God's revelation.

Reformed. A term usually associated with the historic Protestant Reformation, we use it to refer to that tradition which emphasizes the authority of Scripture and the sovereignty of God over all of life.

Relativism. The ideology that suggests that truth and reality are determined by the circumstances. What may be truth in one situation may not be truth in another context; hence there are no universals or absolute truths.

Secularism. A view of life as separate or free from religious beliefs.

Structuralism. The attempt to bring reality into a fixed format, thus giving it objectivity.

Syncretism. The fusing of two or more teachings, for example, the blending of other religious teachings with Christianity in order to make Christianity culturally acceptable.

Systems approach. The view that everything is so intricately put together that each part necessarily affects the whole.

Technology, technism. All the developments of the scientific era.

Worldview. The filters or glasses (which are not necessarily scientifically validated) through which we "see" reality or what we believe to be reality. "Worldview" is our perspective of how things really are, a system by which we interpret things.

Supplementary Bibliography

Adams, Jay E. *Life under the Sun/Son: Counsel from the Book of Ecclesiastes.* n.p.: Timeless Texts, 1999.

Anderson, Walter. *Reality Isn't What It Used to Be.* San Francisco: HarperCollins, 1992.

Barna, George. *The Second Coming of the Church.* Nashville: Word, 1998.

———. *Transforming Children into Spiritual Champions: Why Children Should Be Your Church's #1 Priority.* Ventura, Calif.: Regal, 2003.

———, and Mark Hatch. *Boiling Point: It Only Takes One Degree.* Ventura, Calif.: Regal, 2001.

Barrs, Jerram. *The Heart of Evangelism.* Wheaton, Ill.: Crossway, 2001.

Bellah, Robert, et al. *Habits of the Heart.* Berkeley: University of California Press, 1996.

Bloom, Allan. *The Closing of the American Mind.* New York: Simon and Schuster, 1987.

Brown, Harold O. J. *The Sensate Culture.* Dallas: Word, 1996.

Carson D. A. *Exegetical Fallacies.* 2d ed. Grand Rapids: Baker, 1996.

Colson, Charles. *Against the Night: Living in the New Dark Ages.* Ann Arbor: Servant, 1989.

Dawn, Marva J. *Is It a Lost Cause?* Grand Rapids: Eerdmans, 1997.

———. *Reaching Out Without Dumbing Down.* Grand Rapids: Eerdmans, 1995.

DeGraaf, S. G. *Promise and Deliverance.* 4 vols. St. Catharines, Ont.: Paideia, 1977.

Dumbrell, W. J. *Covenant and Creation: A Theology of the Old Testament Covenants.* Grand Rapids: Baker, 1984.

Ellul, Jacques. *The Presence of the Kingdom.* Colorado Springs: Helmers and Howard, 1989.

Engels, James, and Will Norton. *Contemporary Christian Communications: Its Theory and Practice*. Nashville: Nelson, 1979.

Feinberg, John S. *No One Like Him: The Doctrine of God*. Wheaton, Ill.: Crossway, 2001.

Frame, John M. *The Doctrine of God*. Phillipsburg, N.J.: P&R Publishing, 2002.

———. *The Doctrine of the Knowledge of God*. Phillipsburg, N.J.: Presbyterian and Reformed, 1987.

Gallup, George, Jr., and D. Michael Lindsay. *Surveying the Religious Landscape: Trends in U.S. Beliefs*. Harrisburg, Pa.: Morehouse, 1999.

Gallup, George, Jr., and Timothy Jones. *The Next American Spirituality*. Elgin, Ill.: Cook, 2000.

Gerber, Jerry, et al. *Lifetrends: The Future of Baby Boomers and Other Aging Americans*. New York: Macmillan, 1989.

Grenz, Stanley J., and Roger E. Olson. *Who Needs Theology? An Invitation to Study God*. Downers Grove, Ill.: InterVarsity, 1996.

Guinness, Os. *Time for Truth: Living Free in a World of Lies, Hype, and Spin*. Grand Rapids: Baker, 2000.

Hendriksen, William. *The Covenant of Grace*. Grand Rapids: Baker, 1932.

Henry, Carl F. H. *Twilight of a Great Civilization: The Drift Toward Neo-Paganism*. Westchester, Ill.: Crossway, 1988.

Hesselink, I. John. *On Being Reformed*. 2d ed. New York: Reformed Church Press, 1988.

Heyns, William. *Manual of Reformed Doctrine*. Grand Rapids: Eerdmans, 1926.

Hicks, Rick, and Kathy Hicks. *Boomers, Xers, and Other Strangers: Understanding the Generational Differences That Divide Us*. Wheaton, Ill.: Tyndale, 1999.

Holmes, Arthur. *Contours of a World View*. Downers Grove, Ill.: InterVarsity, 1983.

Hunt, Susan. *Heirs of the Covenant*. Wheaton, Ill.: Crossway, 1998.

Jocz, Jacob. *The Covenant: A Theology of Human Destiny*. Grand Rapids: Eerdmans, 1968.

Jones, Landon. *Great Expectations*. New York: Ballantine Books, 1980.

Lewis, Bernard. *The Crisis of Islam*. New York: Modern Library, 2003.

Lugo, Luis, ed. *Religion, Pluralism, and Public Life: Abraham Kuyper's Legacy for the Twenty-first Century*. Grand Rapids: Eerdmans, 2000.

Marsden, George M. *Reforming Fundamentalism*. Grand Rapids: Eerdmans, 1987.

McIntosh, Gary L. *One Church, Four Generations: Understanding and Reaching All Ages in Your Church*. Grand Rapids: Baker, 2002.

Meek, Esther Lightcap. *Longing to Know: The Philosophy of Knowledge for Ordinary People*. Grand Rapids: Brazos, 2003.

Middleton, J. Richard, and Brian J. Walsh. *Truth Is Stranger Than It Used to Be: Biblical Faith in a Postmodern World*. Downers Grove, Ill.: InterVarsity, 1995.

Moore, T. M. *I Will Be Your God*. Phillipsburg, N.J.: P&R Publishing, 2002.

———. *Redeeming Pop Culture*. Phillipsburg, N.J.: P&R Publishing, 2003.

Moreland, J. P., and William Lane Craig. *Philosophical Foundations for a Christian Worldview*. Downers Grove, Ill.: InterVarsity, 2003.

Neuhaus, Richard John. *Naked Public Square*. Grand Rapids, Eerdmans, 1984.

Patterson, James, and Peter Kim. *The Day America Told the Truth*. Old Tappan, N.J.: Prentice Hall, 1991.

Peterson, Jim. *Lifestyle Discipleship*. Colorado Springs: NavPress, 1994.

Plantinga, Cornelius. *Engaging God's World: A Christian Vision of Faith, Learning, and Living*. Grand Rapids: Eerdmans, 2002.

Regels, Michael. *The Death of the Church*. Grand Rapids: Zondervan, 1995.

Ridderbos, Herman. *The Coming of the Kingdom*. Philadelphia: Presbyterian and Reformed, 1962.

Ringma, Charles. *Resist the Powers*. Colorado Springs: Pinon, 2000.

Rushdoony, Rousas J. *Intellectual Schizophrenia*. Philadelphia: Presbyterian and Reformed, 1961.

Schaeffer, Francis. *The God Who Is There*. Downers Grove, Ill.: InterVarsity, 1998.

Spykman, Gordon. *Reformational Theology: A New Paradigm for Doing Dogmatics*. Grand Rapids: Eerdmans, 1992.

Stevens, R. Paul. *The Other Six Days*. Grand Rapids: Eerdmans, 1999.

Stott, John R. W. *Between Two Worlds*. Grand Rapids: Eerdmans, 1982.

———. *One People*. Downers Grove, Ill.: InterVarsity, 1978.

Strauss, William, and Neil Howe. *Generations: The History of America's Future, 1584 to 2069*. New York: William Morrow, 1991.

Vos, Geerhardus. *Redemption History and Biblical Interpretation*. Edited by Richard B. Gaffin Jr. Phillipsburg, N.J.: Presbyterian and Reformed, 1980.

Walsh, Brian J., and J. Richard Middleton. *The Transforming Vision: Shaping a Christian World View.* Downers Grove, Ill.: InterVarsity, 1984.

Webber, Robert E. *Ancient-Future Evangelism.* Grand Rapids: Baker, 2003.

Webb-Mitchell, Brett. *Christly Gestures: Learning to Be Members of the Body of Christ.* Grand Rapids: Eerdmans, 2003.

Witherington, Ben, III. *The Acts of the Apostles: A Socio-Rhetorical Commentary.* Grand Rapids: Eerdmans, 1998.

Wolters, Albert M. *Creation Regained: Biblical Basics for a Reformational World-view.* Grand Rapids: Eerdmans, 1985.

Wuthnow, Robert. *The Crisis in the Churches: Spiritual Malaise, Fiscal Woe.* New York: Oxford University Press, 1997.

Zorn, Raymond O. *Church and Kingdom.* Philadelphia: Presbyterian and Reformed, 1962.

Index of Scripture

247

Charles H. Dunahoo (M.Div., Columbia Theological Seminary; D.Min., Westminster Theological Seminary) is coordinator for the Committee for Christian Education and Publications of the Presbyterian Church in America, as well as editor of *Equip for Ministry*. He was instrumental in the founding and organization of the PCA denomination, serving on several committees in its formative years.

Dunahoo's experience as an educator includes the pastorate and four years as professor of systematic theology and apologetics at the Atlanta School of Biblical Studies. In his current role he conducts various seminars on Christian education, counseling, family and marriage, and officer training. His consulting with local church leaders and other Christian organizations has taken him across North America and to several foreign countries.